KU-571-910

# Phenomenological Psychology

PEARSON
Education

We work with leading authors to develop the strongest educational materials in psychology, bringing cutting-edge thinking and best learning practice to a global market.

Under a range of well-known imprints, including Prentice Hall, we craft high-quality print and electronic publications which help readers to understand and apply their content, whether studying or at work.

To find out more about the complete range of our publishing, please visit us on the World Wide Web at: **www.pearsoned.co.uk**

# Phenomenological Psychology

## Theory, Research and Method

DARREN LANGDRIDGE
The Open University

PEARSON

Prentice
Hall

Harlow, England • London • New York • Boston • San Francisco • Toronto • Sydney • Singapore • Hong Kong
Tokyo • Seoul • Taipei • New Delhi • Cape Town • Madrid • Mexico City • Amsterdam • Munich • Paris • Milan

**Pearson Education Limited**
Edinburgh Gate
Harlow
Essex CM20 2JE
England

and Associated Companies throughout the world

*Visit us on the World Wide Web at*:
www.pearsoned.co.uk

First published 2007

© Pearson Education Limited 2007

The right of Darren Langdridge to be identified as author of this work has
been asserted by him in accordance with the Copyright, Designs and
Patents Act 1988.

All rights reserved. No part of this publication may be reproduced, stored in
a retrieval system, or transmitted in any form or by any means, electronic,
mechanical, photocopying, recording or otherwise, without either the prior
written permission of the publisher or a licence permitting restricted copying
in the United Kingdom issued by the Copyright Licensing Agency Ltd,
Saffron House, 6–10 Kirby Street, London EC1N 8TS.

All trademarks used herein are the property of their respective owners. The
use of any trademark in this text does not vest in the author or publisher any
trademark ownership rights in such trademarks, nor does the use of such
trademarks imply any affiliation with or endorsement of this book by such owners.

ISBN: 978-0-13-196523-2

**British Library Cataloguing-in-Publication Data**
A catalogue record for this book is available from the British Library

**Library of Congress Cataloging-in-Publication Data**
Langdridge, Darren.
    Phenomenological psychology : theory, research and method / Darren Langdridge.
        p. cm.
    Includes bibliographical references and index.
    ISBN-13: 978-0-13-196523-2
    ISBN-10: 0-13-196523-9
    1. Phenomenological psychology. I. Title.

    BF204.5.L36 2007
    150.19'2--dc22

                                                                    2006051241

10 9 8 7 6 5 4 3
10 09

Typeset in 9.5/13pt Stone Serif by 30
Printed and bound by Ashford Colour Press, Gosport, Houts.

*The publisher's policy is to use paper manufactured from sustainable forests.*

This book is dedicated to Ian,
my past, present and future.

# Guided tour

**Chapter aims** highlight what you should have learnt by the end of the chapter and give you a taste of what you'll be covering

**Biography boxes** explore the contribution of key figures to the field of phenomenology. There are **photographs** throughout the text that bring the subject to life and help to illustrate concepts

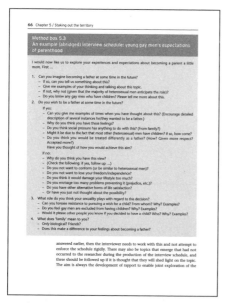

**Method boxes** provide concrete examples of phenomenological methods and approaches

**Study boxes** reflect on a specific study, giving you access to a variety of current literature

**Data boxes** contain examples of raw data that would be used in phenomenological studies

**Analysis boxes** encourage you to reflect on and analyse the data, by examining the evidence using phenomenological methods

**End of chapter summaries** and **further reading** review the key issues and theories in the chapter and give you the tools to move beyond the material covered in the book

# Acknowledgements

I am grateful to Elizabeth Valentine and the BPS for permission to reproduce sections of Langridge, D. (2003). Hermeneutic phenomenology: arguments for a new social psychology. *History and Philosophy of Psychology*, 5(1), pp. 30–45.

   I would like to take this opportunity to thank Trevor Butt, Linda Finlay, Mark Burgess and David Giles for invaluable feedback on earlier drafts of chapters. Special thanks also to Ole Spaten, the students at Aalborg University, staff and students at the University of Huddersfield, London South Bank University and attendees at the Lesbian and Gay Psychology Section Building Partnerships Event 3 for providing me with the opportunity to put theory into practice. I am also grateful to all my colleagues at the Open University for providing me with such a stimulating intellectual home. Thanks also to Morten Fuglevand and Janey Webb at Pearson Education for believing in this project and bringing it to fruition.

   Finally, I would like to thank my family and friends – new and old – for the love and support they have provided throughout this project.

# Publisher's acknowledgements

The publishers are grateful to the following for permission to reproduce copyright material:

Figure 2.1 Bettman / Corbis; 2.2 (top) TM-Photo/zefa/ Corbis; Figure 2.4 Stephen Hird/Reuters/ Corbis; Figure 3.1 and 3.2 Bettmann/ Corbis; Figure 3.5 Georges Pierre/Sygma/Corbis; Figure 3.6 Topfoto; Figure 4.1 Empics; Figure 4.2 Peter M. Fisher/Corbis; Figure 5.1 Tom Stewart/Corbis; Figure 5.3 and 5.4 Corbis.

In some instances we have been unable to trace the owners of copyright material, and we would appreciate any information that would enable us to do so.

# 1 Phenomenological psychology in context

## Chapter aims

- Introduce key terms in qualitative methodology
- Explain the basics of phenomenological psychology
- Position phenomenological psychology within the broader field of qualitative perspectives in psychology
- Outline the structure of the book

I still remember my first lecture in psychology at the University of Sheffield, where I studied for my first degree. I was both excited and anxious: excited because I had managed to get to university and anxious because I did not know whether I would be good enough. The lecture theatre appeared huge, full to the brim with all these confident young women and men, and then there was me, experiencing a nauseating mix of feelings. The lecture began with a warning, a warning that if you were here to understand yourself better, then you were in the wrong place, because we were here to learn about the science of psychology and not ourselves. Oh dear: maybe I was in the wrong place. Luckily, the lecture moved on to spell out the fascinating range of topics that were to be covered in the coming years, and I was hooked. I was proud to be a scientist and to be involved in the study of a new science. During the course of the three years that followed, however, I became increasingly sceptical of this belief in the discipline and myself. This was, at least in part, due to studying philosophy, with the tutors casting doubt on all my claims to know pretty much anything, including the psychology of human nature. All those things I held certain, from my belief in a real world to the possibility of gaining objective knowledge about people, were blown out of the water. This then became the start of a journey to discover a way of 'doing psychology' that was informed by philosophy, and one which would, of course, also illuminate the human condition. As you might already have guessed, this led me to phenomenological psychology, with its focus on understanding lived experience. This story itself is a little study in phenomenological psychology, since it is a description of one person's lived experience – in this case, my own – that is also more generally illuminating about, for instance, the experience of attending university for the first time. The story not only serves to situate me in relation to the subject of this book but also informs both the structure and the content of this book, as I hope will become clear during the course of this introduction.

This book aims to provide comprehensive coverage of one set of qualitative methods, those based on or informed by phenomenological philosophy: commonly known as 'phenomenological psychology'. This is not a new way of doing philosophy or psychological research, however. Phenomenological philosophy emerged over 100 years ago and was first used by psychologists in the 1960s to inform the kind of research that they conducted. The phenomenological approach to psychological research has continued from that point – often ignored by the wider psychology community – but has grown rapidly and started to be taken more seriously in the UK, continental Europe, the USA, Australia and South Africa over the past 20 years or so. This book is a response to that growth and an attempt to provide a single volume on this family of methods, viewed through the lens of British psychology and the methods being employed therein.

## 1.1 Qualitative methods in psychology

Qualitative methods are the methods concerned with the naturalistic description or interpretation of phenomena in terms of the meanings these have for the people experiencing them. This is in contrast to quantitative methods, which are concerned with counting the amount of the phenomenon or some aspect thereof. The focus for many in this field, and especially those engaged in phenomenological psychology, is rich description of some aspect of experience. This is not true for all qualitative researchers, however. For instance, discursive psychologists focus on the action orientation of talk, such as the way we manage to stake an interest in a conversation (e.g. Edwards and Potter, 1992; Potter and Wetherell, 1987) and/or discursive resources, and the way in which language actually constitutes life and, therefore, both allows and limits our possible ways of living in the world (e.g. Henriques *et al.*, 1984; Parker, 1992) rather than focusing on experience described through language.

At the turn of the twenty-first century, social (and also clinical and applied) psychology still continues to be dominated, in the UK, continental Europe, Australia and North America at least, by the (predominantly experimental) social cognitive perspective. This way of understanding psychology has not, however, gone unchallenged (see Burr, 2003, for a good summary of the criticisms), and these challenges have become ever more vigorous and also more readily heard since the 'crisis' in social psychology in the mid-1970s. Qualitative methods have increased in popularity in psychology in recent years, in part as a result of the growing dissatisfaction with quantitative methods among sections of the psychological community. Just a quick examination of the research methods books produced or articles published in academic journals in recent years is testament to the increasing importance of qualitative methods in psychology.

The criticisms of the cognitive perspective involve questions about the realism (the assumption that there is a real knowable world out there that we can study) and essentialism (the belief that there is an essential given core to people that makes them what they are once and for all) at the heart of the cognitive approach to psychology. Furthermore, the failure of many cognitive researchers to take account of the way in which knowledge is a product of both history and culture (constructed through language and our ways of speaking and writing about events) provokes considerable doubt about the findings from this perspective. As a result, people have looked for alternative ways of producing knowledge and investigating human nature. These qualitative alternatives take a critical (i.e. sceptical) stance towards knowledge and the claims we are making about psychology, recognize the influence of history and culture on such claims, and appreciate how we construct such knowledge intersubjectively (i.e. between people) through language.

One of the initial difficulties for many people trying to learn about qualitative methods is the need to understand the huge variety of complex terms. In the following short section, I unpack just a few of the fundamental terms of relevance for all qualitative methods and, in the process, further highlight criticisms of mainstream (i.e. cognitive) approaches to psychology. The first important organizing principle for all research is the _paradigm_. A paradigm is a set of basic beliefs that provide the principles for understanding the world and, hence, the basic principles underpinning research in the social sciences. By and large, these beliefs must be taken 'on trust', argued philosophically, but ultimately are always debatable (if they were not, then the ongoing debates in philosophy about the nature of existence and what we can say we know about this would have been over years ago). Mainstream psychology used to – and to some extent still does – subscribe to a _positivist_ paradigm. A positivist paradigm is one in which there is belief in a real world that we can gain knowledge about, through the use of scientific methods (including, therefore, quantification and the use of statistics). Positivism has, for most social science researchers, been superseded by a _postpositivist_ paradigm, where a real world is still assumed but our knowledge of it is critical (i.e. sceptical) and, therefore, never complete and only an approximation (Guba, 1990). Most mainstream psychological research works within a positivist/postpositivist paradigm, very much like most research in the natural sciences (chemistry, physics and biology), which have formed the model for psychology for many years. Although a positivist/postpositivist paradigm may be appropriate for the natural sciences (although even this has been questioned in recent years), this seems an inappropriate paradigm for psychology and the study of human nature. Consequently, we have seen the appropriation of many different paradigms for psychology, including adoption of the phenomenological paradigm (see below).

All paradigms lead to a set of beliefs about the world and with this invoke another set of terms. Paradigms lead to particular _epistemological_ positions – that is, our position with regard to what we can say we know about something. Epistemology is the branch of philosophy concerned with knowledge and what we can say we know about the world, the relationship between the knower and the known. If we believe in a real world, then we will need to employ a scientific epistemology (where we are objective, detached and value-free) in order to discover truths about the world (or find out how things really are). A phenomenological paradigm would, by contrast, have an epistemological focus on experience or narrative (rather than a real knowable world) and so require ways of capturing this that are subjective and involved. The final two links in this chain are *methodology*, a term referring to the general way to research a topic, and *method*, the specific technique(s) being employed. The methodology that is adopted will be informed by a person's epistemological position. The methodology is in turn likely to influence the type of methods used. Someone subscribing to a positivist scientific methodology is likely to use methods such as experiments, which are designed to remove extraneous factors from the research process. A phenomenological methodology, however, will involve the collection of naturalistic first-person accounts of experience, recognizing the need to account for the influence of the researcher on the data-collection and analytical process. For more on the basics of qualitative theory and method, see Langdridge (2004a).

## 1.2 Phenomenology and phenomenological psychology

The specific focus for phenomenological psychology is a 'return to the things themselves', a famous phrase from the founder of phenomenological philosophy, Edmund Husserl. So, when applying phenomenological philosophy to psychology, we aim to focus on people's perceptions of the world in which they live and what this means to them: a focus on people's lived experience. Phenomenology (i.e. phenomenological philosophy) is a philosophical movement that began in the early 1900s with the work of Edmund Husserl, a German philosopher. It was heralded as a bold and radically new way of doing philosophy, concerned with placing the philosophy of lived experience centre stage. Phenomenology is not, however, a consistent body of thought, and there are many variations with different implications for the way in which we might build on these ideas in order to create a phenomenological psychology. Consequently, there is not one thing we can call phenomenological psychology. Instead, phenomenological psychology should be seen as the label for a family of approaches, which are all informed by phenomenology but with different emphases, depending on the specific strand of phenomenological philosophy that most informs the methodology.

All phenomenologists resist the subject–object dualism that is central to positivism and the scientific project, where we see the separation of the world as it really is and the world as it appears to us through perception. Phenomenologists argue that it does not make sense to think of objects in the world separately from subjectivity and our perception of them. An object enters our reality only when we perceive it, when it is presented to consciousness. Furthermore, our perception varies according to the context, the position of the perceiver in relation to the object and the mood of the perceiver, among other things. There is, therefore, no once-and-for-all knowledge to be found about a real knowable world. Instead, we have a focus on our perception of the world and how this is experienced, recognizing that this will be differently meaningful to different people and even the same person in a different context. Consequently, the aim of phenomenological psychology is to study experience and how the world appears to people. To this end, phenomenological psychology employs a set of methods to enable researchers to elicit rich descriptions of concrete experiences and/or narratives of experiences. These methods are designed to illuminate the lived world of the participant and also, possibly, the lived world of the researcher, along with others who have, or may in the future, experienced something similar.

## 1.3 Outline of the book

Chapter 1
Introduction

**Foundations and philosophical underpinnings**

Chapter 2
Phenomenology

Chapter 3
Existentialism

Chapter 4
Hermeneutics

Chapter 5  Practicalities of carrying out phenomenological research

**Approaches to research**

Chapter 6
Descriptive
approach

Chapter 7
Interpretive
approach

Chapter 8
Narrative
approach

Chapter 9  Key issues, debates and analysis of phenomenological methods

The book begins with three chapters outlining the philosophical foundations of phenomenological psychology. These, in turn, introduce the foundations of phenomenology (Chapter 2), along with the existential (Chapter 3) and hermeneutic (Chapter 4) movements that followed, transformed phenomenology and directly influenced phenomenological methodology. Chapters 2–4 provide details of the philosophical basis for the different varieties of phenomenological thought and how developments in this strand of continental philosophy have involved a shift from what is termed *Husserlian phenomenology* to *existential phenomenology* (or, more often, simply *existentialism*) to *hermeneutic phenomenology* (or, sometimes, *hermeneutic-existential phenomenology*). These ferocious-sounding names are immediately offputting but simply refer to the original philosophy of Edmund Husserl (the founder of phenomenology), a focus on lived existence and the interpretation of meaning, respectively; if you are interested in understanding the world as it is lived and narrated by people – in all its richness, complexity and vitality – then it is worth the effort of understanding the 'tribal language' of phenomenology. The following three chapters serve, I hope, to explain these complex terms, such that the philosophical heart of phenomenology is laid bare for all to understand. These three chapters map on to the three groups of phenomenological methods presented in Chapters 6–8. Chapter 6 focuses on the descriptive approach to phenomenological psychology, which is aligned most closely with the fundamentals of phenomenology presented in Chapter 2, along with ideas from the existentialists (covered in Chapter 3). Chapter 7 moves on to consider more interpretive ways of carrying out phenomenological psychology and is, therefore, aligned more closely with the existential and hermeneutic turns in phenomenological philosophy presented in Chapters 3 and 4, respectively. Chapter 8 introduces a narrative approach to phenomenology that builds directly on the hermeneutic phenomenology of the philosopher Paul Ricoeur, which is discussed in Chapter 3. Chapter 5 is quite different from Chapters 2–4. It is a large chapter providing practical information about a wide variety of issues common to most phenomenological research. There is information about research design, sampling, reflexivity, ethics and the collection of data, among other things. Finally, Chapter 9 is an attempt to provide a phenomenological response to criticisms of this perspective and engage with a number of key debates currently happening among qualitative researchers in psychology (and beyond). Some of these debates are quite complex, and so some sections may not appear terribly important to those readers simply interested in carrying out a piece of phenomenological research. However, I hope that there will be much in this chapter for readers interested in the criticisms levelled at phenomenological psychology and debates about interpretation, language, postmodernism and the future of phenomenological psychology.

When reading this book, it is entirely possible to skip the next three chapters and go straight to the chapters concerned with the practicalities of carrying out phenomenological research without too many problems. Indeed, if time is tight and there is an urgent need for information about how to carry out a phenomenological study, then I would actually recommend skipping the next three chapters to focus immediately on the practicalities of the research process. General detail about design, sampling and the collection of data, among other things, is given in Chapter 5 and the different ways of analysing the data are provided in Chapters 6–8. However, this is not the ideal way of reading this text, for phenomenological psychology, like many qualitative methods, is grounded in philosophy. Understanding the philosophy that informs the method being used will greatly enrich the research carried out. It will also help to ensure that the research is valid and methodologically sound. With this in mind, I would recommend reading through the next three chapters before moving on to the practical chapters that follow. It may be necessary – indeed, desirable – to return to these chapters when reading the later chapters, but the initial grounding in phenomenological philosophy that Chapters 2–4 provide will form the foundations for all further reading and a great base upon which to build knowledge about phenomenological psychology.

You will notice that I use the first person ('I') in this text and also offer my views. Many phenomenological psychologists use 'I' as a contrast to the impersonal style of much mainstream psychology writing and as a challenge to the authority which that implies. Moreover, the use of this more personal voice reflects the recognition within phenomenological psychology of the importance of the researcher in the research process. For us, knowledge is not produced outside history, culture or the particular theoretical perspective being employed. Phenomenological psychologists do not claim to produce the 'truth' – nor do we think this possible – and thus it is up to you – the reader – to determine the value of what is presented rather than take it on trust as the product of an academic 'expert'.

## Summary

Qualitative methods are the methods concerned with the naturalistic description or interpretation of phenomena in terms of the meanings these have for the people experiencing them. Although psychology remains dominated by a quantitative cognitive perspective, there has been growing criticism of this perspective and increasing interest in qualitative alternatives. One of these alternative perspectives is phenomenological psychology. Phenomenological psychology is concerned first and foremost with understanding people's lived experience of the world: a 'return to the things themselves'. There is not one phenomenological psychology, however, but rather a family of methods with a common phenomenological philosophical foundation. The remaining chapters are split into two sections, with the initial chapters concerned with explaining the philosophical foundations of phenomenological psychology and the later chapters describing the practical application of these concepts in psychology.

# 2 Fundamentals of phenomenology

## Chapter aims

- Explain what phenomenological psychology is

- Provide a brief history of phenomenological philosophy and an introduction to the thought of the founder Edmund Husserl

- Introduce the fundamental concepts of phenomenological philosophy: intentionality, noema–noesis, epoché, phenomenological reduction, imaginative variation, essences

This chapter seeks to outline the fundamentals of phenomenology, particularly those features of this philosophical movement that are important for psychology. I begin by attempting to answer the question 'What is phenomenology?' and then move on to tell the history of this movement to provide some context for present-day understandings. After this, I take six key concepts in phenomenology and, in turn, provide clear and succinct descriptions that will form the foundation for their practical application. But first, the following discussion seeks to provide a little more information about the place of phenomenological research methods in psychology.

As mentioned in Chapter 1, the dominant approach to research in psychology is one that is quantitative and positivist/post-positivist. That approach is concerned with the quantification of data through the reduction of psychological phenomena to scores on variables, built on an assumption of a relatively unproblematic relationship between our perception of the world and the world itself. Researchers working within this perspective think that there is ultimately some truth to be discerned about the object of study, whether it is observable behaviours or 'states of mind'. To achieve this, they might conduct experiments involving the manipulation of independent variables so the effect can be measured on dependent variables or design questionnaires to gain answers to questions about attitudes, beliefs and behaviours. The belief is that by collecting data about people in this way, it will tell us what is going on in their heads. Of course, it is not as simple as this, since many psychologists recognize the way in which objects differently accrue meaning depending on the person or people perceiving them and the context in which they are perceived. For instance, one person may perceive the sea as a relaxing or fun thing, evoking memories of wonderful beach holidays in the sunshine, while another person may perceive exactly the same sea as a raging beast that is out of control, ready to drag them out and drown them. The exact same object may mean very different things to different people or even different things to the same person on different occasions and in different contexts (the sea before and after being nearly drowned or the sea when calm versus the sea when stormy or even, simply, the sea when one is in a good mood versus the sea when one is in a bad mood). However, among mainstream psychologists, there is still an underlying belief that through the application of ever more rigorous methods, we can reveal the secrets of our psychology. This perspective has not gone unchallenged, and a particularly powerful and increasingly popular alternative – phenomenological psychology – is, of course, the focus of this book. As will become clear through the next three chapters, a phenomenological approach offers a radical alternative to traditional understandings about what we believe we can know about the world and therefore, by implication, what we believe we can know about human nature. A phenomenological approach to psychological research, in common with many other qualitative perspectives, and in contrast to a quantitative positivist natural science perspective, entails the following:

■ a focus on human experience as a topic in its own right;
■ a concern with meaning and the way in which meaning arises in experience;
■ a focus on description and relationships rather than interpretation and causality (although this distinction will be addressed further and somewhat problematized in the following chapters);
■ recognition of the role of the researcher in the co-construction of the topic under investigation and built on an understanding of the way in which all experience must be understood in context (historical, cultural and personal).

See Study box 2.1 for an example of a phenomenological psychological study on the experience of male rape, which vividly brings to life the horror of this experience and the meaning it has for the men involved. At all times, there is sensitivity to context, with the researchers recognizing the limitations of the study while seeking to reveal the structure of this experience, such that this knowledge might be applied to help the prevention of such crimes, along with the healing process of those who have survived them. This is what phenomenological psychology is all about – rich description of people's experiences, so that we can understand them in new, subtle and different ways and then use this new knowledge to make a difference to the lived world of ourselves and others.

## Study box 2.1

**Pretorius, H.G. & Hull, R.M.** (2005). The experience of male rape in non-institutionalised settings. *Indo-Pacific Journal of Phenomenology*, 5(2), 1–11.

This paper presents the findings from a study of the experience of three men who have survived being raped in non-institutionalized settings. The authors employ a phenomenological method, with a focus on describing, in rich detail, the experiences of the men and the impact that these events have had on their lives. They gathered data through in-depth interviews with the participants and focused on eliciting information about the rape experience and its impact on their lives. The interviews were transcribed verbatim and subjected to a descriptive phenomenological analysis (see Chapters 5 and 6 for more on this method of analysis). The authors structure their findings into five categories: the unexpected assault, the effects of rape on the self, the disclosure of the rape experience, support agencies and life change. These are then described in detail, supplemented by short quotes from the participants, and linked back to previous literature on the topic. The researchers report how the lives of these men were turned upside down by the rape(s), as they became victims needing to redefine and reconstruct what it means to be a man. Conflicting emotions emerged between relief at surviving and anger at what they – and those they loved – had to suffer. Disclosing the rape to others was particularly problematic but also crucially important in enabling the men to move forward and incorporate the rape, and its meaning for them, into their lives. The authors (pp. 8–9) provide the following vivid summary description of the lived experience of male rape and the consequences it had for the lives of these men:

The experience of rape for the victim involves the ultimate intrusion or invasion of his personal space, an intrusion that is not only physical, violating his bodily space, but an intrusion that runs deeper, so deep that it violates the very essence of his sense of self. The rape is an experience that, through forceful subjugation, humiliation and embarrassment, wrestles control of the victim's life from him and places it into the hands of others. It is an event that destroys who and what the victim was, his old self, shattering it into a million pieces and scattering it to the four corners of the earth ... Through disclosure, life can be filled with vitality once again. Through reframing and recontextualizing the rape, the victim can integrate what happened into a new self that takes back control ... The experience of being a victim of rape, however, remains forever a part of the victim's concept of self. It is recognised as ever present and a permanent threat to well-being and health. For others, the rape remains the all-consuming object of their focus, a thief, an embezzler of life's successes, devouring happiness, healing and opportunity.

## 2.1   What is phenomenology?

Phenomenology (a compound of the Greek words *phainomenon* and *logos*) is the study of human experience and the way in which things are perceived as they appear to consciousness. More broadly, phenomenology is the name given to the philosophical movement beginning with Edmund Husserl (1859–1938) and then developed by Martin Heidegger (1889–1976) and his followers. This movement played a central part in philosophical thinking in the twentieth century and has led to many of the current strands of philosophy active today. This philosophical movement also has had an influence on many disciplines, psychology included, and the intersection of phenomenological philosophy and psychology forms the core of this text.

So, the focus is on people's perceptions of the world – or, famously – their perception of the 'things in their appearing'. We are interested in describing the world as it appears to people, and we need to engage in a variety of processes in order to achieve this. There are a variety of methods to enable us to focus on people's experience and I will outline these later in the book. But first it is important to go back to the beginning and identify the philosophical foundation of these methods. That is, we must begin with phenomenological philosophy itself, and work through some rather difficult ideas, in order to understand the way that phenomenology offers something very different from other philosophical movements (and, hence, how phenomenological psychology offers something very different from other psychological approaches). It is important to point out here that not all phenomenological approaches to psychology engage equally with these concepts. The phenomenological focus on experience is key for all phenomenological approaches, and so the discussion of intentionality (see Section 2.3) and the correlation between the way the world appears and our experience of it (see Section 2.4) are relevant to all methods of phenomenological psychology. However, the different methods of phenomenological psychology outlined in Chapters 6–8 do not all employ the epoché (see Section 2.5), phenomenological reduction (see Section 2.6) or imaginative variation (see Section 2.7) or, if they do, may have reworked them so they are barely recognizable. I will return to the use (or not) of these concepts in Chapters 6–8, where I introduce the different methods; for now, what is important is understanding the way in which these concepts form the basis for a phenomenological way of thinking that is different from our everyday way of thinking about ourselves and the world.

## 2.2 History

Figure 2.1 Edmund Husserl: the founder of phenomenology

Edmund Husserl (see Figure 2.1 and Biography box 2.1), the founder of the branch of philosophy known as phenomenology, was a mathematician by training who set out to establish the meaning of the fundamental concepts employed in the different sciences. To do this, he thought it necessary to identify the essential structures of experience that distinguished the sciences and determined the concepts on which they relied. There would, therefore, be a phenomenological physics, geography, psychology and so on. He aimed to establish firmly the fundamental concepts of these disciplines through a rigorous analysis of the way the objects of study (physical processes, geographical features or psychological phenomena) appeared to us in our experience of them. Psychologists later adopted Husserl's methods. They were interested not in distinguishing the sciences from one another through an understanding of their foundational concepts but rather in understanding specific aspects of our human experience of the world.

## Biography box 2.1 Edmund Husserl

Edmund Husserl was born in 1859 in Prossnitz, Moravia (a part of the Austrian empire). His family were assimilated Jews who had lived in the area for centuries. His father, a draper, was seemingly indifferent to his religion, and the young Husserl did not mix with the local Jewish population. Husserl was schooled locally and completed his school-leaving certificate in 1876. He was not a particularly good student, performing at a rather average level in all subjects except mathematics, for which he showed a particular aptitude. Levinas, a well-known philosopher, recounted a tale, which Husserl himself apparently told, of how when he was a young boy he was given a penknife, which he thought was not sharp enough. In his attempt to achieve the perfect blade, he continued to sharpen the knife until there was nothing left: Husserl thought this symbolized his philosophy, as should become clear throughout this chapter. After completing his high-school certificate, Husserl went on to study astronomy at the University of Leipzig, but he also attended lectures on mathematics and physics. Two years later, he went to Berlin and then a little later the University of Vienna to study further. It was at this point that he started to become more interested in philosophy. He was awarded his doctorate in 1882 for his work on pure mathematics. The key moment in the development of Husserl's philosophy was when, through the encouragement of his friend

Masaryk, he attended the lectures of Brentano and began to study the New Testament. He would later claim that his interest in philosophy came about through his desire to pursue religious questions in a non-dogmatic way. Under the tutelage of Brentano, Husserl began his studies in philosophy proper. He was later to draw on the work of Brentano, particularly when developing his ideas about 'intentionality', a key concept in phenomenology (see Section 2.3).

Husserl produced in excess of 20 major publications before and during his 40 years of teaching and researching at the universities of Göttingen and Freiburg. His work has had enormous impact on the, predominantly, French and German philosophers that followed him in the early twentieth century. His development of phenomenology, outlined in *Logical Investigations* ([1900]1970), sought to return to the origins of all knowledge through an examination of how the world appears to human consciousness. The call to return us 'back to the things themselves' has become the rallying cry of the phenomenological movement, since it is only when we return to the things themselves that we recognize how the world is a *lived experience* rather than an object to be studied. This was a profoundly important matter for Husserl, and for him phenomenology represented a radical beginning for philosophy, where we might start to see the world in a new way, as it really is, through lived experience.

Husserl laid the foundations for the phenomenological movement that followed. With the work of Martin Heidegger the movement took an existential turn, with a central focus on understanding existence, which was realized fully with Jean-Paul Sartre, Simone de Beauvoir and Maurice Merleau-Ponty (discussed in detail in Chapter 3). The work of these philosophers dominated the intellectual movement on the continent of Europe in the middle part of the twentieth century, and their legacy remains with us today. More recently still, we have witnessed the (re)emergence of a hermeneutic turn in phenomenology, where there is a concern with interpretation, with the widespread recognition of the work of Hans-Georg Gadamer and Paul Ricoeur (discussed in detail in Chapter 4). In the following two chapters, I introduce the ideas of some of these key thinkers that followed Husserl. Some built on his work while others radically transformed his project to such an extent that Husserl would probably not recognize the enterprise as phenomenology. However, even among those that have been most radical, the foundational concepts introduced in this chapter still stand, albeit often in a more nuanced form.

## 2.3  Intentionality

*Intentionality* is the key feature of consciousness for Husserl. Here, intentionality is not being used in its usual sense, of intending to do something such as go to the gym or bathe the cat. Instead, it refers to the fact that whenever we are conscious (or aware, if you like), it is always to be conscious (or aware) of something. There is always an object of consciousness, whether that is your cat, another person or an idea. So, for instance, when we see something, it does not appear to be in our heads as a projection on the occipital lobes of our brain, but rather out there in the world. Why is this important to phenomenologists? Well, it strikes to the heart of a longstanding debate in philosophy about the notion of a mind being separate from a body. This debate, while not our primary concern as psychologists, has an impact on what we can say about human nature. In brief, over the past few hundred years of philosophy, most notably following the work of Descartes in the seventeenth century, human consciousness has been understood in a very particular way, where we are aware of ourselves, our own thoughts and feelings, and as such our awareness is directed inwards rather than outwards to the things that lead to such thoughts and feelings. With this Cartesian view of consciousness, our consciousness is not 'of' anything; instead, we are caught in what some philosophers have termed an 'egocentric predicament'. Work in neuroscience appears, upon first inspection, to support such a view of consciousness, since it is obvious (surely?) that thinking must occur inside our heads as a result of changes to our brain states. But in spite of this seemingly obvious understanding of consciousness, it presents us all with a predicament about how, if awareness is inner-directed, we can ever come to have contact with the world outside (hence 'egocentric predicament'). Furthermore, how can we ever come to know the world of another person similarly trapped in their own subjectivity? For phenomenologists, however, there is no 'ghost in the machine', to quote Gilbert Ryle (1949), no mind or spirit inhabiting our body and directing our actions. The focus is, instead, on the way consciousness is turned out on to the world, as it intentionally relates to objects in the world. And it is this consciousness of the world, or, more specifically, the relationship between a person's consciousness and the world, that is the object of study for phenomenological psychologists: the public realm of experience.

Phenomenological psychology is thus not concerned with understanding cognition, looking inside people to try to understand what is going on in their heads, as is traditional in much mainstream psychology. Instead, the intentional correlation leads to a focus on the experience of things in their appearing and the way in which they appear to us as we focus our attention on them in consciousness. The mind is, therefore, no longer understood as something that is private to an individual ('a ghost in a machine') but instead recognized as something intrinsically public. With this, the project of psychology becomes one that is based on what occurs between a person and the world they inhabit, including the relationships between people (intersubjectivity), rather than a search for thinking patterns in the brain. As a result of this idea, phenomenological psychology has a central concern with understanding experience and the way in which a person perceives the world they inhabit (Figure 2.2).

Figure 2.2 How might a city worker's perception of the world vary from that of a member of a remote village?

## 2.4 What is experienced (*noema*) and the way it is experienced (*noesis*)

The central role of *intentionality* in phenomenological theory should become even clearer with an understanding of two new terms: *noema* and *noesis*. In traditional philosophy, much of contemporary psychology and also everyday thinking, there is a distinction made between objects and subjects. The subject is the person that comes to know an object. Somewhat crudely, the subject is the person who thinks, acts and perceives, while the object is a thing that can be perceived, often, though not necessarily, a material thing (such as a chair or desk). Husserl, however, argues that all experience is experience of (something) and, with this, seeks to transform the distinction between subjects and objects into a correlation between what is experienced (the *noema*, or *noematic correlate*) and the way it is experienced (the *noesis*, or *noetic correlate*). This correlation is termed *intentionality*. Part of the power of this understanding is the way in which, as in quantitative methods, correlation does not imply cause but simply a relationship. The distinction is between those things of experience that are present to me (such as my computer present principally through vision and touch) in consciousness and the way in which these things are present to me and can, thus, be detected reflexively (such as the keyboard and screen requiring or demanding my attention as tools to facilitate the writing of this book). However, although it is possible to distinguish between the two poles of intentionality, they remain necessarily related, since, to quote Ihde (1986: 42–43), '... every experiencing has its reference or direction towards what is experienced, and, contrarily, every experienced phenomenon refers to or reflects a mode of experiencing to which it is present.' This relationship exists with all experience and not simply perception. For instance, if I imagine rather than really perceive a future success (e.g. as a Nobel Laureate), then my imaginary visual representation of me receiving this honour also possesses its own noematic qualities. I can describe in detail the setting, what I am wearing, how I feel and the company around me, along with much more of this representation. The relationship between noema – that which is experienced – and noesis – the manner in which something is experienced – is universal and inextricable.

Don Ihde (1986) provides a useful diagrammatic description of the relationship between noema and noesis, which, through his elaboration of this diagram, helpfully distinguishes between a transcendental and existential phenomenology. Transcendental refers to being able to go outside experience (stand outside of ourselves 'to view the world from above'), while existential refers to a need to focus on existence (i.e. our experience of the world as it is lived by us). This distinction is important for phenomenological psychologists, but not only phenomenological philosophers, since it speaks to the limits of what we can know about any phenomenon (epistemology). This distinction will arise again in Chapter 5 (and the following four chapters), when I introduce some of the most important approaches to phenomenological psychology in use in the UK today. I shall, therefore, follow Ihde (1986) closely in the following discussion of the correlation between noema and noesis and the distinction between transcendental and existential phenomenology. Ihde (1986: 44) depicts the relationship between noema and noesis thus:

The arrow serves to emphasize the way in which that which is experienced is always experienced in a particular way. In this diagram, we see what has hitherto been missing in our discussion: the person (the subject, ego or 'I') who experiences that which is experienced. This was very much the position that Husserl took at the beginning of his work. He was, however, later to take a transcendental turn, where the subject (or experiencer) was no longer part of the correlation between noema and noesis and was instead able to make a reflexive move (Ihde, 1986) outside of this relationship to view the process from the outside (or above). This move arose in part from the realization that experience consisted of at least two different aspects. If you imagine driving a car on a motorway, you will almost certainly find the experience of driving is such that you will not be thinking much about the process of driving itself. It is unlikely, unless you are very new to driving, that you will be thinking about needing to change gear or turn the steering wheel. Instead, you will be so engaged with the immediate experience of driving that if you do start to think about the process, you may find that your driving suffers. Much of our experience is of this kind, and this straightforward and very involved experience appears to be very different from the experience of thinking about that experience. Thinking about an experience, whether it is driving or any other experience, is of course still an experience itself, but of a very different kind from an experience where you are actively and immediately immersed in that experience. Although this distinction appears obvious, it can lead to difficulties, for with the reflexive move, where we step outside an immediate experience to reflect on that experience, it is easy to believe that we are stepping outside the intentional correlation between noema and noesis. This would lead us to take a 'God's eye view' (Merleau-Ponty, [1945] 1962) of the experience, with the emergence of a 'transcendental I' or 'transcendental ego'. The belief that these two kinds of experience are fundamentally different has been much criticized, with almost all of those that followed Husserl rejecting this aspect of his philosophy. Instead, the phenomenological movement led by Martin Heidegger took an existential turn, where the 'I' remained embedded in the intentional relationship between noema and noesis and, more generally, existence was understood to be founded on an embodied being-in-the-world (the hyphens indicating the way in which it is impossible to separate our being and the world – but more on this in Chapter 3). All perception of the world is, according to this philosophical perspective, therefore grounded in our body in relation to the environment in which we live.

The place of the 'I' in brackets at the noetic pole of the intentional correlation is important. The self-reflective ego (person) does not occupy the principal position in phenomenology. That is, unlike many forms of humanism (approaches where there is the belief that the person is captain of the ship), the person (who experiences) is not the starting point for investigation of the structure of experience. Instead, the noematic pole is the beginning, as it is the first to stand out within experience. Thus, phenomenological investigation must begin with that which first appears in straightforward experience (description of the immediate experience): hence, the call to the 'things themselves'. If, for instance, we were in a wood looking at a fallen branch, the branch would be the initial focus of experience, standing out within my sensory field: the noema. But this is not all there is to an experience. The second move must be towards the noetic pole and the 'how' of experiencing (the reflexive nature of the experience itself). The noetic is possible only through the possibilities provided by the noema, but the noetic provides the figuration of such possibilities. If I return to the branch in the wood and attend to it in my conscious awareness, then how it appears is revealed. Although it was first present to me simply as a branch, I experience it as a sign of ageing and decay, as a source of fuel and home to myriad creatures of the forest floor: the noesis. The final stage is to move to the 'I' that is experiencing and the way in which it (the person) emerges through reflective experience as a consequence of that experience. The 'I' does not reveal the world in advance of experience, upon interrogation, but instead reveals itself through engagement with all that it encounters in the world. That is, we focus on experience of the world as it is lived by people through their own perceptions of the world and, through this, come to understand the person in the act of perceiving.

## 2.5 Epoché

Phenomenological research in psychology is concerned primarily with first-person accounts of life experiences. A phenomenological investigation seeks to describe these accounts and arrive at an understanding of the meanings and essences (or fundamental structure) of experience. The *epoché* (pronounced ae-pockay) is a Greek word used by Husserl ([1931] 1967) to mean the process by which we attempt to abstain from our presuppositions, those preconceived ideas we might have about the things we are investigating. This is sometimes referred to as bracketing. The core of epoché is doubt: not doubt about everything we say we know, but doubt about the natural attitude or the biases of everyday knowledge. Husserl argued that human existence was characterized by the natural attitude. This is our most basic way of experiencing the world, with all our taken-for-granted assumptions in operation. There is little attempt to critically examine our experience or work through all the available possibilities. Instead, we simply get on with life and live it through the natural attitude. Researchers too will operate within the natural attitude and, indeed, most mainstream psychology does, with a simple adoption of quantitative methods and little critical awareness of the way in which this will simply (re)present experience through the natural attitude (rather than revealing what is hidden beyond the natural attitude). Much as a tennis player instinctively runs to and reaches out to play a shot without consciously reflecting on all of the possible alternative ways to play, we live unthinkingly in the natural attitude most of the time (Figure 2.3). As a consequence, much is hidden from view and there is, therefore, much to be revealed through the application of phenomenological methods, which seek to enable us to set aside the natural attitude or, at the very least, become critically aware of the natural attitude and, therefore, gain a greater critical understanding of the assumptions at play in a person's lived experience.

 The aim of the epoché is to enable the researcher to describe the 'things themselves' and (attempt to) set aside our natural attitude or all those assumptions we

Figure 2.3 When you play music, what would happen if you thought about every move you made?

have about the world around us. This is not an easy thing to do. The challenge is to let the things we experience appear in our consciousness as if for the first time. This freshness of vision requires us to become aware of our presumptions and prejudices and then to examine the object of consciousness from different perspectives. The ability to see phenomena from many different perspectives is crucial in uncovering the essence (or fundamental structure) of the phenomena.

How much we can truly bracket off our preconceptions is debated hotly within phenomenology. Critics of the phenomenological approach have challenged the possibility of ever achieving epoché. There are two broad camps within phenomenology that are split over this issue. The transcendental phenomenologists follow Husserl and argue that the epoché is achievable and that it is possible to transcend your own experience of the world, to see it differently, as another person might. The existential phenomenologists follow Heidegger, Sartre and Merleau-Ponty (see Chapter 3) and believe that you should try to achieve epoché but that you can never truly bracket off all your presuppositions and achieve a 'God's eye view'. They stress the grounded and embodied nature of our being in the world. Some descriptive phenomenology (see Chapters 5 and 6) appears to subscribe to the transcendental position, while others working within this particular perspective (e.g. Ashworth, 2003a,b) adopt a more existential position. Whichever position is taken, the aim remains the same: to attempt to bracket off one's preconceptions about the phenomenon being investigated and to be open to a participant's experience through a return to the things themselves in their appearing to consciousness.

## 2.6 The phenomenological reduction

The phenomenological reduction[1] continues the process initiated with the epoché. There are three key elements to this process: description, horizontalization and verification. Once we have begun to see the things as they appear, with our preconceptions bracketed off, we must now describe what we see, not only in terms of our perception but also in terms of our consciousness. Here we aim to

[1] Husserl actually proposed a series of reductions with some confusion over the nature of all of these. The reduction described here is known as the psychological reduction and is the reduction most often used in phenomenological psychology.

capture and describe the total experience of consciousness in as much detail as possible. Unlike much mainstream psychology, which inhabits the natural attitude and, therefore, seeks to interpret the meaning of experiences, the task is simply to describe the general features of some phenomenon, excluding all elements that are not directly within conscious experience. What this requires is repeated reflection on the phenomenon, examination and elucidation, all the time remembering the rule of horizontalization. In phenomenological psychological research, this would involve, for instance, examining the transcript of an interview (or written description) in an attempt to describe how the world appears to a participant with regard to the particular experience being described. This is where we resist the temptation to produce hierarchies of meaning and, instead, treat all detail with equal value. All detail that we perceive must be described, regardless of how mundane it appears, and no particular perception should be privileged at this stage. One should examine minute details and then the whole, for part – whole relationships can help to identify the essence of the phenomenon. In the natural attitude, we are likely to 'verticalize', by thinking that one thing is more important than another. This is resisted as much as possible in phenomenological psychology when attempting to understand the meaning of an experience for a research participant. The key to the reduction is repeated, looking to uncover the layers of meaning inherent in the phenomenon being perceived. Once this process has been conducted, we might begin to formulate tentative hypotheses about hierarchies of meaning and engage in the process of verification. This is where we take our analysis back to the text to check that it makes sense in this context. Once the phenomenon has been examined in this way, the final stage is to write a complete textural description of the experience.

## 2.7 Imaginative variation

There is another stage that may be employed, following the phenomenological reduction, to further elucidate meaning from an experience. Imaginative variation (more properly, 'imaginative free variation') is the process of approaching the phenomenon being experienced from different perspectives by imaginatively varying features of the phenomenon. The idea is a simple one but nonetheless powerful for that. The aim is to imaginatively vary elements of our experience so the essence may come into view and the contingent fade away. So, for instance, one might ask a person to describe the experience of being a patient in a hospital and vary the doctors and nurses such that the doctors become nurses, and vice versa. How would this change the experience of being a patient and enable the participant to perceive the essence of this particular aspect of their experience? I think it would probably enable the participant to see how the profession is gendered but also, more subtly, probably how they give up power differently to doctors and nurses. That is, they become passive recipients of treatments acted upon them with doctors but more active participants in their own care with nurses. It is also likely to show up the way – for the patient – in which nurses appear to operate collectively and doctors singularly, leading to the further embodiment of power in the doctor figure. The possibilities are endless, since one can move away from simply naturalistic variations and, instead, move into the realm of fantasy while retaining that which is being perceived (Figure 2.4). As you can imagine, imaginative variation is potentially a very powerful technique for enabling us to uncover the layers of meaning and invariant properties of an experience. In phenomenological psychology, demographic characteristics lend themselves particularly to this kind of work. But one need not stop with simply reversing gender (or, indeed, attempting to do away with gender altogether), race, class or sexuality. It does require practice to free oneself from the natural attitude to the phenomenon being investigated and imagine other ways of seeing. However, anything and everything is possible if only we are able to see.

**Figure 2.4** Imagine the police dressed as clowns – what impact might this have on the meaning of this image (especially when thinking about the relationship between the police and protestors)?

## 2.8 Essences

The move to identifying essences in phenomenology represents a move from description of individual experience to exploration of the structure underlying such experience. Husserl believed that it was possible on the basis of a single experience to identify the universal structure(s) (essence(s)) underlying the experience. The process of moving from the individual to the universal was termed *eidetic intuition*, which Husserl thought was a spontaneous process in everyday experience. The concept of essences is a controversial one, and some feel Husserl never developed this aspect of phenomenology fully. However, it does represent an important move (for some) from description of individual experience to description of the structures of experience more generally. Although Husserl believed it was possible to discern the essence(s) of an experience from any individual experience, phenomenological psychologists have tended to attempt to discern essences through multiple descriptions from a number of participants. This is effectively a sort of sampling imaginative variation, where the true nature of the essence is revealed through an examination of the form of the experience under investigation from a number of different perspectives.

Husserl thought the ability to identify essences was something that requires considerable effort, since it is very easy to slip back into the *natural attitude*, where our everyday way of seeing the world colours our experience. It is important to recognize any experience not as an individual piece of information but rather as an expression of the essence itself. The focus on essences, in psychological terms at least, represents an attempt to explore those elements that come to make up all experience in such a way that we overcome naturalistic prejudice, where phenomenological exploration of essences is confused with introspection (where we simply look inside ourselves for an understanding of psychology). Essences emerge not through some sense of inner intuition but through rigorous examination and reflection on experience itself as given to consciousness among the participants in an investigation. Epoché, the phenomenological reduction and imaginative variation, described above, provide the method for identifying essences and, hence, the methods for phenomenological psychology, which will be described in detail in Chapters 5–8.

## Summary

Phenomenological psychology is an approach to psychology that draws directly on the phenomenological tradition of philosophy. This involves a focus on human experience and how the things that are perceived appear to the person. Understanding experience involves the psychologist engaging in a series of processes designed to generate rich descriptions of people's lived experiences of the world. With this comes recognition of the way the researcher may have preconceptions about a topic and how it is important to reflect on these and attempt to bracket them off. Phenomenological philosophy began with Edmund Husserl, writing in the late nineteenth century. One of the most important concepts in this branch of philosophy is intentionality, which refers to the fact that whenever we are conscious, we are always conscious of something. This is important for the way it emphasizes the need to attend to people's experience of 'the things in their appearing' and how they appear to consciousness, rather than to search inside people's heads for cognitions. The consequence of intentionality is a move away from a distinction between subjects and objects and, instead, a focus on what is experienced (noema) and the way it is experienced (noesis). Epoché (sometimes referred to as 'bracketing') is a Greek word referring to the process by which we attempt to abstain from our presuppositions and see the 'things in their appearing', as if for the first time. This involves an attempt to set aside the natural attitude, our everyday way of seeing the world. This aspect of phenomenological philosophy is, however, hotly debated, with different views about how possible it is to bracket off preconceptions about an experience. The phenomenological reduction continues the process initiated with the epoché and involves three key elements: description, horizontalization and verification. A further stage may follow the reduction; this is imaginative variation, which is the process of approaching the phenomenon being investigated from different perspectives by imaginatively varying key features. The aim for Husserl, and those phenomenological psychologists adhering to this branch of phenomenology, is to identify the essence of phenomena: the invariant structures underpinning the thing as it appears to perception. Phenomenological psychologists have taken the key ideas from Husserl in attempting to understand human nature. Those phenomenological psychologists most faithful to Husserlian philosophy remain committed to description, epoché and the phenomenological reduction and are discussed in detail in Chapter 6.

## Further reading

Ihde, D. (1986). *Experimental Phenomenology: An Introduction*. Albany, NY: SUNY Press. This is an excellent introductory book, which, through the medium of visual perception, introduces many of the fundamentals of phenomenological philosophy. A very good starting point for the reader wishing to get to grips with the practical nature of phenomenological philosophy.

Kearney, R. (1994). *Modern Movements in European Philosophy*, 2nd edn. Manchester: Manchester University Press. A beautifully written and very clear book providing coverage of the thought of many of the key figures in the phenomenological movement. The book includes chapters on Husserl, Heidegger, Sartre, Merleau-Ponty and Ricoeur, as well as many other continental philosophers.

Moran, D. (2000). *Introduction to Phenomenology*. London: Routledge. An extremely comprehensive if somewhat dense book providing coverage of the thought of many, although not all, phenomenological philosophers.

Sokolowski, R. (2000). *Introduction to Phenomenology*. Cambridge: Cambridge University Press. An interesting book that seeks to introduce phenomenology without much reference to the philosophers upon which the ideas are based. This makes the book very readable, although really only appropriate as an adjunct to another text that provides detail of which philosopher's work relates to which idea.

# 3 Existentialism and phenomenology

## Chapter aims

■ Describe the existential turn in phenomenological philosophy

■ Outline the fundamentals of existential philosophy

■ Introduce key existential ideas, including: lifeworld, *Dasein*, temporality, facticity, mood, being-towards-death, care, authenticity, being-with, discourse, bad faith, body-subject

Husserl ([1936] 1970) prefigured the existential turn in phenomenological philosophy through the concept of the *lifeworld* (*lebenswelt*), which he saw as the basis of all philosophy and human sciences research.[1] The lifeworld is the world as concretely lived, which should be the foundation for all phenomenological psychological investigation. Once again, we see not only how experience is the focus but also how this is grounded in our everyday lived experience, experience in which meaning is prioritized, even though it is invariably hidden through the natural attitude. Uncovering this meaning, therefore, requires that we engage in methods of phenomenology (such as the psychological reduction) to enable us to set aside the natural attitude. Husserl's own work was contradictory, and the emphasis on the lifeworld in his later writing appears to represent a very different position from his earlier transcendental position, where he held the belief that it is possible to stand outside of lived experience – one's own subjective position and the natural attitude – to see things as they really are. However, even late in his writing, where the lifeworld was most central, Husserl still argued that it was possible to transcend our subjectivity, to bracket off aspects of consciousness and reveal the world as it really is. Phenomenological psychologists of every kind are well aware of these issues, with many (e.g. Dahlberg, Drew and Nyström, 2001) seeing the phenomenological reduction as an imperfect process that can never enable pure transcendence, as Husserl believed, but still a valuable method for uncovering at least some of the ways in which the natural attitude conceals our understanding of human nature.

[1] Merleau-Ponty ([1945] 1962) thought that the focus on the lifeworld marked a late existential turn in Husserl's philosophy. However, more recent commentators disagree and simply see this as another layer of meaning, uncovered through the reductions (e.g. Moran 2000).

Husserl's transcendental phenomenology came under sustained critique, principally from philosophers who were themselves once his own students. This led initially to the existential turn in phenomenology, a movement that was to radically supersede the work of Husserl and result in the rise to fame of Sartre and de Beauvoir in the 1950s and 1960s. Later still was the hermeneutic turn, which resulted in a particular interest in interpretation and language – more of which in Chapter 4. The most significant of the existential critics was undoubtedly Martin Heidegger (1889–1976). His work has had a lasting impact on phenomenology and philosophy more generally. However, although Heidegger was undoubtedly the most important philosopher to follow Husserl, and the first real existentialist, the roots of existentialism can be traced back much further to the philosophy of Søren Kierkegaard (1813–1855) and Friedrich Nietzsche (1844–1900).

Husserl's phenomenology clearly provides methods that can be imported into psychology, but the relationship between existentialism, phenomenology and psychology is a little more complicated. The existentialists built on the phenomenological foundations provided by Husserl but were much less concerned with the development of a new philosophical method.[2] Instead, they sought to address fundamental questions about our very existence and the form that this takes. Heidegger, in particular, was not terribly concerned, at least in his earlier work, with what we can say we know about human nature (*epistemology*) but instead was concerned with establishing the truth about our very existence (*ontology*); as such, it is harder to see the relevance of his ideas for phenomenological psychology. In spite of this, Heidegger's work does have implications for both philosophy and psychology, and I hope that you will gain a sense of the implications in the following section. In particular, Heidegger's work opened up phenomenology to interpretation through language in a way that was not seen before. The work of the hermeneutic phenomenologists Gadamer and Ricoeur (discussed in detail in Chapter 4) built on the work of Heidegger in a way that has radical implications for phenomenological psychology (discussed further in Chapters 5 and 8). The existentialists who immediately followed Heidegger – Sartre (1905–1980), Merleau-Ponty (1908–1961) and de Beauvoir (1908–1986) – were, however, concerned primarily with understanding the human condition, and their thought has impacted directly on some contemporary forms of phenomenological psychology, most notably the Sheffield School variation of phenomenological psychology (see Chapters 5 and 6).

In spite of the differences between the existentialists and Husserl, there are also some very important commonalities. Most importantly, the existential phenomenologists all retain the idea from Husserl that human existence is first and foremost *intentional*. The *natural attitude*, of course, serves to hide the essence of this experiencing, and this is where we witness the initial difference between

[2] Of course, Husserl was not simply trying to develop a new method of doing philosophy: he wanted phenomenology to be a radical new beginning to philosophy itself as it returned to its foundations. However, in the process of establishing new foundations for a wide variety of disciplines, he developed his phenomenological method, which is clearly and simply applicable to psychology.

Husserl, who believed it possible to (totally) bracket off the natural attitude, and the existentialists, who thought we were too practically engaged with the world – through the lifeworld – to be able to make such an abstraction. They did, however, all agree that it was certainly necessary to bracket off the scientific natural attitude, dominant in contemporary psychology, if we were to be able to really describe the 'things in their appearing'. So, although it may not be possible to stand outside all of our everyday ways of living in the lifeworld, we are at least able to set aside aspects of the natural attitude, which should include those where we assume a scientific approach will reveal truths about human nature.

In the remainder of this chapter, I provide a brief, and necessarily selective, overview of the work of Heidegger, Sartre and Merleau-Ponty. There are many other significant figures in existential philosophy of course, but the aim here is not to provide the definitive guide to existentialism. Instead, the aim is to provide sufficient theoretical understanding of existentialism to enable the reader to appreciate the existential development of phenomenology and the possible relevance this might have for the practice of phenomenological psychology. But first, I trace the roots of existentialism back to Kierkegaard and Nietzsche and in doing so aim to provide a better understanding of the fundamental issues at stake for the existential movement as a whole.

## 3.1 Fundamentals of existentialism

The foundations of existentialism can be traced back to the work of the Danish philosopher Søren Kierkegaard (1813–1855) (Figure 3.1), his observations about the human struggle for freedom and our need to accept this struggle as an essential part of the human condition. Although there is considerable difficulty in defining who is or is not an existential philosopher, with some central to the project (such as Heidegger) refusing the label themselves, existential philosophy of whatever persuasion is concerned fundamentally with the human struggle for freedom, identified by Kierkegaard, not in some abstract way, but instead through a practical lived approach to philosophy. That is, existentialism should not be simply an intellectual activity but should be something we live and, through living it, learn to live anew. This double concern with freedom and the need to practically engage with philosophy is central to all those in the existential movement since Kierkegaard. The other common strand that can be seen in existentialism is a methodological one: the phenomenological method of Husserl (outlined in Chapter 2). Although this method was (theoretically) transformed by Heidegger, Sartre and Merleau-Ponty, as will become clear in this chapter, it still remains at the heart of existentialism.

**Figure 3.1 Søren Kierkegaard: a founding thinker on existentialism**

I share Warnock's (1970) belief that it is impossible to understand the philosophical project of Kierkegaard without some understanding of his life. Kierkegaard was brought up in a strictly religious household, which he found suffocating. As he grew up, he threw off the straitjacket of this fundamentalist religion and instead sought pleasure and joy. Following this, he lived a very moral life, believing he had found a set of universal moral principles for himself and others. Then, in 1838, Kierkegaard converted to Christianity, finding a new faith in God. These stages were later codified by Kierkegaard as three stages thought to be general to all human development. The first stage, where one is apparently free and enjoying the good life, was termed the *aesthetic* stage. For Kierkegaard, the freedom one perceives in this stage is illusory, as too is the freedom in the next, *ethical*, stage. Here, one is not choosing one's own way of living but subscribing to human (moral) norms and systems. It was only with his conversion to Christianity and discovery of faith in the *religious* stage that Kierkegaard believed he had truly found a way of throwing off the humanistic illusion and discovering what it meant to be free. This developmental model was not simply one of progression through the aesthetic to the ethical to the religious, however. And, indeed, the notion that one needs to reach the religious stage to be free is highly contentious. The key aspect of this stage model is the need to choose to move to a higher stage, to choose to live beyond the norms and expectations of the masses. One cannot be persuaded to be free; one can only choose to live in such a way and, upon making such a choice – not simply an intellectual (rational) choice but rather a true (irrational) – felt – choice about how one wishes to live – recognize the very different way of seeing the world that comes from living free of the constraints and expectations of others.

Kierkegaard's existential mission was to free his readers from the illusion of what he termed *objectivity*. Objectivity, here, refers to the human condition where we accept, and indeed welcome, rules governing the way we live. Anything that is perceived to have a single truth is objective, hence the scientific model of knowing, common to much contemporary psychology, which attempts to predict and control is rejected, as is a morality founded on universal principles, be they religious or legal. Objectivity is most acute in the ethical stage, where people are bound by rules, codified and passed down from teacher to pupil, in effect being nothing more than observers on life, failing to live creatively and with passion. *Subjectivity*, by contrast, involves each person living as an individual, making his or her own choices in life, 'living in inwardness'. But this is not easy, for it is hard to throw off the shackles of objectivity, where one is lost in the mass, and instead face the harsh reality of freedom and choice. With subjectivity, faith is no longer a matter of dogmatism, but what an individual chooses to believe. Similarly, science cannot provide the answers, for the answers it provides are simply illusions based on an objective way of living, neither relevant nor applicable to the concrete individuality of existence that comes from living subjectively. This is because science employs an objective technology, based on the analysis of objects rather than subjects, focused only on what is rational and obscuring the irrational. Humanity, in its highest forms, according to Kierkegaard, involves each person engaging in projects in which they must choose their own path. The psychological project must, therefore, also be radically transformed from one of natural science, grounded in objectivity, to one of human science, grounded in subjectivity.

Nietzsche (1844–1900), like Kierkegaard before him, fought against objectivity and the myth that there were indisputable and identifiable truths in the world. Starting with the principle that God was dead, Nietzsche argued that all meanings are impositions that we make on the world rather than natural discoveries of meaning in the world. This means there is no inherent meaning in life but, instead, the human possibility of creating meaning: there are no facts but only perspectives. With the death of God, we no longer have solid foundations, based on religion, upon which to draw but must create our own path to realize our own potential. The supposed neutrality of science was a particular target for Nietzsche, for even here, he argued, it is impossible to be value-free and simply build up a body of knowledge that will be true for all time. Even the most basic descriptions of the world involve an evaluation of some kind. When, for instance, a psychologist investigates crowd behaviour, implicit in their work is the desire to understand and then control the crowd. And this is the key to the way human beings conceptualize the world, through the desire to control and dominate the world in order to make it more manageable and better suited to their needs: the *will to power*. So, Nietzsche, like Kierkegaard, emphasized freedom and choice, and the necessity to break free of the illusion of objectivity, particularly perpetuated by the language of science. Instead, they both argue that we need to face the anxiety that comes from such uncertainty and live with passion. Psychology also, therefore, needs to become a much less certain (scientific) discipline, recognizing the partial and contingent nature of the knowledge that it produces.

## 3.2  Martin Heidegger

Figure 3.2 Martin Heidegger: a key figure in existential philosophy

Heidegger's (see Biography box 3.1) masterpiece is *Being and Time* ([1927] 1962), and it is here that we best see his critique of Husserl and presentation of his own existential project. Heidegger built on the hermeneutic tradition, which I will talk about in much more detail in Chapter 4, which is concerned with the interpretation of text. In *Being and Time*, Heidegger sought to examine what is – that is, what exists. In the process, he argued that it was not possible for the philosopher to investigate the things in their appearing and identify their essence in a neutral or detached way. For Heidegger, all people, philosophers included, are inseparable from the world they inhabit and, therefore, it is not possible to bracket off one's way of seeing and identify the essence of a phenomenon, as Husserl proposed. Instead, our way of existing must be seen in its historical and cultural context and understood with due regard to the role of language – it must be interpreted and not simply described. So, we still have a phenomenological method, but one that is concerned less with universals – essences of the things in their

## Biography box 3.1   Martin Heidegger

Martin Heidegger (1889–1976) is one of the most important philosophers of the twentieth century. His work has had a profound impact on philosophy and a number of other disciplines. His life, and by implication his work, is not by any means an uncontroversial one. He was born in 1889 in Messkirch in Germany. He was destined for the priesthood, with his early education a preparation for such a vocation. His life course changed dramatically upon being presented with a copy of Brentano's 1862 book *On the Several Senses of Being in Aristotle* by the headmaster of a local school. This book, described by Heidegger as his 'rod and staff', was to be the catalyst for a career in philosophy as he moved from this text to the original Greek texts of Aristotle. Heidegger went on to study theology at Freiburg University while attending the diocesan seminary and here continued his exploration into the meaning of Being, following Brentano. It was also during this time that he discovered hermeneutics – the study of interpretation – through the work of Schleiermacher. After periods of ill-health, which would dog him his entire life, Heidegger returned to study philosophy at Freiburg, gaining his doctorate in 1913. Upon the outbreak of the First World War, he was called up for military service, but he was quickly discharged due to ill-health and instead had to work as a censor in the post office in Freiburg. Heidegger began his study of phenomenology proper when Husserl gained the Chair of Philosophy in Freiburg in 1916 and he became Husserl's assistant in 1919, beginning to lecture to great critical acclaim. It was not until 1927 that Heidegger published *Being and Time*, following pressure to increase his publication output to secure a chair himself. During the years in which he worked with Husserl, their differences became apparent, with Heidegger deeply critical of the transcendental nature of Husserl's phenomenological project, preferring to focus on the lived reality of existence. Husserl, by contrast, thought Heidegger was engaged in

philosophical anthropology and had failed to realize the importance of the transcendental reduction. Over the following years, however, it was Heidegger's position that was to dominate in most philosophical circles. In 1928, Heidegger succeeded Husserl, gaining the Chair in Philosophy at Freiburg University.

It is important to spend a little time discussing Heidegger's involvement in National Socialism. A lot has been written on the involvement of Heidegger in the Nazi Party, and there has been considerable discussion of the relationship between this aspect of his life and his philosophy. There is no doubt about his active involvement in the National Socialist Party and his direct personal involvement in some appalling actions while Rector of Freiburg University, in spite of later attempts to provide rather facile justifications for his actions. Suffice it to say that his role in National Socialism and failure to publicly apologize following the war need to be condemned but should not blind us to his philosophical genius. He demonstrated considerable human failure during and after the Second World War, and this should not be forgotten, but it should not be grounds alone to refuse to engage with his philosophy. Some have gone further to suggest that his philosophy itself demonstrates sympathy with the cause of National Socialism, but I think this position requires the reader to adopt a very particular critical position with regard to the text. My own approach is to bracket off his life when reading his philosophy and to fuse my political horizons with those of the text. That is, although the text provides the horizon of my reading experience, this is only in relation to the fusion (a concept from Gadamer) of this with – a critical awareness of – the horizon of the experience I bring to bear to it when attempting to appropriate the meaning. This position should become clearer when I discuss the work of Gadamer and Ricoeur, the hermeneutic turn in phenomenology, and the appropriation of meaning from text in the next chapter.

## Biography box 2.1  Martin Heidegger

Heidegger's later work was concerned primarily with language as the 'house of Being', having moved from a focus on Being related to *Dasein* (see below) towards Being in general, and in particular poetry as the key to understanding Being. He thought poetry transcended the technical forms of speaking that were beginning to dominate, providing an alternative way of revealing the truth of Being. Heidegger also forged a professional alliance with Medard Boss, conducting the *Zollikon Seminars* in Zurich in 1949, which were concerned with developing an existential approach to psychoanalysis – *Daseinanalysis*. This method of psychoanalysis continues to this day, mostly in Switzerland and Austria, and, in part, led to the development of *existential psychotherapy*, an increasingly popular approach to psychotherapy in the UK and continental Europe (e.g. Cohn, 1997; Spinelli, 2005; van Deurzen-Smith, 1997). Heidegger died in 1976, and his legacy – philosophical, psychological and personal – has remained controversial to this day.

appearing – and, instead, concerned more with interpreting the meaning of the things in their appearing from a position that is always grounded in the things themselves. The philosopher can no longer adopt a God's eye view (as Merleau-Ponty would later say) but must be content with a position in relation to whatever it is they want to understand.

Heidegger has become renowned for the introduction of an entirely new vocabulary in his philosophy and some of the development of new vocabulary is to avoid the misunderstandings that come from reusing a word that already has widespread currency – such as *intentionality* and some of the new vocabulary is due to Heidegger wishing to trace back the meaning of key terms to their Greek origins. This new language can, especially at first, lead the reader to find Heidegger's thinking unbearably perplexing. This feeling, however, can be reduced if one approaches his writing phenomenologically, as if it is appearing for the first time, ready to reveal the truth. Much of it requires an initial 'leap of faith', but once this move has been negotiated successfully, it no longer appears so difficult and, indeed, it becomes difficult to think of the world as you once did.

It is important to begin by highlighting the distinction drawn by Heidegger between the *ontic* and the *ontological*, since this is something that impacts directly on the kind of claims one might make as a result of carrying out phenomenological psychology. Ontological is a term that is familiar to some psychologists and refers simply to Being or existence, with *ontology* being the philosophical study of Being (existence). The *ontic*, by contrast, refers to the particular facts about entities that exist, which are, for Heidegger at least, only those creatures concerned with existence: human beings or, rather, *Dasein*. Most importantly, the ontic is that which can be revealed through empirical investigation, while the ontological is that which can be revealed only through philosophy. No matter how much we empirically investigate *Dasein* we will never be able to say anything more about the ontological status of *Dasein*: This can be achieved only through philosophy, and this was the heart of Heidegger's work. However, we can learn about the facts of existence, or the ontic qualities of *Dasein*, through empirical investigation, and this is the project of phenomenological psychology that is at the heart of this book.

One of the most important concepts developed by Heidegger is *Dasein* (often translated as being-in-the-world), a German word that in everyday use means 'existence' but literally (etymologically speaking) means 'being there' and that has come to stand for man, the person (or subject) in the Heideggerian philosophical project. Heidegger uses the term *Dasein* instead of man (person or subject) in order to allow us to look with fresh eyes at what it means to exist, a uniquely human problem, and also to emphasize a number of features of existence that may be obscured when using a term such as 'man', 'person' or 'subject'. I briefly outline a number of these key features of Dasein, drawing principally on Kearney (1994), that Heidegger argued were fundamental to human existence, below.

### 3.2.1 Temporality

As might be expected given the title of Heidegger's masterpiece (*Being and Time*), temporality – that is, our experience of time – is at the heart of what it means to exist. This is because our understanding in the present always involves our past and a projection of our future: *Dasein* is always projecting itself towards future possibilities. That is, we are not an object such as a stone but rather what we are to become, for here existence is not a noun (such as man or woman) but a verb (*Dasein*), since existence for humanity at least requires us to create it rather than simply live it. We are primarily a dynamic (verb-like), being engaged in the act of 'selving', if you like, and only later might we define ourselves as noun-like (as an intellectual, a working-class man, a psychologist). We are meaning-making machines, always making sense of ourselves and others, even if this is not always in conscious awareness (Figure 3.3).

### 3.2.2 Facticity

Although we create ourselves, there are limits to these choices, since we are thrown into a world that predates us and that limits our possible ways of being: the *facticity* of our existence. Physical, psychological and social factors, our historical situatedness, will all serve to limit our possibilities, but even here these factors do not determine what *Dasein* might or might not be, since *Dasein* can make of this facticity what it chooses.

### 3.2.3 Mood

*Mood*, for Heidegger, refers to a pre-reflective way of experiencing the world – in anguish, fear or guilt, for instance – which is not a psychological phe-

Figure 3.3 Think about how your (and others') conception of yourself changes over time

nomenon first and foremost but rather an ontological phenomenon that results from an awareness of the fear of non-being. Anguish, for instance, frequently experienced as depression, is not simply something that colours our way of living as a result of negative life events but rather is the result of becoming aware of the nothingness of existence. The important issue here is how our experience of the world is first and foremost lived pre-reflectively through a mood and only later understood through reflection.

### 3.2.4 Being-towards-death

The ultimate limit to existence is, of course, death, and this marks the end of all human possibilities. We do not determine the beginning or end of our lives, being thrown into existence at birth with death at the end. Our experience is, therefore, always subject to an awareness of the inescapably finite nature of life and the end of our possibilities. Most of the time we conceal this from ourselves, but when we become aware of our being-towards-death, often through some disruption to our everyday way of living – through bereavement, divorce or unemployment, for instance – we experience anguish (*Angst*) or anxiety, the most fundamental of our moods. But although we cannot choose the circumstances of our birth or death, we can choose how we will face these ontological givens. It is this choice and awareness of the ontological limits on existence that lead to anxiety. If you think of your own life, I am sure there have been difficult choices that brought with them great anxiety: choices to leave a job, to have children, to split up with a partner. Anxiety is exacerbated further through the realization that there is no foundation to life, as Nietzsche argued with his proclamation of the death of God. Life is not intrinsically meaningful and, as such, we alone have the responsibility to make life meaningful as we face the dizzying anxiety of knowing the limits of existence.

### 3.2.5 Care

All being-in-the-world revolves around us being involved in the world, actively engaged in other things and people. This *care* – resulting from *Dasein's* concern for things in the world – stands in contrast to objects that are simply *present-at-hand* and the way in which these things simply occupy space rather than live (or exist) in space. For all people, the facticity of their existence necessitates some concern or care. Of course, there may be times when we do not operate so fully in this mode, for instance when bored or daydreaming, but these are, according to Heidegger, deficient modes of concern where there is less engagement with the things that matter in the world.

### 3.2.6 Authenticity

Authenticity is when *Dasein* no longer takes the world for granted but, instead, recognizes the fundamental reality of being that is being-towards-death and the need to engage in the possibilities of existence. Most of the time, *Dasein* exists inauthentically, hiding from the reality of being-towards-death, through the security that comes from being part of the 'They' (*Das Man*). Acting in the proscribed ways that come with being part of the crowd results in a fixity where *Dasein* no longer lives its possibilities. This fixity obscures the reality of death and in so doing reduces the anguish of existence. But such inauthenticity also results in the foreclosure of possible ways of being and the loss of care for existence itself.

### 3.2.7 Being-with

Up until now, the emphasis has clearly been on the qualities demonstrated by *Dasein* in a seemingly singular form. However, later in *Being and Time* Heidegger is keen to stress the inherently social nature of *Dasein*. For all being-in-the-world is in fact *being-in-the-world-with-others*, all experience is in relation to other people. If I buy a shirt, then I will have bought the shirt from someone; and even if I did not and instead embraced e-commerce, I would still be in relation through communication and also through simply wearing something that someone else has designed. Playing the piano is similarly not solitary, since I will have had to learn how to play and/or be playing music composed by someone else. Even when other people are not around and being engaged with directly, I must acknowledge my relationship to others when I do something or use something (Figure 3.4). For Heidegger, we are inescapably social beings, always in relation with the other, always *being-with* (or *Mitsein*).

### 3.2.8 Discourse

*Discourse*, for Heidegger, is the way in which the meaning of the world is manifested for *Dasein*. The world and, of course, our being-in-the-world is, in effect,

**Figure 3.4** Even though this boy is alone, he is in a social world – someone designed the clothes he is wearing, someone created the hay bale and, most importantly, his experience to date has been in the context of other people

intelligible through discourse, or as Heidegger (1978: 217) would later say, 'Language is the house of Being'. The concern with speech acts (or the functional qualities of language), common to many analytical philosophers (and, indeed, many contemporary psychologists such as *discourse, analysts*), are for Heidegger merely one part of discourse with the more fundamental part the way in which discourse comes to disclose Being. In his later writing, the distinction between language as a prosaic medium designed to simply and effectively communicate information and poetic language offering the possibility of disclosing our being-in-the-world becomes particularly important. Scientific language is designed to make language unambiguous, able to simply and effectively communicate facts about the world, a perfect system of representation. This is a problem for Heidegger, however, since language becomes dead as soon as it is fixed (that is, separated from a speaker or author creatively making it meaningful), narrow and rigid, and, indeed, even here it cannot have meaning outside history. Even the simplest meanings change through history, even when codified in scientific discourse. He argues for the poetic as a way of disclosing the world and transforming existence. Here, poetry is more fundamental because it is creative, metaphorical and novel, authentic if you will, revealing or *unconcealing* more about the world than can ever be revealed through scientific (or artificial) language.

<table>
<tr><td>3.3</td><td>The later existentialists – Sartre, de Beauvoir and Merleau-Ponty</td></tr>
</table>

## 3.3 The later existentialists – Sartre, de Beauvoir and Merleau-Ponty

The existential phenomenological – or simply existential movement, as it became – reached its zenith in the middle of the twentieth century with Jean-Paul Sartre, Simone de Beauvoir (Figure 3.5) and Maurice Merleau-Ponty. These philosophers built on Heidegger's work and further focused attention on understanding existence: hence the term 'existential'. Their work was phenomenological, following in the tradition of Husserl, but was concerned principally with theorizing existence itself. All three emphasized different aspects of existence, though de Beauvoir's work – for instance, *The Second Sex* ([1949] 1997) – is not (generally) thought to be concerned directly with existential philosophy, and for this reason her work will not be considered here. De Beauvoir worked with Sartre her entire life, and there is some debate about her involvement in Sartre's philosophy. Regardless, de Beauvior is recognized in her own right for her work on what it means to be a woman, particularly *The Second Sex*, a brilliant philosophical anthropology of that which is *Other*. I provide a little more detail on the work of Sartre and Merleau-Ponty but would recommend the interested reader explore some of the further reading suggested at the end of this chapter. In spite of the brevity of this coverage, it will provide enough of an insight to enable the reader to understand how these philosophers might have something to say to those of us carrying out phenomenological research in psychology.

Figure 3.5 Jean-Paul Sartre and Simone de Beauvoir: two of the central figures in the existential movement

## 3.4 Sartre, choice and the emptiness of existence

Sartre ([1943] 2003) emphasized the empty nature of consciousness in his magnum opus *Being and Nothingness*. For him, there were no essential qualities to consciousness and human existence is freedom itself. The 'nothingness' of *Being and Nothingness* refers to the emptiness or 'no-thing-ness' of human existence. We are not objects, things, to be studied and measured as we might study and measure objects in the natural sciences. Instead, similar to Heidegger's notion of *Dasein*, consciousness (the self) is not a thing that we are or have but something we constantly create through our lived experience: that is, we do not have freedom but are freedom embodied. We are free to choose who and what we want to be within the limits of the *facticity* of our existence. Sartre stressed the embodied nature of this freedom, since it is only through our bodies that we are able to act on the world. The relationship between consciousness and the world was not causal, however, and Sartre was keen to stress this point, also, in contrast to much of traditional psychology, noting that consciousness was not determined causally by the past. This rupture in causality was because Sartre believed that our present selves were separated from the past by nothingness. We are not beings with a core self, continuing over time relatively unchanged, but rather an emptiness striving to create a sense of self. As a consequence, given identical circumstances, a person could have acted differently. For Sartre ([1943] 1956: 439), humanity is 'condemned to be free', since even to decide not to choose is a choice and no other person, no matter what the circumstances, can control the free will of another.

The facticity of our existence does, of course, place limits on our freedom. So freedom is always freedom bounded by the facticity of our existence, whether that be through bodily limits, the influence of the past or current social relationships. But, even here, it is possible to choose what meaning these limits have, so the past or present never determines who or what someone may be. Because human beings are free, they must also take responsibility for their actions. Being born into poverty may place limits on what a person can achieve, but it is up to that person to decide whether to live their poverty or fight to escape from it. Sartre never suggests this is easy, and a person may fail, but it is always possible to choose and, in so doing, at least strive to live differently.

Sartre believed that we are conscious of our freedom and faced constantly with the anguish that this entails. Because of this, we make efforts to hide ourselves from the anguish, which follows from our freedom and responsibility, through the use of *bad faith* (*mauvaise foi*). Bad faith is self-deception through a desire to pretend that we are not human beings, condemned to be free, but rather like non-conscious objects that never have to choose or justify what they are. In the process, we may, therefore, assume a particular role, as wife, as victim, as boss, to hide ourselves, through the pretence of having no choice, from the anguish at the heart of existence. Sartre ([1943] 2003: 78–79) himself provides some vivid examples of such self-deception, including this classic:

> Take the example of a woman who has consented to go out with a particular man for the first time. She knows very well the intentions which the man who is speaking to her cherishes regarding her. She knows also that it will be necessary sooner or later for her to make a decision. But she does not want to realize the urgency; she concerns herself only with what is respectful and discreet in the attitude of her companion... Now suppose he takes her hand. This act of her companion risks changing the situation by calling for an immediate decision. To leave her hand there is to consent in herself to flirt, to engage herself. To withdraw it is to break the troubled and unstable harmony which gives the hour its charm. The aim is to postpone the moment of decision as long as possible. We know what happens next; the young woman leaves her hand there, but she *does not notice* that she is leaving it. She draws her companion up to the most lofty regions of sentimental speculation; she speaks of Life, of her life, she shows herself in her essential aspect – a personality, a consciousness. And during this time the divorce of the body from the soul is accomplished; the hand rests inert between the warm hands of her companion – neither consenting nor resisting – a thing. We shall say that this woman is in bad faith.

Sartre also believed that each person has an original theme, or *project*, which guides his or her life. We may choose to change this project but, unlike many everyday choices, this is not easy since it represents our fundamental way of seeing ourselves. Our fundamental project, Sartre believes, is formed early in childhood as a vague project of self-realization. The child wants to be an artist, academic, victim or hero and begins to build a life in pursuit of that project. But this fundamental project is something fashioned out of *bad faith*, as something we have to be rather than something we choose to do. Furthermore, Sartre believed that most people spend their entire lives seeking to achieve these fundamental projects, all the time evading the choice and responsibility that recognition of their freedom would entail.

## 3.5 Merleau-Ponty and the body-subject

In spite of the greater fame of Sartre and de Beauvoir and their greater philosophical reputations, it is Merleau-Ponty (Figure 3.6) who has had the greatest direct impact on phenomenological psychology. It is his version of existentialism that underpins much of the work of contemporary phenomenological psychologists. This is probably due, at least in part, to the fact that Merleau-Ponty was not only a philosopher but also a psychologist, occupying the same chair in child psychology that Piaget did. He remained committed to Husserl's phenomenological reduction, where we attempt to bracket off our preconceptions and focus on describing the things in their appearing, but he did not believe it possible to take a God's eye view and produce incontrovertible truths about our experience of phenomena. Instead, he was concerned with spelling out our lived experience, or rather our experience of the *lifeworld* (Husserl's *Lebenswelt*). Merleau-Ponty's

**Figure 3.6 Maurice Merleau-Ponty: one of the most influential existential philosophers**

([1945] 1962) most well-known work, *Phenomenology of Perception*, forms the philosophical foundation of much contemporary work in phenomenological psychology and, as such, is important reading.

> Perception is not a science of the world, it is not even an act, a deliberate taking up of a position; it is the background from which all acts stand out, and is presupposed by them... Truth does not 'inhabit' only 'the inner man', or more accurately, there is no inner man, man is in the world, and only in the world does he know himself.
>
> Merleau-Ponty ([1945] 1962: x–xi)

Merleau-Ponty ([1945] 1962), unlike Sartre, did not think that we were condemned to be free, with freedom as the basis of human action, but rather that freedom results from the way in which we act and take up positions in the world. It is through our actions that we make ourselves and the world we inhabit meaningful and significant, and as our actions become commitments, we create our freedom: 'Because we are in the world, we are *condemned to meaning . . .*' (p. xix). Merleau-Ponty also stresses the *ambiguity of the lifeworld*, resisting the either/or dichotomy embraced by both Kierkegaard and Sartre. Just as human perception demonstrates an inherent ambiguity, so do our ways of living in the world: certainty and causality are rejected, as is the subject–object dualism so prevalent in contemporary psychology (and, indeed, that can also be seen in Sartre – a major problem with his philosophy). People are, for Merleau-Ponty, essentially connected to the world with our embodied consciousness in the in-between, neither in us (in our minds) nor in the world (in the environment). The world becomes meaningful only through our perception of it and this must, therefore, always be our focus.

Merleau-Ponty is particularly well known for the emphasis he places on embodiment (see Study box 3.1 for an example of a phenomenological study, which draws on Merleau-Ponty's thought and has a particular focus on embodiment). Here, the person is understood as a *body-subject*, with consciousness embedded in the body and intentionality that of the body-subject, rather than simply one's consciousness. Subjectivity is not reducible to either consciousness or the material world; instead, he stresses our ambiguous incarnate existence and the way this must not be lost in a phenomenological reduction. The power of the body-subject comes from how the body is on the subject side of the subject–object divide; we speak and think from the body. Merleau-Ponty ([1945] 1962: 203) also stresses the way in which body-subjects occupy a spatial realm, with the body and world intrinsically interlinked:

> Our own body is in the world as the heart is in the organism: it keeps the visible spectacle constantly alive, it breathes life into it and sustains it inwardly, and with it forms a system.

Truth is, therefore, created by this system as a way of making sense of the situations in which we find ourselves: what is true in one situation need not be true in another. However, sometimes, in scientific discourse for instance, we treat these contingent 'truths' as if they were definite, for all time. Merleau-Ponty refers to this process as *sedimentation*, the process whereby knowledge becomes laid down as a solid ground. Sedimentation is similar to Sartre's notion of *mineralization*, where the way in which we summarize the world becomes fixed, as if set in stone.

## Study box 3.1

**Finlay, L.** (2003). The intertwining of body, self and world: a phenomenological study of living with recently diagnosed multiple sclerosis. *Journal of Phenomenological Psychology*, 34 (2), 157–178.

In this study, Linda Finlay seeks to explore the experience of one woman living with recently diagnosed multiple sclerosis. The author emphasizes the grounded nature of the analysis, with themes emerging from the text. Following two hours of interviewing over two days, Finlay reconstructs the story of living with recently diagnosed multiple sclerosis for Ann, her participant. This involves telling the story chronologically (over a period of one year) on behalf of Ann but using Ann's words wherever possible. Following this, four emergent themes are discussed: embodiment, identity and project, relations with others, and living uncertainty. One particularly interesting aspect of Finlay's analysis is the vivid way in which she describes the impact of multiple sclerosis on Ann's experience of her body. Ann experiences a sense of 'bodily alienation' while simultaneously recognizing that she is inescapably embodied. A distinction is drawn in the analysis between the subjective body (or the body as experienced) and the objective body (the body as object), with Ann feeling disconnected from her previously familiar subjective and pre-reflective experience of her body, as her arm, in particular but not exclusively, becomes an object to be observed and scrutinized. Finally, it is probably worth mentioning the overall finding that the study reveals about the profound impact of this illness, not only on the body but also on the relationships between body, self and others. That is, the experience of multiple sclerosis, in this case at least, 'is encountered in the context of her family, relationships, aspirations and history – the intersubjective and social realms of the lifeworld... Ann's experience of multiple sclerosis cannot be separated from her world; specifically from her experience of her family. Just as the multiple sclerosis is 'in' her, it is 'in' her embodied intersubjective relations with others' (p. 172).

Ideas such as these from Merleau-Ponty, and others from Heidegger and Sartre, form a theoretical backdrop for much contemporary work in phenomenological psychology. Not only are the methods of phenomenological psychology informed by these philosophical theories (with a focus on the body-subject, for instance), but also the findings generated may be analysed using these concepts heuristically. That is, we may use these concepts to interrogate our findings to see how, for instance, temporality, spatiality or embodiment are realized in the experiences being described. These concepts then enable greater theoretical analysis of the data and a move from description to interpretation. The existentialists have described something about lived experience that appears to cut across history and culture, as far as we can know, and so vividly reveals the structure of the lifeworld.

## Summary

The existential turn in phenomenological philosophy was prefigured by Husserl's concept of the lifeworld. The lifeworld is the world as concretely lived, and Husserl argued late in his writing that this should be the foundation for all philosophy and, therefore, all human sciences research. The existential movement led by Heidegger, Sartre and Merleau-Ponty resulted in a radical transformation of phenomenological philosophy as they criticized the transcendental aspect of Husserl's philosophy. Instead, these philosophers sought to develop a practical philosophy concerned with understanding the nature of existence itself. In *Being and Time,* Heidegger sought to determine what exists. In the process, he outlined a number of features of *Dasein* – literally the 'there of being' but basically referring to human subjectivity. These included the way in which we all live in time (temporality) in a verb-like way, as meaning-making machines seeking to realize ourselves. Although we are free to choose what we make of life (a key existential concept most elaborated by Sartre), this is within the limits of the facticity of existence. Here, unlike humanism, humankind is not placed centre-stage in some simple isolated fashion but is brought into existence through engagement in the world in relation to others (being-with). Heidegger's work was elaborated further by Sartre and Merleau-Ponty. Sartre emphasized the emptiness of existence (the 'no-thingness' of existence), where there are no essential qualities to human nature, with existence freedom itself: We are 'condemned to be free'. Merleau-Ponty differed from Sartre, thinking that rather than being 'condemned to be free', we are 'condemned to meaning'. For Merleau-Ponty, freedom is not the basis of existence but, instead, the way in which we act and take up positions in the world. Finally, Merleau-Ponty stressed the need to account for the body, understanding the person as a body-subject, with consciousness always embedded in the body. The thought of these philosophers has directly influenced phenomenological psychology of all kinds and, in particular, led to a more interpretive version, as discussed in detail in Chapter 7.

## Further reading

**Kearney, R. (1994).** *Modern Movements in European Philosophy,* **2nd edn. Manchester: Manchester University Press**. A beautifully written and very clear book providing succinct coverage of the thought of many of the key figures in the existential movement. The book includes chapters on Heidegger, Sartre and Merleau-Ponty as well as many other continental philosophers.

**Langer, M. M. (1989).** *Merleau-Ponty's Phenomenology of Perception: A Guide and Commentary.* **Basingstoke: Macmillan Press**. A clear and succinct chapter-by-chapter guide to Merleau-Ponty's masterpiece.

**Merleau-Ponty, M. (1962).** *Phenomenology of Perception* **[trans. C. Smith]. London: Routledge**. The philosophical foundation for a considerable amount of contemporary work in phenomenological psychology and, as such, recommended reading. It is more clearly relevant for psychology and also a more accessible work than *Being and Time* or *Being and Nothingness*. The preface alone is worth reading as an introduction to phenomenology.

**Polt, R. (1999).** *Heidegger: An Introduction.* **London: UCL Press.** A superb introduction to the thought of this very difficult thinker. It is mostly concerned with *Being and Time*, but this will be more than enough for most readers.

**Warnock, M. (1970).** *Existentialism.* **Oxford: Oxford University Press.** A brief and clear, though somewhat partial, introduction to existentialism.

# 4 The hermeneutic turn[1]

## Chapter aims

- Describe the hermeneutic turn in phenomenology

- Outline the work of Gadamer and Ricoeur – two of the most important hermeneutic philosophers

- Discuss the need for interpretation and the distinction between hermeneutics of meaning-recollection and suspicion

- Explain how the hermeneutic philosophy of Ricoeur results in a turn to narrative

There is considerable debate within phenomenology and phenomenological psychology about the need to interpret and employ specific methods of interpretation versus the need to simply describe the things in their appearing (see Chapter 9 for a discussion). So, for instance, some people have been dissatisfied with the very descriptive nature of descriptive phenomenological psychology (see Chapter 6) and argued that it is necessary to be much more interpretative – much more psychological if you will. With this has also come increasing awareness of the way that much, if not all, of our experience can be best understood through the stories we tell of that experience. That is, life as experienced is narratively structured, produced and re-produced. And so, if we are interested in understanding experiences of the lifeworld, we need to explore the stories people tell of their experiences, often with the help of some specific hermeneutic, or method of interpretation.

Following Heidegger and his move to a hermeneutic phenomenology, two philosophers stand out as being particularly important: Hans-Georg Gadamer (1900–2002) and Paul Ricoeur (1913–2005). There are very many similarities between their work, and often the differences seem very minor, especially when viewed from outside the world of hermeneutics. My own work, developing a method of critical narrative analysis (see Chapter 8), builds directly on Ricoeur's middle and later philosophy. In this chapter, I want to introduce some of the

[1] Parts of this chapter were first published in *History and Philosophy of Psychology* (2003), 5(1), pp. 30–45 as 'Hermeneutic phenomenology: arguments for a new social psychology'.

ideas of Gadamer and Ricoeur, although the focus will be mainly on the latter. The reason for this focus is simply that although Gadamer is in many ways the senior of the two philosophers, Ricoeur has addressed some key limitations in Gadamer's work and, as such, Ricoeur's philosophy is, I believe, more complete and certainly more appropriate for a critical phenomenological analysis.

## 4.1  Hans-Georg Gadamer

Gadamer views philosophy as an active and participative enterprise and not something confined to the lone academic. He was deeply influenced by Husserl and Heidegger, and also the work of Dilthey and his concern with the history of *hermeneutics* – the art of interpretation. Following Heidegger and the notion of *facticity*, Gadamer was keen to stress the historically and culturally situated nature of all understanding. Understanding is not about producing a-historical and a-cultural truths about the world – the project of science – but rather something that is situated in a particular space and place, historically and culturally contingent. However, in spite of the cultural and historical distance inherent in all understanding, understanding is the key to human existence. Like Heidegger before him, Gadamer ([1975] 1996) argued that understanding is at the core of human existence. And for Gadamer and the later Heidegger, language is the means through which we gain understanding of the world that we inhabit. Furthermore, Gadamer believes that it is speech, and especially conversation, that is at the heart of all understanding. For him, philosophy itself – and, hence, all meaningful existence – is a conversation leading towards mutual understanding. It is through conversation that the world reveals itself, phenomenologically speaking, as shared understanding reveals the 'things themselves'. Thus, for Gadamer at least, the focus must always be on language and the way in which it can be used through conversation to reveal something that was previously concealed. And that which is revealed comes through a mutual attempt at shared understanding through conversation, where we accept the genuine intentions of the other person whom we wish to understand while also recognizing the very particular situated nature of our own position.

Central to understanding is self-understanding because we always speak from somewhere, from a position dependent on our history and culture. Understanding is therefore always determined by our *pre-judgements*, which are the result of our *effective history*. All understanding is the result of the accumulation of knowledge about the object in question. Objects understood in this way do not simply hold some intrinsic meaning that we must grasp but rather evolve into being for us and our communities through their effective history and the influence they have had for us. Therefore, for Gadamer, our understanding is both enabled and limited by our pre-understanding, but this is not all. Our understanding is also limited by our *horizons*, since all understanding occurs within a certain horizon. However, although we are limited by the horizons of our outlook, these are not fixed but rather are overlapping and developing all the time. For Gadamer believed that we can and do gain mutual understanding and that this is through the *fusion of horizons*, where we acknowledge consensus in our particular worldviews.

Gadamer's greatest work is *Truth and Method* ([1975] 1996), in which he questions how much method might guarantee true understanding, whether in the natural or human sciences. The sciences have been built on the notion that rigorous method provides the guarantee of truth, which the scientist seeks. This idea is a powerful one, which has influenced the social sciences, and particularly psychology, where we see a similar concern with method. However, although Gadamer is sceptical of the value of method, and particularly the scientific method, which inevitably objectifies the world, he is not anti-science. Rather, he argues that scientific method is not the whole truth, and that truth cannot be limited to that which is only knowable through scientific method. Furthermore, Gadamer does not simply advance a negative claim against scientific method as the purveyor of all truth but also advances a positive claim that other aspects of human existence, and in particular art and history, give rise to truth.

Language is, for Gadamer, the essential way in which understanding emerges. Although he argues that all existence is not reducible to language, he does argue, like Ricoeur, that all interpretative understanding of existence comes through language. That is because, following Heidegger, he believes that we are 'meaning-makers' thrown into a world where all possibilities are already experienced interpretations: and these experienced interpretations are all communicated through language. Therefore, full understanding comes about only through language. But language is not simply reflective of experience, simply telling us what people think or feel, but actually brings humanity into existence and, with this, all notions of selfhood and culture, as well as already being infused with the cultural into which one is thrown. It is because of this that he argues that our understanding emerges out of our *tradition*, with its own particular set of *prejudices*, requiring a hermeneutics of meaning-recollection operating in and through conversation and the desire to understand and be understood.

## 4.2 Paul Ricoeur

Ricoeur's work is concerned primarily with interpreting text, and in the following section I introduce a number of key ideas from Ricoeur's elaborate theory of interpretation (see Biography box 4.1). Ricoeur's work provides a theoretical position, which, like Gadamer, recognizes the embodied being-in-the-world of human beings that is beyond and pre-exists language, *and* an interpretative understanding of human nature through language. Neither of these two elements is unique in itself. Existential phenomenology (see Chapter 3) recognizes human beings as embodied creatures beyond language, while certain strands of discursively oriented psychology demonstrate an interpretative understanding of people through their use of language (e.g. Edwards, 1997; Edwards & Potter, 1992; Harré & Gillett, 1994; Henriques *et al.*, 1984; Parker,

Figure 4.1 Paul Ricoeur: a key figure in the hermeneutic turn in phenomenology

1992; Potter & Wetherell, 1987; Wetherell, Taylor & Yates, 2001a,b). However, these positions have traditionally been opposed or at the very least seen to be incompatible. It is important to note, at this point, that phenomenological psychology already recognizes the importance of both existentialism and hermeneutics (van Manen, 1990). Hermeneutic phenomenology, drawing on Heiddegger ([1927] 1962), is concerned with interpretation designed to grasp the understanding of a research participant (see, for instance, the interpretive phenomenology of van Manen, 1990, Chapter 7). Ricoeur (1970) terms this the *hermeneutics of empathy* or *meaning-recollection*. However, existential phenomenology does not incorporate what Ricoeur (1970) termed the *hermeneutics of suspicion*. This is the mode of interpretation, employed by psychoanalysis for instance, that seeks to understand by peeling back the layers of meaning – digging beneath the surface for what is hidden – which may lead to suspicion over the initial empathic account of meaning.

## Biography box 4.1   Paul Ricoeur (1913–2005)

Paul Ricoeur (Figure 4.1) was born in 1913 in Valence, France. Although he has become an internationally renowned philosopher, he kept his life quite private, preferring to be known for his writing. However, in 1998 *Critique and Conviction* was published; in this book, Ricoeur discusses his remarkable life openly and frankly in conversation with François Azouvi and Marc de Launay. Ricoeur's father was an English teacher, but the most significant fact of Ricoeur's childhood was the loss of both parents during the First World War. The end of the war was not a joyous time for him, since he was mourning the loss of his parents, particularly his father, who was still presumed dead, missing in action. With the death of his father, Paul Ricoeur and his sister were taken in by their grandparents, assisted by a young unmarried aunt. His sister died a short time later from tuberculosis, leaving Ricoeur with the sense of an unpaid debt, a theme that has been important in his work, since he felt he was very much the favoured child. These circumstances resulted in an upbringing dominated by reading with very little time for games. Indeed, Ricoeur (1998: 5) remarks that 'school became more a form of

recreation to me than a discipline'. He encountered philosophy proper at Rennes secondary school, where he was inspired by the teaching of Roland Dalbiez. This left a lasting mark on Ricoeur; through the advice of Dalbiez that 'when an obstacle presents itself, you have to confront it, not slip around it; never be afraid to go and see' (Ricoeur, 1998: 7), he decided to pursue a career in philosophy. Having no parents, he needed to complete his studies quickly and entered teaching as soon as he had finished his first degree.

Ricoeur served as an officer during the Second World War but in 1940 was captured by the Germans and imprisoned in a prison camp for officers in Pomerania. Life in the camp was quite remarkable, as the inmates created an intellectual life with a theatre, a stock market (with cigarettes as the standard unit of exchange), a library and a university (with programmes, courses, enrolments and exams). It was during this time that Ricoeur read the work of the existentialist Karl Jaspers and began to translate Husserl's *Ideas*, writing his translation in the margins because they had no paper. Upon Ricoeur's return to Paris at the end of the war, he visited Gabriel Marcel, another key existen-

## Biography box 4.1  Paul Ricoeur (1913-2005)

tial philosopher, who had taught him before the war; his philosophical career began in earnest as he finished his translation of *Ideas*.

Ricoeur's career began with two books on Jaspers, which have never been translated into English, before moving on to the first phase of his career proper, where he reflected on existential questions concerning human will. This period began with *Freedom and Nature: The Voluntary and the Involuntary*, where Ricoeur considers the limits to human will, and also resulted in *Finitude and Guilt*, which is where we see the start of Ricoeur's turn to hermeneutics and the second phase of his writing. This phase was to dominate Ricoeur's

writing for 30 years or so, resulting in works such as *Freud and Philosophy*, and *The Rule of Metaphor*. However, it was with the acclaimed multivolume work *Time and Narrative* (Vol. 1 published in French in 1983) that Ricoeur once again found favour with the philosophical establishment and his thinking arrived in the third phase, a phase concerned with narrative. Ricoeur continued to write up until his death in 2005, producing the acclaimed work *Oneself as Another*, which continues the narrative theme begun in *Time and Narrative*, extending his thinking to construct a 'hermeneutics of the self' and exploring the implications of this for ethics.

### 4.2.1  Discourse, text and action

Ricoeur makes an important distinction between *discourse* and *language*. For Ricoeur, discourse is spoken speech, a synthetic construction of human beings that is not reducible to the words that make it up, whereas language is the system of signs that make up discourse. The basic unit of language is the sign (phonological or lexical), while the basic unit of discourse is the sentence. Breaking down a sentence into its component parts, as the structuralists would have us do, may provide insights into the construction of that sentence, but it simultaneously obscures the meaning inherent in the sentence that is the synthetic construction of a human agent. This distinction between language, which is the focus of classic structuralist analyses, and discourse, which exemplifies the creative action of human agents, is a critical one for hermeneutic phenomenology. Ricoeur delineates this distinction further by identifying four essential traits of discourse. First, discourse is always realized temporally while language operates outside time. Second, discourse always implies the presence of a subject. Behind all discourse there is an 'I' that speaks. In other words, asking the question 'Who is speaking?' makes sense only with discourse and not with language. Third, discourse is always about something. Here we see the symbolic function of language actualized. The active nature of language is exemplified in discourse in that it refers to a world that it claims to describe or represent. Fourth, discourse is always addressed to another person. Although language provides the codes for dialogue, it is only in discourse that we see an interlocutor to whom it is addressed. This dialogic component to discourse is crucial. For it is only while we are engaged in communication that we see the creative use of language in discourse.

Ricoeur makes a further distinction between spoken and written discourse. Here we see the word *text* used to indicate any discourse fixed in writing. This distinction is important, for in writing we see text detached from the conditions of spoken word. That is, the text '... escape[s] from the finite intentional horizon of its author' (Muldoon, 2002: 51). We no longer have a human agent with whom we can engage dialogically. We can no longer argue, question and challenge in order to reach a level of communicative understanding. Instead, the text enters the world of other texts and transcends the psychological, sociological and historical conditions of its own production. The moment of two speakers engaged in dialogue is abolished forever, and we witness the loss of *ostensive reference* – that is, loss of the temporarily agreed reference within the dialogue to a world beyond language. Text enters into relation with other texts, which take the place of the circumstantial reality referred to by living speech. There is still reference to 'reality', but this is now second-order reference, a non-situational reference to a symbolic world. Transcribed interviews, the material for most qualitative analyses, clearly occupy an intermediate position, for they are produced in dialogue with ostensive reference but then fixed in writing, thereby transcending the conditions of their own production.

Let's follow Ricoeur's (1971) lead and unpack the differences between speech and text in more detail through engagement with the four essential components of discourse outlined above. First, unlike language, discourse exists within time. This is clearly different in spoken and written language. In speech, we see the momentary nature of discourse as discursive events are created and then disappear. Ricoeur refers to this as the problem of *fixation*. For language, which is a-temporal, is fixed (through inscription of the alphabet, syntax, etc.) only in order to enable us to fix discourse. And the reason for needing to inscribe discourse is because it disappears in speech. But writing does not serve to fix the speech event itself. It fixes only what is said, or rather the meaning of what is said, in speech. Ricoeur draws on the distinctions made between locutionary (the act *of* saying), illocutionary (that which we do *in* saying) and perlocutionary (that which we do *by* saying) acts from speech-act theory (Austin, 1962; Searle, 1969) in order to further elucidate the distinction between speech and writing. In brief, the locutionary, illocutionary and perlocutionary acts can be understood in terms of inscription as sentences with decreasing effect. That is, less and less of the speech act can be inscribed in text as we move from locutionary through illocutionary to perlocutionary acts. These distinctions are important, for Ricoeur argues that it is necessary to understand the sentence not only as a propositional act but also as a locutionary, illocutionary and even perlocutionary act if we are to truly identify the meaning that is inscribed therein. We must, therefore, attempt to recover the meaning in text at all levels: propositional, locutionary, illocutionary and perlocutionary, in as far as we can.

The second trait of discourse is concerned with how the sentence designates a speaker. Due to the immediate self-referential nature of speech, there is an overlap between the subjective intention of the speaker and the meaning of the discourse. This effectively means that to understand what the discourse means is the same thing as to understand what the speaker means. However, with written discourse, this overlap is no longer present, and we see the dissociation of the author's intention and the meaning of the text. This does not mean that we witness the 'death of the author' (Barthes, 1977), but that the relationship between speaker and discourse are distanced with the text escaping '… the finite horizon lived by its author' (Ricoeur, 1981: 201). When discourse is written rather than spoken, the meaning inscribed by the text becomes more important than the meaning intended by the author, for with writing the text has '... broken its moorings to the psychology of its author' (Ricoeur, 1981: 201).

The third trait of discourse is how it refers to a world, and in spoken discourse this world is that which is common to the interlocutors. Aspects of this world can be shown in dialogue through gesture, adverbs of time and place, and so on. Here the reference is *ostensive*. This ostensive reference disappears in written discourse, but the text still has a reference. The move is from reference to our actual world (*Umwelt*) to that of a symbolic world (*Welt*) produced through reference to all the texts we have encountered previously. Discourse must always be about something – there is always reference to a world – not the ostensive world witnessed in dialogue (*Umwelt*), but a world of texts (*Welt*).

The fourth trait of discourse is that it is addressed to someone. Here, there is a clear distinction between speech and writing, for in speech we are clearly communicating with a particular person or persons but in writing we are potentially communicating with anyone who can read. So in writing, text escapes the lived experience of the author, the limits of ostensive reference and the need to be present 'face to face' with another. There is no longer a visible recipient of the discursive act but instead an invisible reader who becomes the addressee of the discourse.

These traits of discourse, and distinctions between spoken and written discourse, are important for social psychology for a number of reasons. First, interviews and transcripts thereof must, according to this classification, occupy an ambiguous position with regard to the author. An interview is a dialogue in which we can recognize the ostensive reference to our circumstantial reality. We can also see the overlap of authorial meaning and textual meaning. This enables us to work towards uncovering the world of the author in a way that becomes increasingly impossible with written text. However, it is only while in dialogue that this opportunity to appropriate the discursive meaning arises, for once the dialogue is transcribed it marks a break between the author and the interlocutor. At this point we may still be close to identifying the world of the author (the author's psychology, as it were), but this will always be an approximation as we move from interlocutor to reader. The origins of discourse are crucial for Ricoeur as the primacy of the speaking subject is asserted and meaning-recollection is paramount. However, once speech is inscribed, the possibility of capturing the intention of the author fades, such that any appropriation of meaning must always remain an approximation. Another factor that therefore becomes apparent is how all text should be recognized as a valid and valuable source of data concerning our engagement with the world. Qualitative social psychology has tended to rely on the interview,[2] perhaps too much. I think that this is, at least

---

[2] There are exceptions of course. Conversation analysis notably eschews the interview in favour of naturalistic conversation. However, even here, where the tape rather than transcript is the focus of analysis, there is inscription and therefore the erasure of authorial intention. It is just a different form of inscription – an inscription of magnetic particles on plastic rather than pen on paper. No matter, the here and now of two people in dialogue has still gone.

in part, because of the underlying belief that analysis of this material will give us unfettered access to the world of another. However, this naive view not only fails to recognize the need for both empathy and suspicion (see below) but also fails to recognize the process of distanciation that is inevitable once spoken discourse becomes text.

Finally, in this section it is important to mention Ricoeur's (1971) radical move where he conceives of all human action as text. Ricoeur argues, on the basis that (i) human action displays much the same properties as text and (ii) human sciences methodology engages with the same kind of procedures as textual interpretation, that all human action should be understood as text. There is not the space to explore this idea in detail here, but the essence of the argument Ricoeur makes for this bold move concerns the 'specific plurivocity' of meaning and possession of a limited range of possible constructions for both text and human action. Because of the inherent similarity between human action and text, and the existing attempts of the human sciences to understand and interpret such material, Ricoeur argues that reconceptualizing human action as text enables better understanding and interpretation, as one becomes able to employ techniques from hermeneutic phenomenology.

### 4.2.2 Appropriation

**Figure 4.2** A key feature of a hermeneutic analysis is the appropriation of meaning – that is, understanding what a text means

*Appropriation* is the means by which we attempt to explicate meaning (Ricoeur, 1981). But this is not a simple task, for we inevitably struggle against cultural distance and possibly historical alienation. That is, when attempting to understand what a text means, one is often, although not always, faced with the twin difficulty of understanding the text from another culture and/or period in history. The purpose of appropriation is to gain an understanding of a proposed world from the text – not from behind the text but from in front of it through expanding the analyst's own way of seeing the world. Appropriation is the act of capturing the meaning being expressed by a text, not necessarily through identification of the intentions of the author, although this may be approximated, but through 'a fusion of horizons' (a term from Gadamer), where we expand knowledge of ourselves through engagement with the other. But, unlike Gadamer, Ricoeur does not simply believe that this entails capturing meaning at 'face-value'. Ricoeur believes that empathy and suspicion are both necessary means for the appropriation of meaning. We need to understand the text both at 'face-value', as you might expect in any phenomenological encounter, and also through the use of a hermeneutic, or method of interpretation, which enables us to see beyond this surface meaning to hidden meanings beyond.

A key element in the process of appropriation is the notion of *play*, which Ricoeur draws from the work of Gadamer ([1975] 1996). Ricoeur (1981) sees play as the most appropriate 'way of being' when one is engaged in textual analysis. Play, according to Ricoeur, has its own way of being, which is not determined by the consciousness at play. Instead, the essential element in play is the 'to and fro' of play in which, like dance, one is carried away to another realm. So whoever plays is also played and in this activity forgets itself. It is through play that a reader may truly achieve 'a fusion of horizons' with a text. Through suspension of seriousness or everyday reality, we gain the possibility of seeing future horizons or possibilities. This notion of play is clearly understandable if we think of losing ourselves when watching a film at a cinema where, if the film engages us, we may see other ways of being or possible future horizons. We are captured by the meaning of the film within the context of our own horizons. The author (scriptwriter, director and producer) may have intended the film to be tragic, and we may actualize this aspect of the text. But the layers of meaning that are actualized through our playful engagement will be the product of our own unique horizons of meaning as we enter into the symbolic world of the text. Getting to the essence of a film is key, however, for a work of discourse will present worldly possibilities only if we move beyond the anecdotal to the essence buried within.

### 4.2.3 Empathy and suspicion

As stated above, Ricoeur identifies two essential approaches for understanding meaning: a *demythologizing* (or empathic) element and a *demystifying* (or suspicious) element. Demythologizing is the process of empathic engagement where we seek to identify the meaning through a fusion of our horizons. We engage with the text, bringing our *pre-understanding*, our way of seeing the world, into play with that inherent in the text. The demystifying moment, in contrast, is one of suspicion, a revolutionary act, where we seek to identify the meaning hidden beneath the surface, for here the real significance of discourse is never immediate and transparent. Ricoeur (1970) identifies Freud, Marx and Nietzsche as the three 'masters of suspicion'. With all three, meaning is never apparent but instead is beneath the surface and in need of unmasking. Their hermeneutics of suspicion extended to uncovering unconscious motivation, economic modes of production and the will to power, respectively. What Ricoeur believed these three 'masters' demonstrated was the inadequacy of gaining understanding through immediate consciousness alone (meaning-recollection or empathy) – the project of transcendental phenomenology and of course descriptive phenomenological psychology.

### 4.2.4 A critique of the illusions of the subject

The other key idea that I wish to discuss is the need for a critique of what Ricoeur refers to as the *illusions of the subject* when appropriating meaning. Ricoeur is careful to recognize the potential errors of interpretation of appropriation and provides a clear corrective in his work. The principal error that may occur is in understanding appropriation as a form of subjectivism in which we witness the projection of the analyst's subjectivity on to the text. This is where the world view of the analyst dominates that of the text through their active projection of their way of *being-in-the-world* on to the text. This should not be the case, but we always speak from somewhere and the mechanism through which this error is corrected involves subjecting the subject itself to a hermeneutic critique. That is, turning the hermeneutic (method of interpretation) of choice on to the analyst first and foremost. It is not possible to speak from nowhere, to step outside the political world (broadly speaking) that we all inhabit. Even the most innocuous of investigations requires that we ask certain questions and, with that, fail to ask others, thus positioning us in a particular way (politically) in relation to the research we are conducting. All research has an agenda, some obviously political (e.g. work trying to reduce racism), some less obviously so (e.g. work on aggression more generally) but still political, only in a more subtle way (e.g. through the desire to reduce aggression in men underpinning the work). Heidegger and Ricoeur both argue that even when attempting to bracket our preconceptions we speak from somewhere, we always occupy an ideological position even if we are unaware of it. This needs to be recognized in our research and must itself be subjected to a critique that enables us to work better with the text and our analysis of it.

### 4.2.5 Gadamer and Ricoeur

It is worth fleshing out the relationship between Gadamer and Ricoeur a little more at this point before moving on to Ricoeur's latest work on narrative, for there are many similarities but also some crucial differences between their work. Gadamer ([1975] 1996) exemplifies the hermeneutics of empathy or meaning-recollection. His work is concerned with understanding through our 'effective history'. The aim is to reach mutual understanding through a 'fusion of horizons', in

spite of being separated by different horizons of understanding. Gadamer emphasized reason operating within traditions where we need to allow ourselves to be
drawn into a tradition in order to understand it. Two traditions must merge if we
are to understand: the tradition of the text we are reading and our own tradition of
understanding. Like Ricoeur, Gadamer asserts that '... that which can be understood is language' (Gadamer, [1975] 1996: 450), meaning not that there is nothing
beyond language but that things come into being only through language.

Although Ricoeur incorporates aspects of Gadamer's hermeneutics into his
hermeneutic phenomenology (the notion of the fusion of horizons and meaning-
recollection as play, for instance), there are a number of limitations that
Ricoeur's work (indirectly) addresses. First, Gadamer recognizes a hermeneutics
of empathy but not a hermeneutics of suspicion in his work. Critics, following
Habermas, have argued that Gadamer seems to be too tolerant of tradition and
needs to be more critical of prevailing ideologies (Moran, 2000). Second, and
most importantly, his emphasis on consensus and mutual agreement for understanding is thought to be fundamentally flawed (Moran, 2000). As Moran (2000:
286) states, '... a society which has convinced itself the earth is flat may be a
well-regulated harmonious society with full agreement; unfortunately it simply
does not have knowledge, a point Habermas has made forcibly against Gadamer.'
Ricoeur is able to move beyond Gadamer's simple emphasis on tradition and
consensus, without losing the value of tradition and consensus in understanding, by incorporating aspects of Habermas' critique into his own understanding
of tradition. Instead of seeing tradition (Gadamer's position) and the critique of
ideology (Habermas's position) in opposition, he proposes a dialectical relationship between participating in tradition and taking a critical distance from
tradition in all understanding. Ricoeur recognizes that his dialectic does not provide a theoretical solution to the Gadamer–Habermas debate (notably between
the notion of values as things discovered and the notion of values as that which
we choose to adopt) but does provide a practical way out of this difficult
dilemma, which I believe has particular utility for a practical and critical phenomenological analysis of narrative (see Chapter 8).

### 4.2.6 Narrative theory and narrative identities

Ricoeur moves his attention away from classical hermeneutics to narrative in his
later works, *Time and Narrative* (Vols 1–3, 1984, 1985, 1988) and *Oneself as
Another* (1992). Ricoeur believes his work on metaphor and narrative to be
closely linked projects, since it is through these two forms of discourse that we
witness the creation of new meaning, something vital to the human project. In
narrative, new meaning comes about through the synthesis of elements into a
coherent whole, while in metaphor new meaning emerges through novel attri-
butions. Ricoeur argued that it was possible to understand the creation of
meaning intrinsic to humanity only through the analysis of metaphor and narrative, where it becomes possible – analytically speaking – to gain access to the
creative process in action.

Ricoeur argues that stories are constructed to make sense of our lived experience through the organization of disparate elements into meaningful wholes. To this end, in *Time and Narrative*, he distinguishes three forms of time: *cosmological time*, *phenomenological time* and *historical time*. Cosmological time refers to the time of space, the planets and the natural world where time is effectively infinite, dwarfing us and our understanding, through the enormity of scale. Phenomenological time is our immediate experience of time, lived through our finite and, relatively speaking, very short existence. We are bounded by the knowledge of our death and, therefore, we are, as Heidegger stated, beings-towards-death, acutely aware of our limited time on the earth. Bridging the gap between these two notions of time is historical time, which humanity has created in order to better reconcile the irreconcilable, to seal the fissure between our finite experience of time and the infinite time of the cosmos. Historical time achieves this bridging through the inscription of existence on the cosmos by producing *traces*, such as the calendar, documents, archives and records of generations. These traces call for *emplotment*, the creation of a story through narrative, as a trace passed from generation to generation requires a storyteller willing to recount the narrative. However, Ricoeur does not stop with historical narratives but insists that fictional narratives also serve to call the subject into being.

At the human level, narratives serve to situate our experience in (phenomenological) time. This is achieved through the *re-figuration* of episodes, or the *episodic dimension*, where there is a linear representation of episodes in time. This re-figuration leads to the *configurational dimension*, where episodes are creatively transformed into one meaningful whole. In practical terms, the historical present is the focus of hermeneutic reflection and analysis. Through the stories we construct, we build a sense of who we are (and who others are too) – our *narrative identities*. These identities are not based on an indecomposable cogito or an essential self but on a living tissue of narrated stories. Narrative selves will be multiple and contingent, historically and culturally specific, and will therefore be subject to change. But this does not mean a slide into textual reductionism for, importantly, Ricoeur argues that it is human agents (not texts) that change institutions and practices. By this account, the human subject does not disappear beneath the text but rather stands in front of the text, waiting to be revealed through an analysis of the text by the reader. The narrative mode thus permits an analysis of steps through which human beings encounter and transform a tradition.

## Summary

Heidegger began the hermeneutic turn in phenomenological philosophy by stressing how all understanding involves interpretation. Following him, two philosophers stand out as being particularly important: Gadamer and Ricoeur. Gadamer was keen to emphasize the historically and culturally situated nature of all understanding. That is, phenomenological understanding is not about producing a-historical and a-cultural truths about the world and our perception of it but rather about producing knowledge that is historically and culturally contingent. Gadamer believed that philosophy was an enterprise of conversation leading to mutual understanding. Both Gadamer and Ricoeur were keen to stress that we always speak from somewhere, being unable to transcend our historical and cultural position. Ricoeur's work is concerned primarily with interpreting text, and through this he developed an elaborate theory of interpretation. His work, like that of Gadamer, provides a theoretical position that recognizes the embodied being-in-the-world of human being that is beyond and pre-exists language, and an interpretative understanding of human nature through language. Ricoeur identifies two distinct approaches to understanding meaning: a demythologizing (or empathic) element and a demystifying (or suspicious) element. The former – also referred to as a hermeneutic of empathy or meaning-recollection – forms the ground of all phenomenological psychology with a focus on understanding meaning through a fusion of horizons (of reader and text), where we seek to understand the meaning of the text as it appears to us. A hermeneutic of suspicion, by contrast, involves an attempt to dig beneath the surface for hidden meaning as one might do in psychoanalysis. In Ricoeur's later work, he moved his attention away from hermeneutics to narrative. Narratives result from a human attempt to organize (re-figure) disparate elements of experience into meaningful wholes and, through this, bring into being narrative identities, identities based on a living tissue of stories.

## Further reading

Clark, S.H. (1990). *Paul Ricoeur*. London: Routledge. A comprehensive guide to Ricoeur's work. A little difficult at times, but very thorough.

Muldoon, M. (2002). *On Ricoeur*. Belmont, CA: Wadsworth/Thomson Learning. An excellent, clear and accessible guide to the thought of this very difficult thinker.

Ricoeur, P. (1981). *Hermeneutics and the Human Sciences* [ed. and trans. J.B. Thompson]. Cambridge: Cambridge University Press. One of the more accessible collections from Ricoeur and also one of the most relevant for psychology and the social sciences more generally.

# 5 Staking out the territory

## Chapter aims

- Introduce the different approaches to phenomenological psychology
- Outline the fundamentals of qualitative phenomenological research, including research design, sampling, reflexivity, ethics, collecting data through interviews, written descriptions, documentary sources and the Internet, transcription, validity, writing and the use of computers

This chapter is the first of the 'practical' chapters in this text and is designed to provide sufficient grounding in the fundamentals of qualitative phenomenological research, to enable you, the reader, to move comfortably through the next three chapters and actually carry out a research project using one of the approaches here described. Since this text is designed to introduce the reader to both the theory and methods of phenomenological research, that will remain the focus here. There are, however, suggestions for further reading at the end of this chapter, which should allow the interested reader to pursue any of the issues raised elsewhere.

Before moving on to the practicalities of design, data collection and so on, I provide an outline of the different approaches to phenomenological psychology commonly in use today. This should enable you to understand a little more about the structure of the following three chapters and highlight some of the similarities and differences between the different schools of phenomenological psychology. This is necessary for a number of reasons. First, you may want information about only one particular approach to phenomenological psychology, and the following brief guide should help with that choice. Second, the following section will of necessity provide practical information that is more relevant to one approach than another; where this is the case, I seek to make this clear. Finally, the different schools of phenomenological psychology map on to the different philosophical schools outlines in the first three chapters (as I indicated in the introduction), and it seems only fitting to take this opportunity to further emphasize that link.

# The different approaches to phenomenological psychology

## 5.1.1 Descriptive phenomenology

This is the most traditional approach to phenomenological psychology. It emerged in the 1970s at Duquesne (pronounced 'Du-kane') University in the USA, with the work of Amedeo Giorgi, now at Saybrook Graduate School, USA, and colleagues, and, indeed, is sometimes called the Duquesne School empirical-structural phenomenology or Husserlian phenomenological psychology). It is the most classically Husserlian method (see Chapter 2), being focused on identifying the essence of the phenomenon through epoché and the psychological phenomenological reduction, but also builds on existential philosophy (see Chapter 3). There is not one single way of conducting *descriptive phenomenological psychology*, although the approach first advocated by Giorgi and colleagues remains dominant. There are many important figures in this field (such as Les Todres in the UK and Steen Halling in the USA, to name just two) continuing to advance the approach theoretically. A relatively recent version is the *Sheffield School*. This has arisen principally with the work of Peter Ashworth and colleagues at Sheffield Hallam University in the UK. Although it is not yet widely known, it does attempt to build on the work of Giorgi, developing a more explicit focus on existential aspects of the lifeworld. It does this by incorporating a number of the ideas of the existentialists into the analytical process through an additional stage (after descriptive phenomenological work based on the methods of descriptive phenomenology), where the analyst interrogates the description produced through a number of existential givens of the lifeworld (e.g. selfhood, embodiment, temporality, spatiality).

## 5.1.2 Interpretative phenomenological analysis, hermeneutic phenomenology and template analysis

The following approaches are all distinguished from descriptive phenomenology through their greater concern with hermeneutics and interpretation. *Interpretative phenomenological analysis* (IPA) is probably the most widely known approach to phenomenological psychology used by psychologists in the UK today. It was developed by Jonathan Smith, now at Birkbeck College, University of London, in the 1990s. It is informed by phenomenological philosophy, with Smith and Osborn (2003) keen to stress the hermeneutic phenomenological roots of the method. There is less emphasis on description and greater interpretation than in descriptive phenomenology, as well as greater engagement with mainstream (principally social-cognitive) psychological literature. It is particularly popular among health and other applied psychologists. Although the emphasis is on qualitative description, there has not, to date, been a great deal of theoretical work to ground this particular method in phenomenological philosophy. *Hermeneutic phenomenology* (sometimes also called interpretive phenomenology) is another interpretive method that involves a thematic analysis of data and that also builds on the later lifeworld philosophy of Husserl, along with existential (see Chapter 3) and hermeneutic (see Chapter 4) philosophy. This approach is growing in popularity, especially among applied researchers (often in nursing and education). Max Van Manen, a professor of education in Canada, has been one of the key figures in the development of this approach, although many others (such as Nancy Diekelmann) have also been actively involved. Finally, *template analysis* (TA) is a lesser-known approach, which is very similar to IPA, developed by Nigel King at the University of Huddersfield, UK. There are very many similarities to IPA, with the focus on producing a thematic analysis of experience, but also one key difference: the possibility of using a coding frame (template) devised theoretically *a priori* (i.e. before collecting the data). This enables the researcher to specifically explore theoretically important aspects of experience while allowing the meaning in these particular areas to emerge in the analytical process, as is normal in phenomenological research. This is often of great help in applied research, where time and money constraints prevent more general exploration of the data or where strong theoretical grounds are identified for exploring a limited aspect of experience.

### 5.1.3 Critical narrative analysis

The increasing interest in the hermeneutic turn in phenomenology (see Chapter 4) has led to the development of phenomenological narrative methods of data analysis, which draw principally on the philosophy of Gadamer and Ricoeur. My own work is an example of such an approach, where I have attempted to develop a *critical narrative analysis* (CNA), primarily building on the work of Ricoeur, designed to facilitate the exploration of experience through a critical analysis of narrative accounts. This approach shares much in common with other forms of narrative analysis (such as that by Dan McAdams, Michael Murray and Donald Polkinghorne), but with some key differences. There is a focus on identifying narratives and examining them for function and tone as well as their thematic content. Crucially, there is also a critical moment in CNA where the researcher employs imaginative hermeneutics of suspicion to interrogate his or her own way of viewing the topic and the narratives being employed by the participant(s).

The following chapters explore these different approaches to phenomenological psychology in more detail. The next chapter (Chapter 6) focuses on descriptive phenomenology, including detail on the Sheffield School variation. Chapter 7 outlines interpretive approaches to phenomenological psychology, including IPA, hermeneutic phenomenology and TA. Finally, Chapter 8 introduces the processes involved in carrying out a CNA.

## 5.2 Research design

Phenomenological studies are usually, although not always, qualitative research projects designed to understand more about the experience of some phenomenon. Appropriate research questions are therefore open-ended questions seeking to understand more about a particular topic rather than attempt to explain or identify causes for phenomena. There have been studies on (for instance):

- the experience of social anxiety (Fischer, 1974);
- the experience of being a victim of crime (Wertz, 1985);
- gay men's understandings of safer sex and sexuality (Flowers *et al.*, 1997);
- identity change during the transition to motherhood (Smith, 1999);
- adaptation to diabetic renal disease (King *et al.*, 2002);
- the role of insight in psychotherapy (Todres, 2002);
- living with multiple sclerosis (Finlay, 2003);
- embodiment and disembodiment in childbirth (Akrich & Pasveer, 2004);
- the construction of sadomasochistic sexual identities (Langdridge & Butt, 2004).

It would be highly unusual to seek explanations or to pose specific questions (especially hypotheses) at the start of a phenomenological research study that might lead to specific predictions. Chapters 2–4 outline the philosophical underpinnings of phenomenological psychology and the way in which it offers a radical alternative to more traditional 'scientific' approaches that seek to reduce phenomena to discrete variables in order to explain and predict. More usually in phenomenological psychology, a researcher frames a question, based on his or her reading of the extant literature, that seeks to explore some experience (e.g. experience of acute infection) or a particular aspect of an experience (e.g. how someone found the hospital and medical professionals when experiencing an acute infection). This does not mean that the researcher enters the field without an agenda. This is impossible and, I would argue, undesirable. The researcher may or may not seek to collaborate with his or her participants in order to formulate the study questions, but regardless the researcher will have an agenda. However, unlike much traditional research, this agenda will result in open-ended research questions designed to discover the qualities of the phenomenon being investigated, and in the process the questions may need to be amended and refined.

## 5.3 Sampling

The primary method of sampling in descriptive phenomenology is *maximum variation sampling*, where the researcher seeks out participants who have a common experience but who vary on as wide a variety of demographic characteristics as possible (Polkinghorne, 1989). So, a researcher may seek to recruit participants who share an experience (such as social anxiety) but who differ on key demographic variables (e.g. age, sex, ethnicity, etc.) thought to be important to the topic under investigation. Of course, it is not always possible to determine which demographic characteristics might be relevant and, indeed, these are likely to vary according to the particular participants recruited. Furthermore, it may be practically impossible to recruit sufficient participants in order to maximize the variation. As is typical in all research, compromise is likely to be necessary, and although the recruitment process may be guided by the principle of maximum variation, this is unlikely to be achieved fully. The principle underpinning this approach to sampling is that with such variation, it should become possible (in the analytical stage) to ascertain those aspects of the experience that are invariant across perception (the *essence(s)* of the phenomenon) and those that vary across perception. Sample sizes are usually very small due to the time-consuming nature of the analytical process.

IPA, hermeneutic phenomenology, TA and narrative approaches are less likely to employ maximum variation sampling. Instead, the sampling is likely to be *purposive* and *homogeneous*. That is, participants are recruited who share the experience at the heart of the investigation and, if possible, do not vary significantly across demographic characteristics. The aim is to recruit a sample of people such that the researcher can make claims about these people and their particular shared experience. Studies are therefore *idiographic*, and there will be little attempt to generalize beyond this particular sample. Here, the aim is not to maximize variation in the hope of uncovering the invariant structural properties of the phenomenon but instead to develop detailed descriptions of the experience of a small number of people who all share that experience. The sample is purposive because you purposely set out to recruit only those people who share the experience being investigated. Researchers seek out a fairly homogeneous sample, since it is not really possible to garner a random sample or indeed a representative sample. Of course, the nature of the sample in any study will depend on the topic being investigated, the interests of the researcher and the constraints of the study. If the topic is very specific, such as the experience of transitioning from man to woman, then the sample is likely to consist of participants sharing this particular experience regardless of other background characteristics. However, with a more common experience, such as the transition to motherhood, it might be possible to focus on a particular group of women, such as single women or young women, and attempt to understand the detail of their particular experience.

Student projects employing any phenomenological method are likely to be small, with no more than six participants. However, it is perfectly possible to carry out a worthwhile research project with just one participant or indeed tens of participants. As always, the research process must be driven by a combination of theoretical/methodological demands and practical constraints. As long as you take account of both and justify the decisions made, then the research should stand up to public scrutiny. The most important factor is the quality of the data; this is, of course, a matter of judgement, but that need not be a solo affair, since such judgements can and will be informed by the norms in the discipline.

## 5.4 Reflexivity

*Reflexivity* is often mentioned as being crucial in qualitative research but rarely taken really seriously. Very simply, reflexivity is the term for the process in which researchers are conscious of and reflective about the ways in which their questions, methods and very own subject position (as white/black, middle class/working class, heterosexual/homosexual, insider/outsider, etc.) might impact on the psychological knowledge produced in a research study. This process of recognition of the role of the researcher in co-producing psychological knowledge stands in stark contrast to the tradition of the researcher as detached observer in search of some objective truth. Instead, most qualitative approaches to research, including phenomenological approaches, seek to recognize the way in which knowledge is always a co-construction, reflecting the choices and questions the researcher makes and brings as much as the experience of the participants being recounted. Method box 5.1 presents a series of fairly basic questions that all researchers should ask when engaged in any research. In fact, I would argue that a researcher should ask these questions at least three times: before beginning the study, during the study, and once the study has been completed but the research not yet written up. At each of these stages, a researcher can potentially stop the research or amend the questions and/or methods in light of reflections on reflexive issues.

## Method box 5.1
## Questions to encourage a reflexive approach to research

Below are a series of questions that a researcher might wish to reflect on in the context of a research project taking reflexive issues seriously:

1. Why am I carrying out this study?
2. What do I hope to achieve with this research?
3. What is my relationship to the topic being investigated?
   - Am I an insider or outsider?
   - Do I empathize with the participants and their experience?
4. Who am I, and how might I influence the research I am conducting in terms of age, sex, class, ethnicity, sexuality, disability and any other relevant cultural, political or social factors?
5. How do I feel about the work?
   - Are there external pressures influencing the work?
6. How will my subject position influencing the analysis?
7. How might the outside world influencing the presentation of findings?
8. How might the findings impact on the participants?
   - Might they lead to harm and, if so, how can I justify this happening?
9. How might the findings impact on the discipline and my career in it?
   - Might they lead to personal problems, and how prepared am I to deal with these should they arise?
10. How might the findings impact on wider understandings of the topic?
    - How might your colleagues respond to the research?
    - What would the newspapers make of the research?
    - Does the research have any implications for future funding (of similar research and/or related organizations)?
    - What political implications might arise as a result of the research?

Reflexivity becomes especially important when a researcher seeks to study vulnerable people and communities, especially if they are not someone who has experienced the issue or a member of the community being studied. In these circumstances, there are dangers in misrepresenting the people and communities being studied and constructing a subject or topic that reflects your own position (as an outsider), such that those being studied no longer recognize themselves or the communities to which they belong. This danger is particularly pertinent when employing hermeneutics of suspicion (see Chapters 4, 8 and 9), especially if they are being employed with people and communities about which there is little care (see Langdridge & Flowers (2005) and Flowers & Langdridge (in press) for more on a very real published example of where an author employed a psychoanalytic hermeneutic of suspicion on gay men with, I would argue, horrifying results). In these circumstances, I think it vital that the researcher interrogates his or her motivation for pursuing such an investigation and engages seriously with the possible implications that might result from carrying out such a study.

So far, this discussion of reflexivity has concentrated on the *personal* (the effect of the individual) and *functional* (the influence of one's role as a researcher) varieties of reflexivity (see Wilkinson (1988) for a typology and discussion). The third type of reflexivity discussed by Wilkinson, she terms *disciplinary reflexivity* and entails a critical stance towards the research in the context of debates about theory and method. The danger of personal and functional forms of reflexivity is the way in which they tend to draw on a realist epistemology in which the author is brought into the analysis to (objectively) validate the findings (Gough, 2003). One particular version of reflexivity designed to tackle this problem is called *epistemic reflexivity* (White, 1997) and involves a critical stance towards academic discourse itself. Here we see an attempt to be critically aware of the way in which academic discourse – even in discussions about reflexivity such as this one – serve to position the author as expert and the information presented as truth. This is often achieved through the use of scientific discourse, with the author adopting a detached objective stance (as I am here). Some authors have sought to disrupt this particular way of writing through the introduction of multiple voices, personal commentary and creative writing, among other things (see Gough (2003) for a summary). Heidegger's ([1947] 1993) move, late in his philosophy, to an analysis of the way in which poetry might be a more revealing form of discourse than technical discourse (see Chapter 9) clearly prefigures and/or supports this particular reflexive process. There have been criticisms (e.g. Gough, 2003) of this form of reflexivity, however, for the way in which it can be rather self-indulgent, more concerned with style than substance. Although I recognize the need to examine the process of knowledge construction itself (cf. Ashmore, 1989), I think there is a danger in a reflexive infinite regression, with a shift in focus from the topic of interest to a rather excessive interest in the accounting procedures of academic discourse itself. It is clearly important to be aware of the way in which the discourse we use has particular effects, but, as Gough (2003: 31) states:

> A balance is required between opening and closure, between deconstruction and reconstruction, between recognising our qualitative analyses as constructed (and per-

haps using some devices from art and literature to deconstruct our analysis), and – temporarily at least – settling for a version of analysis with which we are satisfied, which we think makes a valid theoretical and/or political point...

The final issue worth reflecting on in this section is the way in which we might demonstrate reflexivity to the readers of our research. Much of the time a researcher will state in a publication that he or she has been aware of reflexive issues, and that is it. Indeed, in many descriptive phenomenological studies, there might not even be this level of recognition, given the arguably false belief in the possibility of bracketing off our preconceptions about a topic (see Chapters 2–4 for more on the theoretical background to these issues). I think this is a mistake and want to argue that if we are really taking reflexivity seriously, then we must make much greater effort to involve the reader in the reflexive process. Of course, this is not easy, given the demands of working within the constraints of journal publishing, but even so I still believe there are possibilities for taking issues of reflexivity more seriously. First, it is important to inform the reader of the position of the researcher with regard to the specific topic being investigated. This information must be sufficient for a reader to be able to tune into the particular position of the researcher and the ways in which this position might have influenced the findings. Furthermore, this information needs to be provided before the presentation of the findings. Second, issues of reflexivity should not then be forgotten as if the confessional abdicates responsibility. During the analysis, it is important for researchers to bring themselves into the analytical process as necessary. Finally, it is always valuable for researchers to reflect on the findings and implications at the very end of a project and on how their own position influences the work. I recognize that this is a counsel of perfection and, as always, there will need to be compromise, and this applies as much to issues of reflexivity as any other part of the research process.

## 5.5 Ethics

Ethics have grown in importance over recent years in the social sciences. Some of this growth is very welcome as the history of the social sciences, and psychology in particular, is littered with ethical abuses that would make your hair stand on end. However, some of this growth has not been so welcome, as we stand witness to the growth in a litigation culture, partly inherited from the USA, along with a growing paranoia about the fragility of humanity, which has led to unnecessary and unwarranted increases in ethical concerns at the cost of research itself. In the following section, I return to these controversial issues some more as I seek to provide further information on ethics in general (although this will be necessarily brief) and ethics specific to the phenomenological psychology research process.

The bottom line for most people engaged in psychological research, of any kind, in the UK is the ethical guidelines published by the British Psychological Society (BPS). Indeed, if you are a member of the BPS, as I am, then it is a professional requirement to take these guidelines very seriously indeed. Thankfully, these guidelines are quite sensible, produced by psychologists and built on an accumulated knowledge base. In Method box 5.2, I briefly outline the key issues from these guidelines.

## Method box 5.2
## British Psychological Society ethical guidelines

Below are some of the key ethical issues discussed in the BPS ethical guidelines (available to download from www.bps.org.uk).

### Consent

Consent is perhaps the most fundamental of all ethical principles. It is also, fortunately, not something that is generally a problem with phenomenological research, where it is the norm to provide participants with full knowledge about the nature of the research in the process of securing their agreement to participate. It is vital that participants are given sufficient information about the study and their involvement in order to enable them to provide informed consent to participate. If participants are under 16 years of age, then their consent should still be sought, but that of their guardian should also be sought. Similarly, if adult participants are unable to give informed consent (if they have severe learning difficulties, for instance), then it is still important to seek their consent as best as is possible as well as that of their guardian and/or other person able to appreciate the possible impact of the study on the participant.

Once a person has consented, this does not mean that this is granted for eternity, however. Participants always retain the right to withdraw their consent at any stage of the research process (even when the data-collection phase has ended and the analysis is being written up). It is important that this is made clear to participants and that they feel able to not consent in the first place and then to withdraw their consent if they no longer feel able to participate in the research. This is, of course, difficult for researchers, who often find it challenging to recruit participants, but people who volunteer their time and effort are doing us an enormous favour and it is important that we do not forget this in our efforts to progress our research.

### Confidentiality and anonymity

As a general principle, all information gathered from a participant should remain confidential unless it is absolutely necessary to break this rule. This position should be made clear to anyone agreeing to participate in a research project. There is also the possibility in some research projects for participants to remain anonymous. This is very unlikely to be the case with phenomenological research, where close and often continuing contact with participants is invariably the norm. However, even here it is important that the identities of one's participants are not made obvious when publishing the findings (in whatever form). All efforts should be made to maintain confidentiality within a research team and to protect one's participants by anonymizing the information they provide when it is made public.

### Discomfort and harm

The BPS guidelines make it very clear that it is the prime responsibility of the researcher to protect the participants from physical and mental harm in any research study. Although physical harm is unlikely to be an issue for phenomenological research, mental harm is something that must be considered. The guidelines state that, normally, the risk of harm must not be greater than that which a person may experience in everyday life. This is a tricky thing to measure, but in general all efforts must be made to

## Method box 5.2
## British Psychological Society ethical guidelines

minimize the risk of participation in any study. In general, this will not be a problem for phenomenological research, although issues might arise if one chooses to research 'sensitive' issues. What constitutes a 'sensitive' issue is controversial, and something that is often used by people uncomfortable with a topic to prevent legitimate research in that area. However, in spite of this, it is still the primary responsibility of the researcher to prevent any discomfort or harm, and so care should be taken when researching topics that people may find embarrassing or difficult to talk about. One method commonly used in phenomenological research is to send the participant the questions that will be asked. They will then be able to judge whether the issue is a sensitive one for them and choose to participate (or not) after being informed fully about the nature of the study.

### Deception
Deception remains commonplace is psychological research. It is not the norm in phenomenological research, where it is much more usual for researcher and participant(s) to work openly and honestly towards a common goal. If, however, it proves necessary to deceive one's participants about the true nature of the research, then there should be strong grounds for such deception and full debriefing following the deception if at all possible.

In addition to the issues mentioned in Method box 5.2, *invasion of privacy* is an ethical issue worthy of consideration for some phenomenological research. In particular, it is relevant for researchers using forms of participant (or even non-participant) observation. The right to privacy is generally very important, and researchers need to think long and hard about studies in which there might be an invasion of privacy. Invasion of privacy does not occur only with observational methods of course. It is also a possibility when interviewing if an interviewer is not sufficiently sensitive to a participant and the participant's desire to not talk about particular issues. Consent is no defence in such circumstances, especially given that it is unusual (although less unusual in phenomenological research than in much other research) to provide participants with interview questions in advance of an interview. It is, therefore, important that an interviewer is sensitive to the needs of an interviewee to not answer questions and to maintain privacy around particular aspects of his or her life. Observational methods, particularly covert participant observation, are, however, methods most likely to raise concerns about invasion of privacy. Indeed, the reduction in research using participant observation is probably related in part to the ethical concerns that research of this kind often raises. The key, as always with ethical concerns, is to think through the possible implications of one's actions as a researcher following a particular course in advance of starting the research. It is important not to remain embedded in one's own way of understanding risk though; your participants are very likely to find different things a problem from you, and although that may sound rather obvious, it is amazing how often people rely on their own understandings of the world, and their place in it, to frame their understandings of how other people may experience the world. For good phenomenological psychologists, this is of course quite wrong, as the heart of the phenomenological project is the ability to explore how the world appears to another person, and this is as relevant when considering invasion of privacy, or for that matter any other ethical concern, as it is when engaged in the analytical process itself.

*Ethics committees* are something that researchers are very likely to come into contact with and, if we are honest, something most of us dread coming into contact with. It would be very unusual these days for research to be conducted in an academic or medical setting where a research proposal wasn't first scrutinized by an ethics committee. It is, therefore, necessary for all researchers to become familiar with the procedures of the institutions where they work and to learn about the ways in which it is possible to manage one's involvement with ethics committees in the best possible way. It is also important to know how best to present work in order to maximize the chances of smooth passage through such committees. A very great deal of phenomenological research will raise few ethical concerns. However, if you choose to research 'sensitive' issues, as I do, then you are more likely to find yourself needing to justify the work and to assure the committee that there are adequate safeguards in place for participants and researcher, especially concerning confidentiality, consent and invasion of privacy. The reason for the scare quotes around 'sensitive' is very relevant here. Although some issues are rightly recognized as 'sensitive' topics, being likely to raise difficult feelings, many topics are categorized as 'sensitive' simply because they are topics that members of ethics committees may find unfamiliar, threatening or even repulsive. There are still, unfortunately, many people on ethics committees who, whether through naivety or malicious intent, baulk at the idea of research with some 'sensitive' issues and populations and, as a consequence, raise the threshold for safety, such that researchers have to provide greater justification and reassurance than they would have had they been researching more mundane topics. A good example, and one that I know very well, is research concerned with sexuality and, in particular, sexual minority populations. I have found myself being asked to provide quite extraordinary levels of detail and reassurance when researching the wishes of young gay men to become parents. I do not find the thought of young gay men choosing to be parents unfamiliar, threatening or repulsive, and I do not think it is a particularly sensitive topic. However, simply because the topic concerns the interests of a minority group, I have had to go to extraordinary lengths to justify such work. My work on sadomasochism has met with even more resistance. Of course, the level of resistance in many ways is a result of the way in which ethical decisions reflect wider personal, organizational, institutional and societal ease or dis-ease with an issue, and there is, therefore, no easy answer. All I can do here is raise the issue to prepare researchers and urge anyone interested in researching such a 'sensitive' topic not to let faux ethical concerns prevent their research from happening.

## 5.6  Collecting data 1: interviews

### 5.6.1  Interviewing and phenomenological research

Interviews (Figure 5.1) are generally classified according to whether they are one of three types: *structured*, *semi-structured* or *unstructured*. The structured interview will not be considered further here, since it is not an appropriate form of data collection for a phenomenological psychological study. The structured interview is effectively a guided questionnaire and, as such, not designed to elicit meanings, the core of phenomenological psychology. The closed response options foreclose the possibility of exploration, and it is only through exploration of ideas and events that understanding of meaning emerges.

The most common interview used in phenomenological research, and indeed in all qualitative research, is the semi-structured interview. This approach to interviewing has a long history in psychology and represents a trade-off between consistency and flexibility that best meets the needs of many qualitative researchers. Consistency is maintained through the use of an interview schedule consisting of a series of questions and prompts designed to elicit the maximum possible information (see Method box 5.3). As can be seen from the example in Method box 5.3, the questions tap different aspects of the experience being explored. They should not be treated too rigidly, however. It is important in semi-structured interviewing that the interviewer works with his or her questions in the light of the conversation that occurs with the interviewee. If questions are

Figure 5.1 Interviewing is a particularly important method for collecting data in phenomenological research

**Method box 5.3**
**An example (abridged) interview schedule: young gay men's expectations of parenthood**

I would now like us to explore your experiences and expectations about becoming a parent a little more. First ...

1. Can you imagine becoming a father at some time in the future?
   - If so, can you tell us something about this?
   - Give me examples of your thinking and talking about this topic.
   - If not, why not (given that the majority of heterosexual men anticipate the role)?
   - Do you know any gay men who have children? Please tell me more about this.

2. Do you wish to be a father at some time in the future?

   If yes:
   - Can you give me examples of times when you have thought about this? (Encourage detailed description of several instances he/they wanted to be a father.)
   - Why do you think you have these feelings?
   - Do you think social pressure has anything to do with this? (From family?)
   - Might it be due to the fact that most other (heterosexual) men have children? If so, how come?
   - Do you think you would be treated differently as a father? (How? Given more respect? Accepted more?)
   Have you thought of how you would achieve this aim?

   If no:
   - Why do you think you have this view?
   - (Check the following: if yes, follow up ...)
   - Do you not want to conform (or be similar to heterosexual men)?
   - Do you not want to lose your freedom/independence?
   - Do you think it would damage your lifestyle too much?
   - Do you envisage too many problems preventing it (prejudice, etc.)?
   - Do you have other alternative forms of life satisfaction?
   - Or have you just not thought about the possibility?

3. What role do you think your sexuality plays with regard to this decision?
   - Can you foresee resistance to pursuing a wish for a child? From whom? Why? Examples?
   - Do you feel gay men are excluded from having children? Why? Examples?
   - Would it please other people you know if you decided to have a child? Who? Why? Examples?

4. What does 'family' mean to you?
   - Only biological? Friends?
   - Does this make a difference to your feelings about becoming a father?

answered earlier, then the interviewer needs to work with this and not attempt to enforce the schedule rigidly. There may also be topics that emerge that had not occurred to the researcher during the production of the interview schedule, and these should be followed up if it is thought that they will shed light on the topic. The aim is always the development of rapport to enable joint exploration of the participant's world view concerning the topic; the schedule is merely a guide to enable the researcher to do this as effectively as possible given the constraints of time and money that the researcher (and the participants) inevitably faces.

The construction of an interview schedule is an important part of the process and needs considerable thought, discussion with fellow students/colleagues and, ideally, *piloting* (testing out an early version for feedback). It is important to begin by considering the range of issues to be explored within the broad remit of the topic being researched. With some thought (and often after reviewing the literature), it should be possible to identify a number of key issues (either conceptual or theoretical) that will form the overarching structure to the interview. In the abridged interview schedule shown in Method box 5.3, the interview is structured conceptually (although with a number of theoretical concerns about, for instance, the impact of fatherhood on the sense of identity), with a number of key topics identified (thoughts about fatherhood, desire to be a father, impact of sexuality, etc.). Once a number of topics have been identified, it is important to structure the interview schedule appropriately. It would be usual to structure the interview in the most logical manner possible, with questions flowing naturally from one to another. This may need to be tempered by the desire to tackle more difficult questions later so as not to push an interviewee too hard too soon. It is important to generate rapport, and presenting an interviewee with challenging questions before he or she has had time to settle in to the interview process may well prove counterproductive. Once the topics have been identified and structured appropriately, it is necessary to generate the specific questions for each topic. Invariably, the questions will be *funnelled* from the most general to the most specific. This is to allow the interviewee to focus on his or her concerns rather than the interviewer's, at least at first. Very often with a talkative interviewee, the more specific questions will be unnecessary, as the interviewee answers them all in the course of providing an answer to the initial question. In this case, simply skip the questions and just encourage the participant to keep talking, using the usual prompts and encouragers ('yes', 'go on', 'interesting', 'tell me more', etc.). It is important when writing interview questions that they are clear and simple. Although there is room for clarification in an interview situation, it is always best not to confuse or intimidate an interviewee. Try to keep questions neutral rather than particularly value-laden. Try also to avoid technical language unless you know the interviewee is familiar with the language. And, of course, always use open rather than closed questions – that is, questions that encourage expansive answers rather than simple yes/no answers. With some thought and piloting, it should be possible to construct an interview schedule that will work and avoid these problems. Furthermore, with practice, constructing an interview schedule will become second nature.

The semi-structured interview is not the only choice of interview available to the phenomenological researcher. Unstructured interviews also offer the potential of exploring people's experiences, perhaps even more so than do semi-structured interviews. Unstructured interviews are, however, tricky things to manage, and especially to manage well. The construction of an interview schedule and the consistent application that is vital with semi-structured inter-viewing provides a structure to support the researcher and the collection of good-quality data. Without these structures, there is a greater likelihood of fail-ing to achieve the aims of a study. So what does an unstructured interview entail? Essentially, the researcher is likely to have very little to help guide the interview: the researcher's own agenda concerning the topic he or she wishes to discuss and maybe a few notes to act as an aide-mémoire. Very often, an inter-viewer asks a question to frame the discussion and to focus attention on the topic of interest and then works with the interviewee to explore the interviewee's understanding. This may involve the interviewer picking up on responses and asking for further detail or clarification and asking further questions as and when appropriate. The interview is very likely to be conversational in style, and this is arguably the major advantage of unstructured interviews over semi-structured interviews. If the participant becomes engaged in conversation very naturally, then there is the very real possibility of rapport and, with this, more open and honest responses along with greater richness. However, without considerable practice, these ideals may never be achieved – it is surprisingly difficult to engage in a conversation in a very natural way with a research agenda in the back-ground. One way of increasing the likelihood of rapport and rich responses covering the full range of the topic is to conduct a series of unstructured inter-views, ideally spaced sufficiently apart to enable the researcher to listen (and perhaps transcribe) the previous interview and then to use this as a springboard for the follow-up interview or interviews. Repeated exposure to an interviewer is likely in itself to increase rapport and enable greater exploration of the topic. The costs, in terms of time and finance, for both researcher and participant of engaging in repeated interviews often, however, preclude the possibility of such elaborate data-collection processes, and it is probably for this reason alone that the semi-structured interview has come to dominate qualitative research in the social sciences.

### 5.6.2 The interview process

Interviewing is a skill that requires practice, and there is no substitute for this. It is possible to practise with friends and colleagues, of course, and so avoid at least some of the discomfort (and wasted effort) that may arise with the real thing if you are unprepared. I do recommend that you find the time to practise inter-viewing if it is not something you are already experienced with. Ideally, practise with a more skilled friend or colleague, who will be able to point out weaknesses that you can work on before you carry out the interviews proper. I have spent a lot of time in practice interviews with my students, and I believe that this has ultimately led to much better-quality interviews in the end.

It is important to have the right equipment available when conducting inter-views. Most often this is a tape recorder. Recording equipment is getting better and cheaper all the time, and it is no longer necessary to spend a fortune on equipment to tape-record interviews with a good enough level of sound quality.

The key is to use equipment that will enable the easy transcription of data (see below). Poor recording equipment results in transcription becoming a very difficult process that is error-prone and inaccurate. More and more researchers are exploring the use of digital recording devices. These are often more expensive but do produce very high-quality recordings. The problem, however, is that foot-operated transcription machines are readily available for tape-recorded data but less so for digital media. If you are considering the use of digital equipment, then investigate the ease or difficulty of transcribing given the hardware available to you. The other factor that is important when considering equipment is reliability and ease of operation. It is vital that the equipment does not break down in the middle of an interview (some interviewers use two tape recorders to protect themselves against this possibility) and that you do not struggle to operate the equipment. Whenever conducting a series of interviews, it is important to check your recording equipment thoroughly first and to carry spare tapes, batteries and, if possible, microphone and tape recorder.

The interview should, ideally, be a relaxed affair, enjoyable in many cases for both interviewer and interviewee. This can be achieved best if you take the time to put the interviewee at ease and then continue to monitor his or her state throughout the interview. Work at your interviewee's pace, slowing down or speeding up where necessary. Allow time for people to chat, wander off the subject, and so on. It is not necessary to maintain a steely grip on the proceedings; this will only lead to tension. If an interviewee starts talking about an issue you had listed later in your schedule, then go with it and, if necessary, return to where you were later. By and large, it is always best to avoid interrupting someone when they are talking. If, however, they wander completely off the subject and seem unlikely to return, it may well be necessary to gently remind them of the need to return to the questions. When asking questions, make sure you ask only one at a time. Keep things simple and clear at all times and check regularly whether things are clear to the interviewee. If the interviewee appears confused or distressed, then respond to this directly by asking whether everything is okay. Do not leave things and hope for the best. Finally, do not be afraid of silence. As long as a silence is constructive, there should be no problem. This is something that you must judge carefully, since some silence will be uncomfortable. People need time to think, however, particularly if they have just been asked a novel or challenging question. Give participants time to think and allow the silence. Be watchful, however, of the awkward silence where the participant simply has nothing more to say.

### 5.6.3 The body in phenomenological interviewing

Finlay (2006) has stressed the need to attend to issues of embodiment in the interview process. She correctly highlights the absence of the body in much phenomenological research, in spite of the existential foundations (see Chapter 3) at the heart of the phenomenological psychological perspective. Drawing principally on the work of Merleau-Ponty (see Chapter 3), Finlay (2006) argues persuasively that researchers need to attend reflexively to both their own and their participants' bodies. To this end, she identifies three distinct aspects of embodiment that may be attended to within the interview process: *bodily empathy, embodied self-awareness* and *embodied intersubjectivity*. Bodily empathy involves the researcher paying particular attention to a participant's movements and general demeanour. It is made clear, however, that this does not involve a simple behavioural reading of gestures but instead involves an appreciation of the embodied relationship between researcher and participant. Embodied self-awareness involves the examination of the researcher's own embodied response, where we interrogate our own bodily experience throughout the research process. Embodied intersubjectivity requires us to attend to the 'in between', that which occurs between researcher and researched. Finlay (2006) provides vivid examples for all three aspects of embodiment and, through the use of Merleau-Ponty, highlights the need for working with bodies in phenomenological psychology. Whether the tripartite distinction is necessary is debatable, but it may prove helpful in focusing attention on different aspects of embodiment in the research process. The challenge for all researchers working phenomenologically now becomes one of how they do (or do not) deal with issues of embodiment in the research process.

### 5.6.4 Online interviewing

Interviews can also be conducted via the telephone, email or Internet relay chat (IRC) rather than face to face. These ways of conducting interviews may be especially valuable with geographically distant interviewees and with people who feel more comfortable using more anonymous forms of communication. There are currently two main methods of conducting online interviews. The first and simplest is through email where messages are sent between the interviewer and participant at agreed points (asynchronous communication). The second is IRC, where the interviewer and participant are online at the same time, communicating in real time through online chat software (synchronous communication). This approach mirrors face-to-face interviewing more clearly but is more personally and technologically demanding than email interviewing.

The arguments above about the central role of the body in coming to know the other clearly offer a profound challenge for the practice of online interviewing. With online interviewing, there is a rupture between self and other, especially with regard to the body. There is no longer the opportunity to perceive the presence of the other through the full range of senses available. Of course, the other may be conjured up in the imagination of the participant and/or interviewer, but the corporeality featured in the imaginary must remain imaginary. If the body is central to phenomenological psychology, then online interviewing must necessarily be a form of compromised research practice, justified only by the practical constraints of conducting research in a world of limited resources. In the following section, I, however, explore this issue further, with reference to (i) Heidegger's (2001) distinction between bodies and corporeal things and (ii)

Figure 5.2 The Internet is becoming an increasingly important way of collecting data for qualitative research

the growth of systems of cyber-communication that seek to return the body to an online relationship between self and other. This work builds on the arguments made in Chapter 3, so it is important to have read that chapter before continuing with this section.

Heidegger ([1927] 1962) spends remarkably little time discussing the body in *Being and Time*. The reasons for this become apparent in the *Zollikon Seminars*, where Heidegger (2001: 231) concedes 'the bodily [*das Leibliche*] is the most difficult [to understand]', in spite of the fact that it is the foundation for all being-in-the-world. It is important to note, however, that Heidegger (2001) is not talking about 'the body' but about 'the bodily', and the distinction he draws between corporeality (*Körper*, or corporeal things) and bodies (*Leib*, or the bodily) is what I wish to discuss here, since I believe it provides the potential for a radical move in understanding the role of the body in online research practice.

Heidegger (2001) draws the distinction between *corporeal things* and *the body* in the *Zollikon Seminars* as he tries to answer the question 'What does it mean to be here?' That is, how do we understand what it means to be here in an embodied way in any particular space? Heidegger questions whether the limits of a corporeal body need coincide with the sense of embodied selfhood that we all possess. The corporeal thing stops and is bounded by the skin, whereas our sense of embodied selfhood may extend beyond this 'bodily limit'. Heidegger uses the example of pointing, where our sense of *bodiliness* does not stop at the fingertip but, instead, stretches out beyond the skin to the object captured in our gaze.

Murray's (2004) work on the experience of living with an artificial limb – conducted using email interviews – provides further support for this distinction. He describes how people experience a prosthesis as an extension of the body and its absence as the total absence of that aspect of bodiliness. To clarify the distinction further, and to answer the objections to the making of such a distinction, Heidegger traces our current use of (French and German) language back to the distinction made in the Greek language between dead and living bodies, seeing the Greek language as the origin of Western thought. With this, Heidegger once again challenges our everyday understanding, this time of embodiment. For the phenomenology of the body in the West, in these late modern times, is founded on a very particular individualistic biological understanding of what it means to be embodied.

The distinction between corporeal things and bodies complicates the notion of attending to the body in online research and provides one possible answer to the absence of the (corporeal) body. For, if Heidegger (2001) is right to draw a distinction between that bounded by the skin and our 'bodiliness', then even in online interviewing we are likely to see bodiliness in action. Admittedly, this will be principally through text, but as soon as one moves away from the notion of the body and towards bodiliness, then the ability to conjure up a sense of embodied subjectivity in text emerges. Of course, writers of great literature have always known this and have been able to communicate a sense of space and place in text. It must, therefore, be possible to work with the medium of text with a participant to co-create a sense of our mutual bodiliness or a 'fusion of bodily horizons' (Langdridge, 2005). This may not have the richness of great literature but, instead, it will have an immediacy of communication, a sense of shared accomplishment, as researcher and researched work together to create a sense of embodied meaning within the constraints of the online research setting.

There is another way in which bodiliness is starting to be worked through in cyberspace: through the use of *avatars*. Avatars are computer-generated representations of selves, images created or simply appropriated by cyber-subjects in order to represent them in a particular place at a particular time. These images are most often still, but with increasing technology we see the emergence of moving images and the growth of virtual-reality and three-dimensional representations. Avatars represent a very postmodern (Lyotard, [1979] 2004) turn in the representation of identities, as people appropriate the images of others or create their own, employ fantastical images blurring and merging the boundaries of what it means to be human and present different images and identities at different times and/or in different places. Understanding 'the code' (Baudrillard, 1993), where the distinction between original and copy becomes redundant, is central in this paradoxical world. Here *re*-production, rather than production, is crucial as cyber-subjects appropriate identities not as copies of natural originals but rather as a formula or binary code.

Avatars, therefore, have the potential to facilitate a greater sense of bodiliness in cyberspace, for there is now more than text available to communicate one's sense of embodiment, mood or identity. Avatar users may be blocked or crowded and feel a real sense of bodily power or invasion. Users may also move their images in synchrony with another to dance, while others may express their emotions through movement of their avatar. Suler (1999) describes further aspects of bodiliness that may be communicated through the use of avatars:

> A key component of this physical awareness involves the dynamics of personal space, not unlike face-to-face relationships. Users instinctively feel that the area on and immediately around their avatar is *their* personal zone. Step on it without invitation, and they quickly ask, then demand you to get off. Persist, and some people will holler for a wizard to discipline you. If members don't interpret your behavior as an invasion, they will experience it as an intimate advance. Simply to move towards and stand next to someone is seen as an act of friendship, or more. Snuggling and climbing onto someone's icon ('piggybacking') may convey warm, sexual, or romantic feelings. They can very subtly create emotional bonds. If someone's snuggling goes on for too long, or is not what you want at all, you may feel restricted, suffocated, and hesitant to move away for fear of hurting feelings. Right or wrong, other people may think that you two are an 'item.' The emotional depth of these non-verbal behaviors can be quite amazing. As in face-to-face interactions, they may provide glimpses into underlying feelings and attitudes that are not being expressed verbally.

Future possibilities are limited only by technology, and the rapid advances in graphical processing have been staggering. There are already attempts to engage with avatars in the mental-health field (e.g. Anthony & Lawson, 2002). Although text will remain, for the time being at least, the principal medium of communication, it can now be supplemented by images that may further reduce perceived gaps between face-to-face and online interviewing. Furthermore, these technological innovations, if accompanied by widespread social change, may in turn influence our everyday understandings and experience of our bodies in such a way that Heidegger's (2001) notion of bodiliness becomes perceived en masse as the phenomenological ground for our embodied way of being-the-world.

### 5.6.5 Transcription

Transcription is a vital part of a phenomenological study when data have been collected through interviews. Unlike discourse analysis, however, phenomenological psychology projects tend to work with a relatively simple level of transcription. The focus is nearly always on producing a transcript that, in effect, provides the analyst with a verbatim account of the interview. This will include 'ums' and 'ahs' but normally not any finer level of detail. Discourse and conversation analysts by contrast will employ some version of a Jefferson version of transcription, which includes detail of pauses (timed precisely), overlaps in speech, intonation and much more (see Hutchby and Wooffitt (1998) for more on this and the conversation analytical method). It is extremely time-consuming to produce this level of transcript and, given the focus on the content of speech that is at the heart of most phenomenological approaches, also unnecessary. See Method box 5.4 for an example of a transcript produced for a phenomenological level of analysis.

## Method box 5.4
## An example (abridged transcript)

**Participant 1 – male, 18 years, 18 December 2001**

[First half of interview cut]

*Int:*     Right. OK, I want to go on to now it's about expectations about fatherhood. I would now     1
like to explore your experiences and expectations about becoming a parent. Firstly, can
you imagine becoming a father at some time in the future?

*Par:*     Definitely! Yep – ermm – the current situation is that I've just bought my first home and
I've just lost my job. Ermm – so certainly from the financial point of view alone I wouldn't    5
consider having a child at the moment. There's a lot of things that need to be done with
the house – ermm – I don't feel that … I'm certainly emotionally ready to have a child but
not financially. I wouldn't want to bring a child into the world at the moment obviously,
because of the uncertainty in the future. Certainly the emotional support would be there
– that wouldn't be a problem. And the love and the affection and spending time with the    10
child wouldn't bother me in the slightest – that would always be there.

*Int:*     OK, can you give me examples of when you've actually been thinking and talking about
this topic. You know times when you've thought …

*Par:*     Well, recently – ermm – probably – err – around this time last year, I found out that a gay
couple of mine … two gay men that I know quite well were about to become … we'll say    15
a dad between them – ermm – they've known a couple of gay women that have been
together quite a while who've for several years been unsuccessful with IVF treatment,
because they so desperately wanted a child to bring up together.

    20

Even the simple level of transcription required for phenomenological research raises important questions, however. First, just how much detail is needed? Do we include every 'ermm', or do we erase these aspects of speech, given that we are predominantly concerned with content? Second, do we correct what is spoken in order to improve clarity – clean up the data if you will, lose the colloquialisms, the grammatical errors or mispronunciations? In general, I think it wise to stay as close to the speech of the participant as possible. The transcript is itself a move away from the immediacy of the interaction, with a consequent loss of information. It seems somewhat foolish, therefore, to lose further information that may have a bearing on meaning for the sake of grammatical purity. It is also (arguably) disrespectful to one's participants to 'clean up' their language. This does, of course, then raise the argument that perhaps we should follow the discourse and conversation analysts with their desire to capture the maximum amount of information possible when converting the spoken word into text and adopt a system like the Jefferson system for transcription. Although there is a serious debate to be had, I think the fact that phenomenological methods do not employ methods of analysis that work at the micro-level of discourse or conversation analysis means it is practically unnecessary to transcribe to that level of detail (see Chapter 9 for more on this). The focus of phenomenology is experience and the meaning this has for one's participants, and although the intricacies of language may have something to say about the accounts being produced, they are not the focus of a study in phenomenological psychology.

## 5.7 Collecting data 2: written accounts

### 5.7.1 Concrete descriptions of experience

Interviews are by no means the only method of data analysis suitable for phenomenological studies. Indeed, self-written descriptive accounts have been the mainstay of a considerable amount of descriptive phenomenological work. In essence, this involves the researcher providing the participants with some instructions asking them to produce a written document describing in as much detail as possible an experience of interest to the researcher (see Method box 5.5).

The key with this form of data analysis is to provide sufficient information and encouragement to participants so they produce detailed accounts of their experience. It requires considerable effort to produce something of the detail needed for a good phenomenological analysis, and this will require the selection of suitable participants and then the active encouragement of their efforts. Participants will, of course, also need to be able to write or type, although it is possible to provide tape recorders for people to speak into if they have physical disabilities preventing them from writing or typing. They will then, however, be unable to edit the material.

Very often, researchers combine this written collection of data with interviews. Initial data describing an experience can be elicited using this method, and then a short time later (a week or two) a semi-structured interview can be conducted, designed to encourage participants to elaborate on and clarify the written material they have provided. This is a particularly appealing method, since it encourages active reflection on the topic under investigation between the production of the written account and the interview. The written component gives participants the opportunity to tell their own story, while the interview allows researchers to explore topics of particular interest.

### 5.7.2 (Auto)biographical writing and diaries

In more narratively oriented forms of phenomenology, such as critical narrative analysis (see Chapter 8), it may be appropriate to explore participants' life stories. This can be a particularly rich avenue for research, producing unexpected insights and links that could never have been predicted. Of course, interviews can be conducted in a way so that life histories are told in full or in part. It is simply necessary to structure the schedule in a way that encourages the telling of a life story. This may involve participants being asked simply to tell their story (as it relates to the topic of interest) chronologically or to structure their

## Method box 5.5
## An example of a concrete written description (including prompt information)

### The experience of acute infection: hepatitis A

Thank you for agreeing to take part in this study of the experience of acute infections. All information you provide will be treated confidentially and will be anonymized before being read by anyone other than the researcher (Dr Darren Langdridge, The Open University) or used in any publications arising from the research. The information you provide below will form the basis of an informal interview to be conducted one week after you submit your written account.

I would be grateful if you could describe your experience of being infected with hepatitis A below. Please recount the experience in as much detail as possible, including the experience of the illness prior to and after diagnosis. This should include information about your thoughts and feelings about the experience of this particular illness as well as concrete detail about symptoms and effects of the illness itself.

*After a heavy night out, I awoke with what I thought was a monster hangover, headache, body ache, dehydrated and feeling nauseous. This was Saturday morning. Knowing what to do, I tried to take on fluids and eat a little, but things did not settle well. Through the day the hangover faded but I still felt ill – nausea, fever, sweating, dizziness, tingly skin, shivering and diarrhoea.*

*We were on a weekend break in Prague. I wanted to see some of the city with my partner, keep him company and to be a pleasant person to be with.*

*We were now aware that I did not have just an extended hangover. I felt that I was going down with some virus, flu or something and this was just bad timing.*

*Seeing the sights and eating out was a bit of a chore. I was tired, didn't want to eat or drink so really had to force myself to drink and eat a little. I managed some food in the evening but was not much company afterwards. The evening was fairly cold. I was well wrapped up but was shivering so violently at times it was painful. On returning to the hotel, I was so tired and cold I just wanted to sleep but soon woke up drenched in sweat.*

*The next day I felt worse and did not want to venture far from the hotel, suffering badly from vomiting, headaches, sweating, shivering, dizziness and diarrhoea in all possible combinations. I also felt incredibly tired.*

*The next day was the flight home. With monumental effort, I managed the taxi journey to the airport, the sight and smell of smoked salmon sandwiches on the plane and the drive home from the airport. Once home, I must have just wanted to sleep.*

*Next morning (Tuesday), I was awake first thing to make an appointment at the doctor's. A couple of hours later I was explaining my symptoms to the doctor, including being unable to keep food down and brown unpleasant-smelling urine – a locum GP. Being a very infrequent visitor to the doctor's and being fairly aware of health issues, I would have expected to be taken a little more seriously. Yes, I knew I had a fever and it was probably some virus or other. The outcome was go away and keep taking fluids; if you don't get better, come back.*

*The rest of that day and the following day, my symptoms seemed to worsen. A little comfort from being at home but I had not eaten for days. I was very concerned that I was not pulling through and felt to be getting weaker.*

*[cont.]*

story in the form of a book, with chapters for different periods in their life. Further guidance can be found in Chapter 8 and in the further reading list at the end of this chapter.

Life-story data can also be collected from existing writing and especially from diaries. Many people keep records of their lives, although few are published. This material does, however, provide a rich source of data (Figure 5.3). There are a

**Figure 5.3** Diaries and other forms of autobiographical writing have long been used as a valuable source of data in phenomenological research

number of important considerations to bear in mind if the writing comes from a source outside your control. First, it is important to ask why the person kept the diary. Was it for publication or for purely personal purposes? That is, was the person writing for themselves or for others, or some mix of the two? Then it becomes important to ascertain how much editing has taken place. It is very rare that a diary will appear in print completely unexpurgated. If it has been edited, then it is important to ask by whom and for what purpose and, most importantly, what was cut out. It may in some circumstances be possible to negotiate access to material that has not been published (see Butt and Langdridge (2003) for an example of a theoretically driven analysis of Kenneth Williams' diaries).

It may also be possible to work with one or, very rarely, more than one participant willing to write out the story of their life on their own or with you and/or to keep diaries recording those aspects of life they deem important. This would undoubtedly be a complicated procedure requiring a very high level of commitment on the part of the participant and a very good relationship between participant and researcher. Finally, of course, it is possible to write autobiographically. This circumvents some of the problems inherent in working with participants (dropout, lack of enthusiasm, etc.) while introducing problems unique to this form of data collection. If you are thinking of engaging in this form of data analysis, then it will be wise to think through the following eight questions and evaluate your responses critically and honestly:

1. What is it that I have to say about my life that will be relevant for psychological research?
2. Will I be telling a story that really adds (when analysed) to social scientific knowledge? Or will it simply be an indulgence?

3. How willing am I to disclose all necessary (in terms of the aims of the research) aspects of my life to the public gaze?

4. What impact might it have on those close to me if I do disclose aspects of my life?

5. Am I able to keep a critical distance between those aspects of my life I wish to disclose and those aspects that I do not wish to disclose?

6. Will it be possible for me to work in a systematic way when analysing the data?

7. Do I have the commitment necessary for the research to be worthwhile?

8. Are there better ways of collecting data relevant to the research questions that I have discounted for the perceived ease (and possibly pleasure) of conducting an autobiographical piece of research?

## 5.8   Collecting data 3: other sources of text and observation

### 5.8.1   Documents

I have already touched on this above when discussing the possibility of using diaries and autobiographies as a source of textual material for phenomenological analysis. There are, however, many more sources of text that might form the basis of a phenomenological investigation. Perhaps the most obvious source of text is the mass media: books, newspapers, magazines, television programmes and films (Figure 5.4). There is a mass of information circulating in contemporary society, and there is, therefore, the opportunity to interrogate such information. Of course, for phenomenological researchers predominantly interested in people's experience,

**Figure 5.4  There is a never-ending source of data in the mass media, reports and books**

such sources of text are most likely to be used in addition to, rather than instead of, more conventional forms of data collection. It is worth noting that more narratively oriented forms of analysis (e.g. CNA) may well be suitable for the analysis of the mass media. Confronted with such a mass of information, the researcher has to work systematically, sampling appropriately and then analysing the material in the same way in which one might analyse an interview transcript. Most often, researchers will seek to identify themes and stories in these sources of text as they try to shed light on whatever topic is at stake.

Another source of text that can prove useful in phenomenological research comes from official documents, both state and private in origin. The introduction of legislation, for instance, often generates vast quantities of text that provides often unique insights into contemporary issues in our sociopolitical life. Public inquiries, consultation exercises and so on all require the accumulation of information leading to the production of the final report. Often, the final report is a rather lifeless affair, but the material accumulated in the process of generating the report can be rich and detailed, providing valuable insights about many different topics. Of particular note here is the need to gain access to this information. This can be very difficult but is not impossible if a clear programme of research using the material is identified, along with some outcomes that might benefit those bodies with a vested interest in the archive that you wish to access.

### 5.8.2 The Internet

It is worth mentioning the way in which the Internet might be a valuable source of data. My own research on sadomasochism (Langdridge & Butt, 2004, 2005) began through an analysis of 'enthusiast' Internet sites where people were telling their own stories. This is probably the easiest of all ways of using the Internet for the generation of data. Open-access sites are a feature of this information media and there are, therefore, few difficulties ethically or practically involved in working with this massively underutilized source of data. This is not, of course, the only way in which one can work with the Internet to generate data. Also of note here, albeit briefly, is the use of observational techniques in chat rooms, where a researcher might simply observe the communications, recording them in most cases, or might actively involve him- or herself in the online chat. This can be a particularly fruitful way of gaining access to difficult-to-reach minority populations and garnering real-life conversational data that are tremendously rich. This kind of work does, however, raise a large number of ethical and practical difficulties and should not be undertaken lightly. Mann and Stewart (2000) provide valuable advice on a vast range of issues pertinent to qualitative research and the Internet.

### 5.8.3 Observation

Observation is another method that can be used to collect phenomenological data. It is used less commonly than interviews of written descriptions, but it is a useful method, particularly in situations where interviews or written descriptions may be inappropriate or difficult to conduct. Indeed, I think observation is an underused method of data collection and one, if carried out well, that can add valuable insights into the lifeworld of one's participants. Observation used for phenomenological data collection is most likely to be a form of *close observation* (Van Manen, 1990), more commonly known as *participant observation*. The aim is to enter the lifeworld of the participant in order to better understand and describe it, while still maintaining a critical (hermeneutic) distance to enable reflection on the experience. Van Manen (1990) suggests this process is like the author on the lookout for new stories. The observational researcher should keep notes of his or her experiences, in the form of concrete descriptions, personal reflections in a research diary and anecdotes (see Chapter 9 for more on the use of anecdote in phenomenological psychology). Participant observation is not an easy method of data collection, however, and researchers are likely to require training to enable them to gather good-quality data and adhere to the ethical standards required (see Section 5.5).

## 5.9   Quality: adopting a systematic approach to research

### 5.9.1   Analytical rigour

A large number of researchers do not know how to carry out research properly and/or feel that it is not necessary to be as rigorous with qualitative research as it is with quantitative research. On the contrary, it is absolutely vital that qualitative research is conducted in a systematic and rigorous manner. This is necessary in order to prevent the worse excesses of the projection of the researcher's own subjectivity into the research itself and also to maximize the possibility of discovering that which was otherwise hidden in the data. In the following chapters, it will become obvious that rigour, produced through the systematic application of key methodological principles, is an essential part of the qualitative (phenomenological) research process. More information is given in Chapter 9 on quality and phenomenological psychology, but some of the key issues are briefly mentioned below.

### 5.9.2   Producing a persuasive account

This is probably the most important aspect of the quality-assurance process. In essence, all researchers seek to produce an account of the phenomenon that they have investigated that is persuasive to one or more audiences. Most often the audience will be fellow academics who read research papers, but, depending on the nature of the research, the audience may also be service users, policy-makers and so on. With the theoretical recognition that 'there are no facts only perspectives' (the aim of the Nietzschean 'overman', able to see the world from his own perspective) comes an acknowledgement that methods for validating the quality of research must move away from a natural-science model of truth. Although there might not be any objectively verifiable facts, especially when investigating human nature, there will still be some perspectives that appear to be more relevant, more insightful and, therefore, more persuasive. One's peers play a significant role in this process, as they critically interrogate findings through collegial discussions, conference papers, the review process involved in academic publication and, finally, critical response to a published paper. There are, therefore, many opportunities to assess the persuasiveness of the work and to make adjustments to the process (through a change either in the analytical process or in the method of interpretation) as necessary.

### 5.9.3  Collaborative working

This was touched on above through mention of collegial discussions, but there is clearly a place for engaging in collaborative working as a deliberate strategy for quality assurance. In addition to the usual benefits that come from working together on a project with colleagues, there arises the opportunity to work critically with each member of the team in such a way that academic rigour is maximized and assured. This way of working does not mean that you will be arriving at some truth but that you will better enable active reflection on both process and content, thus maximizing the chance that findings will be robust and persuasive.

### 5.9.4  Participant feedback

Finally, it is worth mentioning the possibility of seeking participant feedback on work. In reality, most researchers seek participant validation of their work rather than feedback, which is of particular theoretical concern for some (see below). This is a somewhat controversial strategy, but it may in some circumstances offer another way of critically evaluating the quality of the research conducted. If we are taking people's experiences seriously, then it is perhaps no surprise that we might want to return to our participants and explore our findings with them, gaining feedback on whether they feel their experience has been rendered accurately and, one hopes, illuminated further. There are some concerns with this, however. First, on a very practical level, if one wishes to receive participant feedback, then one will have to produce materials that are intelligible to the participants. Very often, academic writing is written for fellow academics and this may, therefore, require the researcher to rewrite reports in everyday language (not a bad project in itself) and/or spend considerable time with the participants, talking through the full nature of the project and research process. This is, unfortunately, very often not possible given the practical constraints under which most of us work. Second, there are important issues to bear in mind about the relative power of researcher and participant and the ability of a participant to provide honest feedback. Participants may find it too difficult to criticize a researcher because of fear of offending the researcher or causing them problems (especially when researchers come back to participants at the end of a project). This difficulty can be overcome to some extent through the active involvement of participants throughout the research process, although this raises new difficulties of its own of course. Finally, there is a more theoretically derived concern about seeking participant feedback. First, and at a very simple level, people may not be able to adopt a meta-perspective on their own experience (step outside the natural attitude), being embodied beings-in-the-world, inseparable from their own experience. Asking someone to stand back from their experience and adopt a God's eye perspective is very likely asking the impossible, unless one subscribes to a Husserlian belief that this is possible of course. Most often, people have a partial perspective, sometimes able to distance themselves from a particular experience, while at other times unable to manage any critical distance at all. Second, and much more controversially, if one sees a role for a hermeneutic of suspicion (see Chapters 4 and 8), then one must recognize that this is because it is thought necessary to engage interpretatively with the text in a way that takes it beyond the description that emerged from the participant. Participants may or may not, therefore, recognize themselves when subjected to such interpretation, and the utility of working with participant feedback would be somewhat questionable under these circumstances. In the end, a researcher will need to make a judgement in the light of these issues about the value of working, or not working, with participant feedback. If the choice is not to return to the participants, then it becomes ever more important to interrogate the motivation behind this decision; and if it proves to be motivated by a sense of shame at facing the participants, then the research should be called into question in the most serious way.

## 5.10 Writing and communicating your findings

Qualitative research requires a different method of presentation than quantitative research. The scientific report format that is the mainstay of most psychological research, modelled as it is on reports produced in the natural sciences, does not facilitate the presentation of findings from phenomenological research. Instead, researchers use a variety of different presentation formats depending on their theoretical perspective. Detail on the different forms of presentation is given in the following chapters when the different phenomenological perspectives are described in turn. However, in brief, IPA and TA will tend to use a modified form of the standard scientific report, with variations only in the presentation of method and findings. More narratively oriented work can also be presented using the modified form of report or by presentation in a biographical narrative form, with the chronological presentation of an individual case or cases. Descriptive phenomenological studies often contain features expected in the traditional scientific research report, such as the literature review, but they tend to depart from the traditional scientific report in the presentation of findings. With these approaches, the findings consist of the description of an individual experience and short-paragraph summaries of the structure of the experience being described across all the participants. There is much less attempt to link these findings with the extant literature, although this is changing; instead, there is a strong focus on simply describing the key properties of the experience that is the focus of the study. Like much in psychology, however, there are no hard and fast rules about the method of presentation. It is, of course, vital that the findings are presented in a clear way and that priority is given to representing the experience being described. Beyond this, it is up to the individual researcher to best judge what format will suit their work and also what format is demanded of them, depending on where they wish to publish the work. There is often little choice, since academic journals dictate the precise format required to publish.

## 5.11 The use of computers in phenomenological research

Information technology is increasingly used to facilitate qualitative research. Unlike statistics software, however, qualitative data analysis software (QDAS) does not carry out the analysis for you. Instead, it merely assists in the manipulation of data and the production of the findings. It is, therefore, more akin to word-processing software than to statistics software. Some phenomenological psychologists do make use of QDAS, while others prefer to stay with simple paper-and-pen methods, either because it is not thought worth the effort to learn how to use the software or, more importantly, it is thought that such software imposes restrictions on the type of analysis that is possible and/or takes the researcher further away from the experience being described.

One of the most popular packages, and one of the most useful for phenomenological research, is NVivo™. This package enables the manipulation of data at a fine level, which is ideal for phenomenological work. It is also clear and simple to use. However, the software does require some time to learn and will, to some extent, restrict the way a analyst can work. This may be acceptable for studies using IPA or TA, since these approaches employ fairly traditional modes of coding and data manipulation, although there is not much evidence for the growth in use of such software among IPA researchers. Descriptive and hermeneutic phenomenology, as well as critical narrative analysis, demand greater flexibility, and although it is possible to use QDAS when carrying out an analysis from any of these perspectives, it may not be particularly helpful or desirable. Ultimately, you will need to decide for yourself whether it is worth the effort to learn one of the available packages and whether this will impact negatively on the analytical process. Guidance for further reading on QDAS, and in particular NVivo, is given in the further reading list at the end of this chapter. What is key in all phenomenological psychology, regardless of whether QDAS is used, however, is the central need to remain focused on the experience of the people participating in the study rather than the methods used to explicate this.

## Summary

Phenomenological approaches to psychology can be split broadly into three categories: descriptive phenomenology, interpretive phenomenology and narrative analyses. Phenomenological research is invariably qualitative, designed to understand more about a particular topic rather than to explain or identify causes for its occurrence. Samples are usually small, with different sampling methods being used according to the particular type of phenomenological psychology being undertaken. Reflexivity – broadly understood – is important in all qualitative research, and this includes phenomenological psychology. Reflexivity is the term for the process whereby researchers are critically aware of the ways in which their questions, methods and subject position may impact on the knowledge being produced. This chapter also explored the need for ethical research and outlined key features of the BPS guidelines for ethical research. This includes the need for informed consent, minimization of harm and discomfort and need for the protection of privacy. Methods of data collection are wide and varied, although semi-structured interviews and written concrete descriptions of experiences are most commonly employed. Finally, it is important to note that phenomenological research needs to be presented differently from quantitative research, with different formats used depending on the type of phenomenological psychology being employed.

## Further reading

Finlay, L. & Gough. B. (eds) (2003). *Reflexivity: A Practical Guide for Researchers in Health and Social Science.* **Oxford: Blackwell**. An excellent book on this important issue. There are good general chapters by the editors, along with contributions on a wide range of topics related to reflexivity.

Gibbs, G.R. (2002). *Qualitative Data Analysis: Explorations with NVivo.* **Buckingham: Open University Press**. A comprehensive book for researchers interested in learning one of the most popular software packages for the qualitative analysis of data.

Kvale, S. (1996). *InterViews: An Introduction to Qualitative Research Interviewing.* **London: Sage**. A classic text on interviewing, which takes a phenomenological approach to interviewing. Comprehensive, although a little dry at times.

Mann, C. and Stewart, F. (2000). *Internet Communication and Qualitative Research: A Handbook for Researching Online.* **London: Sage**. Getting a little dated but still that rare thing – a book on the topic of using the Internet for qualitative research that provides information that may actually assist researchers in conducting their research.

Plummer, K. (2001). *Documents of Life 2: An Invitation to a Critical Humanism.* **London: Sage**. Now in a second edition, this classic text, although sociological rather than psychological, provides invaluable information and advice on conducting ethnographic life-history research in a wonderfully engaging style.

# 6 A focus on the things themselves: descriptive phenomenology

## Chapter aims

- Introduce descriptive phenomenological psychology

- Outline the practical issues involved in conducting descriptive phenomenological studies, including data collection, method, analysis and presentation of findings

- Provide a comprehensive worked example of a descriptive phenomenological analysis

This chapter introduces the first main approach to phenomenological psychology to be covered in this book: *descriptive phenomenological psychology* (or, simply, *descriptive phenomenology*). In the main, the focus of this chapter will be on Giorgi's method of descriptive phenomenology (Giorgi, 1985; Giorgi & Giorgi, 2003). This approach (sometimes known as the Duquesne School) is the oldest and most established form of phenomenological psychology. It is not, however, the most popular phenomenological approach in the UK in psychology (although it is well known in other disciplines, such as nursing). I also include discussion of one variation of this approach to descriptive phenomenology: the *Sheffield School variation*. This variation builds on the work of Giorgi and others, being based on a descriptive analysis of the lifeworld, but bringing a number of existential givens explicitly and systematically into the analytic process (see Ashworth, 2003a,b). There have been many variations on method over the years, with phenomenological psychologists generally reluctant to reduce phenomenological psychology to mechanical procedures. This is discussed further in Chapter 9 and should be borne in mind when reading this chapter and those that follow. Although I provide a step-by-step guide to phenomenological methods, for the sake of clarity and ease of learning, in this book, this information should be seen as heuristic (as a guide) rather than definitive.

Phenomenological methods of data analysis are concerned primarily with lived experience, whether that is an experience of being a victim of crime or an experience of playing a game of soccer. This particular focus stems from the philosophical underpinnings established by Husserl and the move away from a subject–object dualism towards a *noema* (the what of experience)–*noesis* (the how of experience) correlation (see Chapter 2). The core of descriptive phenomenology is a return to 'the things themselves'. This phenomenological approach is the most Husserlian of all the methods presented in this book and adheres quite rigidly to a set of methods inspired by Husserlian philosophy. It emerged in the 1970s at Duquesne University with the work of Amedeo Giorgi and colleagues and continues to be employed by researchers across a wide variety of disciplines today. Descriptive phenomenological psychologists are concerned not with explaining phenomena but rather with describing phenomena. There is no attempt to find the underlying causes of some psychological phenomenon as is common in much mainstream (cognitive) social psychology. It is enough (and, indeed, arguably all that is possible philosophically speaking) to simply describe the 'things in their appearing'. In practice, this results in (i) a focus on first-person accounts of experience, (ii) an analysis that seeks to discern the underlying structure of an experience and (iii) the production of findings that describe both the universal structure (*essence*) of the experience and individual idiosyncratic meanings.

Descriptive phenomenological studies have been conducted on:

- the perception of learning (Colaizzi, 1971);
- the phenomenology of being anxious (Fischer, 1974);
- the structure of thinking in chess (Aanstoos, 1983; 1985);
- the experience of being a victim of crime (Wertz, 1985);
- self-deception (Fischer, 1985);
- life boredom (Bargdill, 2000);
- insight in psychotherapy (Todres, 2002).

The Sheffield School has emerged as an interesting new variation, still grounded in the desire to focus on 'the things themselves' and the description of the life-world (central in the later Husserlian writing), but systematically augmented by the philosophy of a number of existential philosophers. The focus is, therefore, description of the participant's lifeworld, as is the case with all descriptive phenomenology, but the analytical process also entails examination of seven structures or 'fractions' thought to be essential features of the lifeworld: selfhood, sociality, embodiment, temporality, spatiality, project and discourse. These fractions are used as a heuristic to guide the analysis in order to gain greater understanding of the lifeworld with regard to a particular topic and group of participants. Further detail on this method of analysis is presented in Section 6.5, following description of Giorgi's method of descriptive phenomenology.

Sheffield School studies have been conducted on:

- female experiences of the body in club culture (Hinchliff, 2001);
- meanings of plagiarism (Ashworth, Freewood & Macdonald, 2003);
- the lifeworld of a person with Alzheimer's disease (Ashworth & Ashworth, 2003).

## Data collection

The ideal method of sampling in descriptive phenomenology is maximum variation sampling, where the researcher seeks out participants who have a common experience but who vary on as wide a variety of demographic characteristics as possible. The principle is that with such variation, it should become possible (in the analytical stage – see below) to ascertain those aspects of the experience that are invariant across perception (the essential structure underpinning all experiences of the same kind) and those that vary across perception (that vary across people and are, therefore, idiosyncratic). Sample sizes are usually very small (around five or six, and sometimes fewer, participants for most research conducted individually) due to the time-consuming nature of the analytical process.

As mentioned in Chapter 5, the data-collection method of choice is the retrospective concrete description of experience and/or in-depth interviews. To reiterate (for full details see Chapter 5), this method of data collection involves the researcher asking participants to write an account of an experience that they have had, ideally an experience that was relatively recent. An example of a possible protocol for such data collection is given in Data box 6.1 (pp. 93–94) along with the description of the experience that was obtained as a result. Other researchers include the instruction that participants should write as if writing for someone who has no knowledge of the experience that they are recounting. However, not all researchers provide as much priming material and, following a brief introduction to the nature of the research project, simply ask a participant to 'describe a situation where ...' (see Data box 6.1 on pp. 93–94) for an example).

The written concrete description is not the only method of data collection used, however. Aanstoos (1985) devised the 'talking aloud technique' for his research on the structure of thinking in chess. This method involves the researcher instructing participants to vocalize their thinking when actively engaged in the task or experience that is the focus of the investigation. Aanstoos (1985) worked with five chess players, getting them to speak their thoughts while playing a game of chess (wearing headphones so as not to disturb their opponents and interfere with the natural play). Their talking aloud was tape-recorded and then transcribed to form the written data for analysis.

Although concrete description and talking aloud are the most appropriate forms of data collection for descriptive phenomenology, it is possible to employ semi-structured or unstructured interviews. Here, of course, the focus would be on the description of some lived experience, with the interviewer aiming to elicit the maximum amount of information about the topic at hand. Once the interview had been transcribed, it would be necessary for the analyst to identify the meaning units (described in full below) and then chronologically reconstruct the narrative of the experience being recounted. It is usual for written accounts to be structured chronologically – as lived – and it is, therefore, unnecessary for the researcher to reconstruct the narrative. However, the dialogical nature of interviews is likely to lead to much greater fragmentation of the story being recounted and, therefore, the need to chronologically reconstruct the story as part of the analytical procedure. Interviews may also be used to supplement written concrete descriptions. Here, the interview will be structured by the description of the participant, with the participant simply being asked to expand on what he or she has already written line (or unit of meaning) by line. This transcribed material can then be incorporated into the participant's description to make a more elaborate description for analysis.

The Sheffield School similarly focuses on first-person accounts but, in line with a great deal of contemporary qualitative research, tends to favour semi-structured interviews, in practice at least, if not because of any theoretical preference. However, since no firm guidance has been issued, and given the same focus on first-person accounts, it would appear that the methods of data collection should be similar.

## 6.2 Method

There are four stages to a descriptive phenomenological analysis (Giorgi, 1985; Giorgi & Giorgi, 2003): reading for overall meaning, identifying meaning units, assessing the psychological significance of meaning units, and synthesizing meaning units and presenting a structural description. I shall go through each of the four stages below in more detail and in Section 6.4 provide a fully worked example to further aid understanding.

The first stage is relatively straightforward and rather obvious. As is common in a great deal of qualitative research, one of the first things to do when beginning an analysis is to read through the text to try to grasp an overall sense of what the text means. The first stage requires the analyst to read (and probably re-read several times) the description of experience that is the focus of the analysis. This will need to be done individually for all the participants. If written descriptions are the source of data, then this stage will need to be attended to very carefully. If interviews are being used, then the process of transcription (provided it is done by the analyst of course) very much entails the sort of close reading required. However, transcription alone will not be enough, because although it brings the person doing the transcription much closer to the data, it does not encourage the sort of global reading required here. This stage should be done within the context of the epoché and as such involves the bracketing of one's preconceptions about the topic. The extent to which bracketing is a meaningful concept is contentious. However, the epoché is attended to seriously by versions of descriptive phenomenological psychology. And, with this in mind, it is important to make every effort to read the text with a sense of discovery, avoiding the temptation to impose meaning by engaging in the phenomenological reduction (see Chapter 2) – that is, describing what appears to consciousness, horizontalizing that which appears (initially at least), engaging in imaginative variation and finally verification (of the meaning of the text with the text itself) throughout the analytical process from the first stage to the last.

The second stage of analysis is where the text is broken down into smaller units of meaning. The analyst needs to work through the text systematically and attempt to discern discrete meaning-units. When trying to determine the units of meaning, the analyst should be limited by two horizons to the meaning that they construe. The first, for psychological projects at least, is that the analyst will need to adopt a *psychological attitude* towards the text. That is, as one reads the text to discern meaning-units, it is necessary to do this with an eye for where the experience relates to issues appropriate for a psychological investigation. So, one might notice emotions, beliefs or behaviours but not be unduly interested in organizational dynamics unless they impact directly on the participant's psychology. Of course, if one were conducting a sociology or education project, one might adopt a different attitude and attend to different aspects of the experience. The second limit to the analysis of the text concerns the topic and the *set* of which it is an example. That is, if one were researching the experience of acute illness, then that would be the focus when identifying discrete units of meaning. There may be interesting information on a variety of other topics, but because it is necessary in any study to set boundaries, if those other topics are not relevant to the set that is the focus of the study, then they will be of little consequence in the analysis. This stage is not particularly easy but, like many other methods, becomes easier with practice. Very often a participant will structure his or her own writing (or talk) in discrete units of meaning through the use of line or paragraph breaks in writing or pauses in talk. These changes should be attended to in the analytical process but should not be allowed to dominate, as not all breaks – in talk or text – indicate a change of meaning.

One other issue worth mentioning here is the argument that Giorgi (1985) makes, following Gurwitsch (1964), that meaning-units should be understood as *constituents* rather than *elements* of the whole. Constituents are those parts of a piece of text whose meaning can only be understood in context, while elements are those parts whose meaning can be understood independent of the context. Very crudely, a word would be an example of a constituent, for its meaning may change depending on the context (the sentence of which it is a part), while a letter is an example of an element, as the meaning does not change according to context (where it is in a word). This distinction is important for aiding the analysis itself (as well as alerting the researcher to the importance of context for meaning). Even though this second stage involves breaking down the text into discrete units, these units accrue meaning only through the context in which they occur. The context moves from the sentences around those that comprise the unit out to the paragraphs and indeed the text as a whole. Part–whole relationships, therefore, become important as they provide vital information for understanding meaning.

The third stage involves assessing the meaning units for their psychological significance. Some units will have no particular psychological meaning and so will be ignored, while others will be psychologically meaningful. Multiple reading of the meaning units, reflecting and engaging in imaginative variation (see Chapter 2) are all ways of determining the psychological (or, indeed, sociological or educative) meaning of the discrete units identified in the previous step. What is important at this stage is the move from idiosyncratic detail to more general meaning. One must not abstract too much or move to engage with grand psychological theories (whether cognitive or psychoanalytical). It is important to stay close to the data and the meaning that emerges there, rather than to constrain the meaning by engagement with any particular theoretical perspective.

The final (fourth) stage concerns first the production of individual structural descriptions for each participant and then one (or more if necessary) general structural description. This involves an attempt to synthesize the psychological units of meaning by identifying the key elements for the phenomenon being described and then writing this up as a brief (chronological) account for each participant (the individual structural description). Following the production of these individual structural descriptions, it is necessary to identify the invariant properties across the descriptions (referring back to the meaning-units where necessary) to produce a general (psychological) structural description. In many cases, it will be possible to produce only one general structural description. However, sometimes this will not be possible, for important information may be lost as the experiences described are so very different. The final general structural description is the culmination of the analytical work described so far and represents the essence (invariant core common to all similar experiences) of the phenomenon being investigated. This can then form the basis of further discussion with reference to the extant literature and individual structural descriptions where appropriate.

See Study box 6.1 for an example of a descriptive phenomenological study on the phenomenology of daydreaming. The box provides detail of the methods used, which are fairly typical of research from this particular theoretical perspective, as well as a brief description of the findings. The study boxes in this chapter, and indeed in the following chapters, should be seen not only as brief summaries of studies designed to further enable understanding of what can be achieved using different methods but also recommendations for further reading. A great deal will be gained in understanding of the methods explained in this book if it is supplemented by the original works summarized in the study boxes.

## 6.3   Presenting findings

There are a variety of ways of presenting the findings in descriptive phenomenology. In an ideal world, one would want to present the individual structural descriptions along with the general structural description and discussion of the findings. However, given the space constraints within which we must all work, it is not common to see detail of the individual structural descriptions in anything other than PhD dissertations. More usually, a Giorgi-style study will begin with a review of the literature, as is common with most research reports, and a statement about the need for more empirical descriptive work on the topic. This is likely to be followed by some discussion of method, including detail of the participants and method of data collection. Published research papers vary in how much information is provided about the participants, with the minimum usually being details about the age, sex, ethnicity and occupation of the participant. However, it is increasingly common for mini-biographies to be provided for all the participants

## Study box 6.1

**Morley, J.** (1998). The private theater: a phenomenological investigation of daydreaming. *Journal of Phenomenological Psychology*, 29(1), 116–134.

In this study, the author sought to explore the meaning of daydreaming in five participants using a descriptive phenomenological method. The author thought the extant literature to be 'deficient in accounting for the ambiguity inherent to the phenomenon and lacking in concrete empirical descriptions' (p. 116). Participants were asked to think of a recent daydream and produce a written description of everything that happened in the daydream, including what brought them out of it. The researcher interviewed the participants following the production of the written accounts to further facilitate the production of the daydream narrative. The two were then edited together to provide a detailed chronological account of the experience for a meaning-unit analysis designed to enable the production of individual situated structural descriptions for each participant and (ideally) one general structural description appropriate for the phenomenon. The author presented one individual situated structural description in the paper along with the general structural description and discussion of the findings. The author found that daydreaming involved multiple self–world relationships. These included three identifiable subject positions: the habitual subject, the enacting subject and the directing spectator. The habitual subject position was where the daydreamer was habitually involved in their environment (e.g. driving a car) while simultaneously being preoccupied with 'another world', that of the daydream. The enacting subject concerned the way in which the daydreamer perceived him- or herself to be acting as the chief protagonist, acting out his or her previously restricted desire. Finally, the directing spectator position describes the ambiguous position of simultaneous attachment and detachment with the daydream. Morley found that the daydream collapsed many of the dualisms that are present in our 'natural attitude' to the world, such as the dualisms between subject and object, mind and body, cognition and emotion, and the real and the imaginary. It was this complex structure – rather than any substantive content of daydreams – that emerged as the central finding of the study, providing a valuable insight into this everyday phenomenon.

in a study to better enable the reader to see the ways in which maximum variation sampling has been employed and to provide some reassurance about the validity of the general structural description. The findings are then presented and generally will include either a summary of an individual description of the experience being studied or one full individual structural description followed by the general structural description generated for all the participants. As mentioned above, there may be more than one general structural description if one is not sufficient to capture the experience in its entirety. The final discussion is likely to involve some theoretical discussion of the findings and further discussion of the way in which the structural descriptions illuminate the topic. There will also usually be a final statement of the conclusions of the study. A Sheffield School study will need to be presented in a somewhat different form, given the focus on the fractions of the lifeworld in the analysis. This is discussed in Section 6.5.

See Study box 6.2 for a descriptive phenomenological study on the structure of being bored – something that is probably familiar to us all.

## Study box 6.2

**Bargdill, R.** (2000). The study of life boredom. *Journal of Phenomenological Psychology*, 31(2), 188–219.

Being bored is something that we will all experience at least once in our lifetime. In this study, Richard Bargdill investigated the experience of life boredom (where people are bored with life in general, rather than specific moments as is more common) in six participants. Like the research described in Study box 6.1, this study employed descriptions and interviews and then Giorgi's method of analysis to ascertain the structure of life boredom. However, the findings were presented in a slightly different format here, as the author provided supporting quotes in between paragraphs of the general structural description (much as quotes would be used to support the presentation of findings in a thematic analysis). The findings revealed that the most important feature of the experience of life boredom was emotional ambivalence. That is, Bargdill found that his participants, while previously having a clear life goal (when they were not bored with life), now were conflicted and divided about life and the path they were taking. Part of this conflict involved participants simultaneously feeling anger and blame towards the world and others as well as themselves. With this self-directed anger came a sense of shame and general loss of confidence, further reducing the likelihood of change. In his discussion, Bargdill makes some interesting comparisons between boredom and depression, as traditionally understood from a cognitive perspective, highlighting a number of similarities and differences, most notably the way in which people who are bored do not have a negative view of themselves. In conclusion, Bargdill suggests that boredom is equivalent to the freeze response (in the 'fight, flight or freeze response' that we have to danger), with people failing to make their own lives meaningful and instead waiting for others to do this for them. He concludes: 'They are in purgatory waiting and dependent on other people's prayers. As if they have seen Medusa, they stagnate, solidify. They are no longer in motion. They are aware, but paralysed. They are bored.' (p. 204).

## 6.4   Descriptive phenomenological analysis: the experience of acute infection

In the following section, I present a full worked example of a descriptive phenomenological analysis focusing on the experience of being infected with hepatitis A. Hepatitis A is an acute viral infection that results in inflammation of the liver. The virus is present in faeces and, therefore, most often transmitted via food through poor hygiene or intimate personal contact (often of a sexual nature). The illness is acute and lasts for between two weeks and two months. There is no medical treatment, and the patient must simply rest, avoid alcohol and eat a healthy, well-balanced diet. Once recovered, the person will have no further symptoms and will be immune from hepatitis A for life. Data box 6.1 shows an elicitation protocol for studying the experience of being infected with hepatitis A, along with the response from one person who had recently recovered from the illness. The original text is as written and not corrected for errors, grammar or spelling. Although some descriptive phenomenologists may correct a participant's language, I think it important to stay with what is written as written, rather than introduce further distance between the analyst and original experience as described.

As you can see, this participant provided a full description of his experience. He also structured his account with headings and paragraphs, which aided the analysis. The first stage of analysis involved reading and re-reading the text within the epoché to determine the overall meaning. This study did not involve formal follow-up interviews (although there was some informal discussion of the description to clarify a few matters), so there was no need to transcribe and incorporate this into the written description. The second stage (the meaning-unit analysis) required me (as the

---

## Data box 6.1
## Written concrete description from a study of the experience of acute infection

### Participant 1 – male, white, British, 34 years

Thank you for agreeing to take part in this study of the experience of acute infections. All information you provide will be treated confidentially and will be anonymized before being read by anyone other than the researcher (Dr Darren Langdridge, The Open University) or used in any publications arising from the research. The information you provide below will form the basis of an informal interview to be conducted one week after you submit your written account.

I would be grateful if you could describe your experience of being infected with hepatitis A below. Please recount the experience in as much detail as possible, including the experience of the illness prior to and after diagnosis. This should include information about your thoughts and feelings about the experience of this particular illness as well as concrete detail about symptoms and effects of the illness itself.

*After a heavy night out I awoke with what I thought was a monster hangover, headache, body ache, dehydrated and feeling nauseous. This was Saturday morning. / Knowing what to do I tried to take on fluids and eat a little but things did not settle well. Through the day the hangover faded but I still felt ill – nausea, fever, sweating, dizziness, tingly skin shivering and diarrhoea. / We were on a weekend break in Prague. I wanted to see some of the city with my partner, keep him company and to be a pleasant person to be with. / We were now aware that I did not have just an extended hangover, I felt that I was going down with some virus, flu or something and this was just bad timing. /*

*Seeing the sights and eating out was a bit of a chore, I was tired didn't want to eat or drink so really had to force myself to drink and eat a little. I managed some food in the evening but was not much company afterwards. The evening was fairly cold. I was well wrapped up but was shivering so violently at times it was painful. On returning to the hotel I was so tired and cold I just wanted to sleep but soon woke up drenched in sweat. /*

*The next day I felt worse and did not want to venture far from the hotel suffering badly from vomiting, headaches, sweating, shivering dizziness and diarrhoea in all possible combinations. I also felt incredibly tired. /*

*The next day was the flight home. With monumental effort I managed the taxi journey to the airport, the sight and smell of smoked salmon sandwiches on the plane and the drive home from the airport. Once home I must have just wanted to sleep. /*

*Next morning (Tuesday) I was awake first thing to make an appointment at the doctors. A couple of hour later I was explaining my symptoms to the doctor including being unable to keep food down and brown unpleasant smelling urine, a locum GP. / Being a very infrequent visitor to the doctors and being fairly aware of health issues I would have expected to be taken a little more seriously. Yes I new I had a fever and it was probably some virus or other. The outcome was 'go away and keep taking fluids', if you don't get better come back. /*

*The rest of that day and the following day my symptoms seemed to worsen, A little comfort from being at home but I had not eaten for days. I was very concerned that I was not pulling through and felt to be getting weaker. On*

→

## Data box 6.1
## Written concrete description from a study of the experience of acute infection

*Thursday morning I was back at the GP. My main concern was that I was barely eating and felt that I was losing strength, strength that I needed to fight the illness. After a short discussion about symptoms the GP stated that I looked a bit jaundice and gave me the option of having some bloods sent off for testing or trying to get me in to see somebody at the hospital. I returned to the waiting room whilst she made a phone call. An hour later I was walking very slowly, with my partner, towards the infectious diseases unit at the hospital. /*

**The Hospital Infectious Diseases Ward**

*After what seemed like an extremely long journey from home we arrived at the nurse's station. After a little booking in I was shown to a room. This ward had individual en-suite rooms each with a TV the bathroom was painted yellow so it was impossible to judge what colour my eyes and skin were. After a while a phlebotomist arrived to take some samples, about a dozen of them. I had my throat swabbed and a student nurse came and took a history and I was given a little food. /*

*I spent about three days in hospital, these were long tedious and uncomfortable. I am not sure who I saw when or in what order. Was given regular meals and tea and biscuits. I had regular visits to take temperature and BP and blood was taken daily, but not so many vials now. All my bodily products were collected for analysis, so occasionally I would push the call button and a cheery rotund assistant would come and take away a bottle or pan.*

*I had daily visits from consultants, doctors and medical students in various numbers and combinations. I had various glands prodded and squeezed. / I was asked where I had been over the previous months, what I had eaten, and many personal questions. The problem was being narrowed down to Hep A, B or Weil's disease. I always felt that there was a slightly accusative tone to the medics questions and advice, sort of 'what have you been up to to catch this' and 'what else may you have been exposed to.' /*

*Over the couple of days in hospital I began to feel less bad, but certainly not better. I was eating, not a great deal and still felt nauseous after food, and feeling tired. As there was no treatment I could be offered and my condition was not critical I was discharged on the Sunday, being told to take it easy and no exertion or stress. I got home Sunday afternoon and rested Sunday and Monday. I was much more comfortable at home. / Robert, realising now that I was actually very ill had come out of stop messing about and spoiling the holiday mode and was being very supportive, this change had occurred some time the previous week. /*

*The hospital called, I had Hep A, this was good news, an acute illness and full recovery, much better than the chronic alternatives. Knowing the transmission route made me feel sick and dirty though. /*

*Later in the week I returned to hospital for more blood tests and got a sick note for a month. My manager was surprisingly concerned and sympathetic, I had always been healthy and took time off extremely rarely, now I was off for at least 6 weeks.*

*For the next few weeks I rested around the house and did odd bits, I was still easily tired. / One afternoon a man from the council public health service called. He had been notified by the hospital as I had a notifiable disease. Again a series of questions, where had I been and what had I eaten, all to make sure that there was no local outbreak. /*

*I had a few more blood tests, results returned to normal, some indicators had been good the whole time showing that I was generally strong and fit. I was eventually discharged in mid December. / The medical staff at the hospital had always seamed a bit detached and cold and clinical. A doctor friend had always been more helpful and supportive to me and especially to Robert. /*

analyst) to identify the discrete units of meaning (while adopting a psychological attitude and set concerned with the experience of an acute infection). These units are marked on the description in Data box 6.1 using slashes to indicate changes in meaning. In practice, this stage requires multiple readings and corrections until there is a sense of feeling fairly certain about the units that have been identified.

The next stage is presented in Analysis box 6.1. Although this form of presentation is being used here to facilitate understanding, it is a useful way of working through the data if you have access to electronic text (and so can paste it into a table) or have the time and/or resources available to transcribe the written description (and/or interview). The left-hand column is the original text broken down into 22 units of meaning (numbered). The middle column is the translation of the original text into less idiosyncratic language. The right-hand column is the further translation into language representing the psychological significance of the units. Giorgi and Giorgi (2003) state that there is no limit to the number of translations necessary to identify the psychological significance and then produce structural descriptions, but it would be rare to need more than these two translations in practice. The right-hand column also involves some initial synthesis of meaning-units as they are combined to represent larger units of psychological meaning.

It should be apparent from Analysis box 6.1 where I have decided that the meaning changes (within the context of a psychological attitude and set concerned with hepatitis A) and therefore where the text needs to be broken into discrete units. The choice to include some units (and not others) in the right-hand column representing the translation of meaning units into their psychological significance is perhaps not so clear and worthy of further discussion. Meaning-unit 8 concerning the flight home from the holiday is a good example of a unit of meaning, which, while reflecting something significant about the experience for this participant, is about the intersection of travel and illness rather than the experience of hepatitis A alone. That is, if this participant had experienced this illness when not on holiday, there would not be any discussion of flying, the 'monumental effort' involved and the smell of smoked-salmon sandwiches, and so this meaning-unit is idiosyncratic and not of psychological significance within the context of this study. That is, the psychological set limiting the focus here concerns the desire to understand the structure of the lived experience of infection with hepatitis A in general, and so meanings beyond this set will be excluded from the structural description. Meaning-unit 13 is also interesting, for here is a section with considerable descriptive detail, where the essence, psychologically speaking, is much simpler and concerns the large number of medical interventions that the participant had to endure. The detail, however vivid, was not particularly revealing of the psychology of the experience being investigated. By contrast, the following meaning-unit (unit 14) highlights the confining and disorienting nature of being in hospital with only the meals providing any sense of familiarity and structure, clearly showing something important about the experience that may have implications for improving services. The next meaning-unit (unit 15) is also revealing, highlighting the potential for embarrassment through intrusive questioning. It is, however, unclear exactly what the participant meant here (and later, in unit 18, when receiving a diagnosis). I discovered through an informal interview that the participant realized that the source of infection must have been a casual sexual partner and this was why he was ambivalent about the diagnosis.

## Analysis box 6.1
## Meaning-unit analysis

| Original text | Description by meaning unit | Psychological significance |
|---|---|---|
| (1) After a heavy night out I awoke with what I thought was a monster hangover, headache, body ache, dehydrated and feeling nauseous. This was Saturday morning. | *P woke up following a night drinking heavily with the symptoms he thought made up a bad hangover.* | *(1) + (2) + (3) + (5) P experienced familiar symptoms that did not worry him initially. However, as his symptoms worsened and persisted, after discussion with his partner, P had to revise his self-diagnosis and, as a result, became more concerned about his condition.* |
| (2) Knowing what to do I tried to take on fluids and eat a little but things did not settle well. | *P was familiar with the symptoms of a hangover and acted to ameliorate the effects in his usual manner. This did not have the desired effect, however.* | |
| (3) Through the day the hangover faded but I still felt ill – nausea, fever, sweating, dizziness, tingly skin shivering and diarrhoea. | *P recognized the hangover symptoms were lessening as the day went on but still felt ill.* | |
| (4) We were on a weekend break in Prague. I wanted to see some of the city with my partner, keep him company and to be a pleasant person to be with. | *P was on holiday so wished to see some of the city and be good company for his partner.* | |
| (5) We were now aware that I did not have just an extended hangover, I felt that I was going down with some virus, flu or something and this was just bad timing. | *Both P and his partner were becoming aware that the symptoms he was experiencing no longer represented a hangover and instead assumed it was something different but fairly familiar, such as a cold or flu.* | |
| (6) Seeing the sights and eating out was a bit of a chore, I was tired didn't want to eat or drink so really had to force myself to drink and eat a little. I managed some food in the evening but was not much company afterwards. The evening was fairly cold. I was well wrapped up but | *P continued to try to act as he would normally on holiday but found it a strain as his symptoms were worsening. Eating and drinking were particularly difficult. P also recognized that he was not good company for his partner.* | *As the symptoms worsened, P found it increasingly difficult to act as he might do normally on holiday and found it particularly difficult to maintain good relations with his partner.* |

## Analysis box 6.1
## Meaning-unit analysis

| Original text | Description by meaning unit | Psychological significance |
|---|---|---|
| was shivering so violently at times it was painful. On returning to the hotel I was so tired and cold I just wanted to sleep but soon woke up drenched in sweat. | | |
| (7) The next day I felt worse and did not want to venture far from the hotel suffering badly from vomiting, headaches, sweating, shivering dizziness and diarrhoea in all possible combinations. I also felt incredibly tired. | *P continued to feel worse (with a variety of symptoms) and, as a result, stayed in his hotel room.* | |
| (8) The next day was the flight home. With monumental effort I managed the taxi journey to the airport, the sight and smell of smoked salmon sandwiches on the plane and the drive home from the airport. Once home I must have just wanted to sleep. | *P was due to fly home from holiday and had to make a huge effort to travel (via taxi and plane). Once home, P simply wanted to sleep.* | |
| (9) Next morning (Tuesday) I was awake first thing to make an appointment at the doctors. A couple of hour later I was explaining my symptoms to the doctor including being unable to keep food down and brown unpleasant smelling urine, a locum GP. | *P awoke and decided to see his doctor. He explained his symptoms to the doctor, who was not his usual medical professional.* | *Since the symptoms continued to persist, P sought advice from his doctor.* |
| (10) Being a very infrequent visitor to the doctors and being fairly aware of health issues I would have expected to be taken a little more seriously. Yes I new I had a fever and it was probably some virus or other. The outcome was 'go away and keep taking fluids, if you don't get better come back'. | *P did not regularly visit the doctor and was therefore surprised when he felt the doctor did not treat him as seriously as he thought his symptoms warranted. He was sent home and told to continue acting as he had been until the illness subsided of its own accord.* | *P found he did not receive the treatment expected from the doctor he saw. In particular, he did not feel that the doctor recognized the seriousness of his symptoms.* |

→

**Analysis box 6.1**
**Continued**

| Original text | Description by meaning unit | Psychological significance |
|---|---|---|
| (11) The rest of that day and the following day my symptoms seemed to worsen, A little comfort from being at home but I had not eaten for days. I was very concerned that I was not pulling through and felt to be getting weaker. | *P became increasingly worried as the symptoms worsened (and he felt weaker), rather than lessened, as he might have expected if he had a familiar cold or virus.* | *(11) + (12) As P continued to feel worse, he once again sought medical advice and this time found the doctor appeared to recognize the seriousness of the condition.* |
| (12) On Thursday morning I was back at the GP. My main concern was that I was barely eating and felt that I was losing strength, strength that I needed to fight the illness. After a short discussion about symptoms the GP stated that I looked a bit jaundice and gave me the option of having some bloods sent off for testing or trying to get me in to see somebody at the hospital. I returned to the waiting room whilst she made a phone call. An hour later I was walking very slowly, with my partner, towards the infectious diseases unit at the hospital. | *P returned to his doctor as a result of his concern over the worsening of his symptoms. This doctor, unlike the last one, recognized the seriousness of the symptoms and identified a further symptom (jaundice), which acted to help diagnose the condition. As a result, P was admitted to the infectious diseases ward of the hospital, accompanied by his partner.* | |
| (13) After what seemed like an extremely long journey from home we arrived at the nurse's station. After a little booking in I was shown to a room. This ward had individual en-suite rooms each with a TV the bathroom was painted yellow so it was impossible to judge what colour my eyes and skin were. After a while a phlebotomist arrived to take some samples, about a dozen of them. I had my throat swabbed and a student nurse came and took a history and I was given a little food. | *The journey to the hospital was a struggle. Upon arrival, P was assigned a private room. Soon after, P had blood taken and his throat swabbed. He then had his medical history taken by a student nurse and had something to eat.* | *P experienced a large number of medical interventions upon admittance to hospital.* |

## Analysis box 6.1
## Continued

| Original text | Description by meaning unit | Psychological significance |
|---|---|---|
| (14) I spent about three days in hospital, these were long tedious and uncomfortable. I am not sure who I saw when or in what order. Was given regular meals and tea and biscuits. I had regular visits to take temperature and BP and blood was taken daily, but not so many vials now. All my bodily products were collected for analysis, so occasionally I would push the call button and a cheery rotund assistant would come and take away a bottle or pan. I had daily visits from consultants, doctors and medical students in various numbers and combinations. I had various glands prodded and squeezed. | *P spent a number of days in hospital, which he found tedious and uncomfortable. He lost track of the medical professionals that he saw. Food and drink were, however, regular. P had repeated medical interventions to collect body products for analysis and assess his current health status.* | *The experience of hospital was both confining and disorienting, with multiple visits from different medical staff. Only the meals provided familiarity and structure.* |
| (15) I was asked where I had been over the previous months, what I had eaten, and many personal questions. The problem was being narrowed down to Hep A, B or Weil's disease. I always felt that there was a slightly accusative tone to the medics questions and advice, sort of 'what have you been up to to catch this' and 'what else may you have been exposed to.' | *Questions were asked of P about his activities over the proceeding time period in order to help diagnose the condition. P found the questions personal and the tone of those asking the questions accusative (implying that he was responsible for bringing about this illness through improper activities).* | *When being questioned in hospital, P felt he was being accused of bringing on his own illness through inappropriate behaviour.* |
| (16) Over the couple of days in hospital I began to feel less bad, but certainly not better. I was eating, not a great deal and still felt nauseous after food, and feeling tired. As there was no treatment I could be offered and my condition was not critical I was discharged on the Sunday, being told to take it easy and no | *The symptoms P was experiencing began to lessen, but he still did not feel well, continuing to feel tired and nauseous. Because there was no hospital treatment, P was discharged to return home. He felt much more comfortable at home.* | *In spite of the symptoms persisting, P was discharged as no treatment could be offered. He was much more comfortable at home.* |

→

## Analysis box 6.1
## Continued

| Original text | Description by meaning unit | Psychological significance |
| --- | --- | --- |
| exertion or stress. I got home Sunday afternoon and rested Sunday and Monday. I was much more comfortable at home. | | |
| (17) Robert, realising now that I was actually very ill had come out of stop messing about and spoiling the holiday mode and was being very supportive, this change had occurred some time the previous week. | P found that the attitude of his partner towards his experience had changed. P felt his partner had finally recognized the seriousness of the condition and became more supportive. | P felt that being admitted to hospital had an impact on his partner, who, as a result, was now more supportive and sympathetic. |
| (18) The hospital called, I had Hep A, this was good news, an acute illness and full recovery, much better than the chronic alternatives. Knowing the transmission route made me feel sick and dirty though. | P finally received a diagnosis over the telephone for his condition. He was relieved to receive this diagnosis, as he now knew what he had and what the prognosis was. P did, however, feel dirty as a result of now knowing how he had caught the disease. | P had ambivalent feelings about the diagnosis he received. He was relieved to know what he had and that it was an acute condition not likely to have any long-term effects but also somewhat disgusted as this also revealed the likely source of the illness. |
| (19) Later in the week I returned to hospital for more blood tests and got a sick note for a month. My manager was surprisingly concerned and sympathetic, I had always been healthy and took time off extremely rarely, now I was off for at least 6 weeks. For the next few weeks I rested around the house and did odd bits, I was still easily tired. | P had to undergo further tests at the hospital and was then given leave from work by the doctor. P was surprised to find his manager sympathetic. He thought this might have been due in part to him normally being very fit and healthy. P remained weak for a number of weeks. | |
| (20) One afternoon a man from the council public health service called. He had been notified by the hospital as I had a notifiable disease. Again a series of questions, where had I been and what had I eaten, all to make sure that there was no local outbreak. | During the period of recovery at home, P received a visit from a public health official. He once again had to answer a series of questions in order to assure the official that there was no local outbreak of the disease. | Even when P was discharged from hospital, he still had to answer further questions about the likely source of the illness he was experiencing. |

## Analysis box 6.1
### Continued

| Original text | Description by meaning unit | Psychological significance |
|---|---|---|
| (21) I had a few more blood tests, results returned to normal, some indicators had been good the whole time showing that I was generally strong and fit. I was eventually discharged in mid December. | *After a further period of time, P found that his test results were normal and that he was healthy again (leading to his full discharge from the care of medical professionals).* | *Test results acted as the final confirmation of health and resulted in P's final discharge from the care of the medical professionals.* |
| (22) The medical staff at the hospital had always seamed a bit detached and cold and clinical. A doctor friend had always been more helpful and supportive to me and especially to Robert. | *In retrospect, P felt the hospital staff he had encountered were cold and clinical. This was in contrast to a friend who was a doctor, who had been more supportive, particularly to P's partner.* | *Looking back, P did not feel the medical staff he encountered had been as caring as he expected. This was in contrast to a friend, who was a doctor, who had been particularly supportive.* |

One of the limits of written descriptions is the inability to question the participant. It is perhaps not surprising that a large number of studies employ follow-up interviews to clarify the written concrete descriptions. Here, however, a simple informal interview was sufficient to clarify understanding where necessary. And, by knowing the possibility of sexual contact being implicated in the transmission of infection here, greater understanding is gained of how this participant must have felt particularly vulnerable when being questioned about his illness. Again, this insight has important implications for improving the way in which medical practitioners interact with patients when dealing with infectious diseases of this kind. Many other insights are demonstrated in this example: the way in which hospital admission was important for the participant's partner recognizing the seriousness of the condition and changing his behaviour (unit 17); the ongoing nature of the illness and need to continue to deal with intrusive questioning (unit 20); the way in which tests confirmed the subjective feelings of health of the participant (unit 21); and the participant's overall feeling that the medical staff he encountered had not been as caring as he had hoped (unit 22). Although I have sought to be rigorous and systematic in identifying meaning-units, this process is subjective and others may identify different units of meaning. Phenomenological analyses require creativity while working systematically through the text, such that none of the detail goes unnoticed.

The final (fourth) stage involves working through the psychologically significant meaning units to produce the individual structural description for this participant's experience of being infected with hepatitis A (see Analysis box 6.2). Redundancy is removed along with idiosyncratic variation in an attempt to produce a description containing the invariant properties of the experience – that is,

## Analysis box 6.2
## Individual structural description of the experience of acute infection

For the participant in this study, the experience of hepatitis A began with symptoms that were familiar. Initially, he put these symptoms down to his own prior activities and therefore did not worry about them. However, as the symptoms failed to subside, he had to revise his self-diagnosis, through discussion with a significant other, and conclude that he had a more enduring illness, but still one with which he was familiar. As time passed and his symptoms still did not improve, P sought advice from his doctor. However, he did not feel he was treated seriously and felt disappointed that the doctor did not seem to grasp the seriousness of the condition. With the further passing of time, P began to think there must be something more seriously wrong and so once again sought the advice of his doctor. He saw a different doctor this time, whom he felt acknowledged the seriousness of his symptoms, which led to him being hospitalized immediately. When in hospital, P experienced a large number of medical interventions and, as a result, he found hospital to be both confining and disorienting, with only meals providing a regular and familiar structure. P found the questions he was asked in hospital intrusive and accusative, with a sense that he was held responsible for bringing about his own illness through inappropriate sexual behaviour. As there was no treatment possible, P was discharged home, where he felt much more comfortable. As a result of the hospital admission, P felt his partner finally fully acknowledged the seriousness of his condition and, as a result, was more supportive and sympathetic. The consequent diagnosis led to ambivalent feelings, with P both relieved at the knowledge that his illness was acute and not harmful in the long term but also somewhat disgusted, as this revealed the likely transmission route of the illness. Even after leaving hospital, P found he had to answer further questions about the likely source of his illness. It was only when he received positive test results, confirming his own sense of wellbeing, that he was discharged fully from the care of the medical professionals. Looking back, P felt he had not received the level of care he expected from the medical professionals that he had encountered.

a description that would be appropriate for anyone experiencing the same event. This is not always possible of course, as there may be important differences in people's experiences, but descriptive phenomenology usually involves the production of essential structures where possible.

If a study involved more than one participant, this analytical procedure would need to be followed for all the descriptions provided by the participants. It is only when all the individual (sometimes called 'situated') structural descriptions have been produced that an attempt is made to further translate the experience into more general language in order to produce a general structural description that encompasses all the individual structural descriptions. Examples of general structural descriptions can be found in the papers described in the study boxes in this chapter. In many ways, they are similar to individual structural descriptions, except that they are more general, more abstract and less idiosyncratic. The key is to work creatively in order to identify those features of the experience that do not vary across participants and separate these out from those features that do vary.

The implications of this work are also important and need to be discussed. In this case, a number of features are worth highlighting. First, the process of self-diagnosis versus diagnosis by a professional is highly salient here. The findings reveal a tension between the self-knowledge of the person with an acute infection (experienced bodily in a different way from other everyday infections) and the 'expert' knowledge of the healthcare professional. Had the patient been treated differently, with greater respect for his own understanding of his body, then diagnosis may have been possible sooner. However, this suggestion must be weighed against the way in which a diagnosis only became possible over time, with the failure of the symptoms to subside, suggesting that a careful watch-and-wait approach by the medical professional may be fruitful. The difficulties associated with being in an infectious-diseases ward also became clear. Being admitted to hospital validated the seriousness of the illness (to self and others) but also led to confusion and disorientation. Meal times provided some normalizing activity, but other ways of providing a regular day-to-day structure (such as regular visits of the same staff) may well be helpful in reducing the sense of confusion experienced in such a situation. Finally, it is worth mentioning the stigma associated with hepatitis A and how this appears linked to possible routes of transmission. In this case, the fact that the mode of transmission may have been sexual led the participant to feel 'dirty', with a perception that the questions asked of him were intrusive and accusative. Greater sensitivity when questioning patients about an infection such as hepatitis A, with potentially stigmatizing routes of transmission, may improve the experience of care for patients admitted to hospital as a result of this disease.

## 6.5  Sheffield School analysis

The initial stages of a Sheffield School analysis are the same as those described above (Ashworth, 2003b). That is, following data collection, stages 1, 2 and, to a certain extent, 3 of Giorgi's method of analysis are followed rigorously. Stage 3 may or may not involve the translation into psychological units of meaning, depending on the study and wishes of the analyst. Regardless, it is only at this point that the Sheffield School departs, analytically speaking, from Giorgi's approach to descriptive phenomenology. Once the meaning-units have been discerned, it becomes necessary to work through these using the seven fractions of the lifeworld as a heuristic to aid interpretation. There is no attempt to produce a general structural description, with much more consideration being given to the individual experience across the fractions of the lifeworld.

The seven fractions of the lifeworld (selfhood, sociality, embodiment, temporality, spatiality, project, discourse) proposed by Ashworth (2003a,b) warrant some further discussion here. These fractions come from the work of phenomenological and existential philosophers, including Husserl, Heidegger, Merleau-Ponty and Sartre (see Chapters 2 and 3). Ashworth (2003a,b) recognizes that he is not the first to talk of these essential aspects of experience and that other writers have mentioned some aspects, such as spatiality or temporality, but never all the features Ashworth contends that the existentialists mark out as intrinsic aspects of all experience. Ashworth (2003a) is also keen to stress the need to avoid what he thinks are more speculative features, such as being-towards-death.[1] Merleau-

Ponty acts as the primary inspiration for the seven fractions, and Ashworth (2003a,b) describes each fraction through quotations from his work. In brief, selfhood refers to that aspect of experience that might impact on a person's sense of agency, presence and voice. Here, selfhood is not something individual but rather something inextricably social or that which emerges between people in interaction. Sociality concerns the way in which a situation affects a person's relations with others, as all situations are intrinsically intersubjective. Embodiment relates to how the body features in experience, including consideration of sex, sexuality, disabilities, etc. Temporality refers to the way in which we are always living in time and how a person's sense of time might serve to underpin the experience being described. Spatiality concerns a person's understanding of space and place. Project is that aspect of a situation that relates to a person's ability to carry out activities that they have committed to and that they believe are central in their life. Finally, discourse concerns the set of language terms (discourses) drawn on from the wider culture in order to describe an experience. Although the Sheffield School recognizes the arguments of Heidegger about 'language being the house of Being', it strongly resists any attempt to reduce the lifeworld to language, with the attendant loss of a conscious agent and focus on experience.

The seven fractions are used to interrogate the text and, specifically, the meaning-units identified in the first three stages of analysis. There is no expectation that all will be obviously present or of equal importance; however, given that they are essential features of the lifeworld, they should always be relevant to understanding. Each individual account is examined using the seven fractions, and then generalities are identified. However, unlike much descriptive phenomenology, no attempt is made to identify the *essence* (invariant properties) of the phenomenon. Instead, the preference is on capturing the variability and individual experience while recognizing that common structures may emerge from the data during the process of analysis. See Study box 6.3 for an example of a Sheffield School study concerned with the meanings of plagiarism for university students in the UK.

Sheffield School studies will, therefore, need to be written up and presented differently from other forms of descriptive phenomenology. The standard qualitative format will be used for the introduction and method sections but, since there is no longer a general structural description, the write-up of a Sheffield School study is not going to culminate in a summary statement of this kind. Instead, studies employing this methodology will present one or more individual accounts of experience (presented either chronologically or in terms of the fractions of the lifeworld) in the findings section, followed by a more general discussion section, structured by the fractions of the lifeworld. It will not always be necessary to use all seven fractions, since some will be more or less relevant to

[1] The Sheffield School believes that, in spite of Heidegger's ([1927] 1962) arguments, this aspect of the lifeworld is more speculative and less immediately apparent than those other aspects delineated here. I, however, think the distinction is a difficult one to sustain and think the analyst could recognize the role of being-towards-death as another fraction of the lifeworld.

## Study box 6.3

**Ashworth, P., Freewood, M. & Macdonald, R. (2003).** The student lifeworld and the meanings of plagiarism. *Journal of Phenomenological Psychology*, 34(2), 257–278.

Plagiarism is an increasing problem, especially in higher education. However, although there are ongoing attempts to tackle this problem, there has been a lack of work concerned with understanding what plagiarism means to students themselves. This paper by Peter Ashworth and colleagues seeks to redress this by studying the meaning of plagiarism among 12 students at a UK university. Semi-structured interviews were conducted and the transcripts analysed using the Duquesne School method. This involved working through the transcripts in order to identify meaning-units after reading to ascertain the overall meaning of the account presented by the participant. Once this initial stage had been completed, the meaning-units were interrogated using the seven fractions of the lifeworld (selfhood, sociality, embodiment, temporality, spatiality, project, discourse) proposed by Ashworth (2003a,b) as a heuristic to further explore the meanings being presented. The authors chose to present three individual accounts structured by some (but not all) of the fractions and then to discuss the common structure of plagiarism across all seven fractions. Since the fractions proposed are heuristic, some will be more relevant than others, depending on the topic. In this case, the individual descriptions were discussed in terms of selfhood, discourse, sociality and project. The three different accounts of plagiarism discussed in the paper variously emphasized anxiety due to the shame of being found to have been plagiaristic by accident, academic development moving from dependence to independence and originality, and disciplinary differences in understandings of plagiarism. What was clear overall, however, was the need for students to be introduced to academic culture, such that they understood why plagiarism was an issue and in what specific contexts. That is, in the light of these findings, it seemed appropriate not to produce university-wide guidelines but rather to focus attention on enculturation, with individual classroom teachers encouraged to do this work as best befits the requirements of their respective disciplines.

any particular topic. This will be followed by a conclusion as appropriate. More information on this variation of descriptive phenomenology (along with Giorgi's approach) can be found in the suggestions for further reading at the end of this chapter.

## Summary

Descriptive phenomenological psychology is the name for one of the earliest applications of phenomenological philosophy to psychology. This approach remains faithful to Husserl's philosophy and as such involves a search for essences following epoché and a phenomenological reduction. This chapter focused on the work of Giorgi and provided details of the method, including a fully worked example of the experience of acute infection. Data are usually collected through written concrete descriptions or semi-structured interviews. There are four stages to the descriptive phenomenological method of Giorgi: reading for overall meaning, identifying meaning-units, assessing the psychological significance of meaning-units, and synthesizing meaning-units and presenting a structural description. The text is systematically coded for units of meaning before moving on to assess their psychological meaning. Following this, the analyst moves from idiosyncratic to more general meaning as they synthesize the units of meaning to produce an individual structural description of the experience. This process is conducted on one case and then repeated for all other cases. One variation of this method is described: the Sheffield School. This approach supplements a meaning-unit analysis with an examination of the data across the fractions of the lifeworld (selfhood, sociality, embodiment, temporality, spatiality, project, discourse). Although descriptive phenomenological psychology was one of the earliest approaches to phenomenological psychology and continues to be used to produce detailed descriptions of phenomena, it is not as popular as interpretive approaches to phenomenological psychology (discussed in Chapter 7).

## Further reading

Ashworth, P. (2003). An approach to phenomenological psychology: the contingencies of the lifeworld. *Journal of Phenomenological Psychology*, 34(2), 145–156. Entire contents of this special issue on the Sheffield School. Comprehensive coverage of the Sheffield School method and variations of it, as applied to a number of contemporary issues.

Giorgi, A. (ed.) (1985). *Phenomenology and Psychological Research*. Pittsburgh, PA: Duquesne University Press. A classic statement of the Duquesne School method along with details of a number of early studies using the method.

Giorgi, A. & Giorgi, B. (2003). Phenomenology. In J. A. Smith (ed.) *Qualitative Psychology: A Practical Guide to Research Methods*. London: Sage. A more recent description of the Duquesne approach to phenomenological psychology.

Moustakas, C. (1994). *Phenomenological Research Methods*. London: Sage. This book provides comprehensive information about the philosophy and practice of the approach to descriptive phenomenology taken by Moustakas.

# 7 Interpretation and meaning: IPA, hermeneutic phenomenology and template analysis

## Chapter aims

- Introduce interpretive phenomenological psychology

- Outline the practical issues involved in conducting interpretive phenomenological analyses, including data collection, method, analysis and presentation of findings

- Provide a comprehensive worked example of an interpretative phenomenological analysis

Three more phenomenological methods are introduced in this chapter: *interpretative phenomenological analysis* (IPA), *hermeneutic phenomenology* and *template analysis* (TA). In the main, this chapter focuses on IPA rather than hermeneutic phenomenology or TA. IPA is probably the most widely known approach to phenomenological psychology among psychologists in the UK today. There is less emphasis on description than would be seen with descriptive phenomenology and greater engagement with mainstream (principally social–cognitive) psychological literature. Although critics have argued that IPA does not appear to be terribly different from thematic analysis or some versions of grounded theory (e.g. Willig, 2001), it has grown in popularity very rapidly, particularly among applied (and, especially, health) psychologists.

The focus of IPA studies is on how people perceive an experience, or rather what any particular experience means for them: a focus on the lifeworld. Researchers do not enter the research process with a predetermined research hypothesis, although they will have a more general question that they wish to explore. The focus on experience and the meaning it has for the participants marks out IPA as a phenomenological method (see Chapter 2). The focus is clearly on the experience of the lifeworld, which is the core of all phenomenological inquiry. IPA has emerged as an alternative to descriptive phenomenological psychology (see Chapter 6), initially designed to bridge the divide between cognitive and discursive psychologies (Smith, 1996). The aim of all IPA studies is the detailed exploration of a participant's view of the topic under investigation. However, the role of the researcher is recognized through the way in which the analyst interprets a participant's understanding. Smith and Osborn (2003) refer to the use of a *double hermeneutic,* with the researcher trying to make sense of the sense-making activities of the participant. Studies are inductive, grounded in the data rather than pre-existing theory, and invariably idiographic, focusing, initially at least, on a single case before moving on to other cases and more general-knowledge claims.

The tendency to associate IPA with cognition (e.g. Smith and Osborn, 2003) is, however, unfortunate given the avowed phenomenological foundations of the method. Other commentators have also raised concerns over this issue (Willig, 2001). Smith and Osborn (2003: 52) state that 'IPA shares with the cognitive psychology and social cognition approaches in social and clinical psychology (Fiske and Taylor, 1991) a concern with mental processes'. A desire to focus on cognition is at odds with phenomenological philosophy and rejection of a mind–body dualism and the 'ghost in the machine'. As explained in Chapter 2, the concern with experience comes about as a result of the focus on the intentional relationship between noema and noesis, rather than between mental processes and behaviour. It is clear that talk of cognition represents a desire to position IPA between traditional experimental cognitive social psychology and discursive approaches, especially in health psychology, but it does make it difficult to ground IPA in phenomenological philosophy and/or recognize it as a true phenomenological method. Thankfully, in practice, this rather odd theoretical claim makes little difference, with most researchers remaining focused on understanding the meaning of experience and resisting the urge to speculate about cognitive processes. But it does highlight some theoretical inconsistencies, which need to be resolved if this method is to continue to grow and develop. I would prefer to see the claim that IPA is concerned with cognition dropped and the method positioned clearly – once and for all – as a form of hermeneutic phenomenology, grounded in the philosophy of the later Husserl, Heidegger and Gadamer. This would better reflect most contemporary IPA practice and provide the necessary link between theory and practice. Until that time, I am sure most IPA researchers will continue to work as they always have done, ignoring any link to cognitive psychology and, instead, exploring the lifeworld of their participants in a manner typical of the phenomenological research tradition.

IPA studies have been conducted on:

- gay men's thoughts about safer sex (Flowers *et al.*, 1997);
- how women's identities change through the transition to motherhood (Smith, 1999);
- what it means to be conceived through donor insemination (Turner & Coyle, 2000);
- the perception of medical technologies among people with genetic conditions (Chapman, 2002).

Hermeneutic phenomenology (sometimes called interpretive phenomenology – not to be confused with IPA) is not one method but a small family of methods, principally based on the philosophy of the later Husserl (with the development of the lifeworld), Heidegger (see Chapter 3) and Gadamer (see Chapter 4). I will concentrate on the hermeneutic phenomenology of Max Van Manen (1990) in this chapter, as it represents one of the most complete and popular hermeneutic methods. Like IPA, these methods focus on understanding the meaning of experience (by searching for themes), with greater interpretative engagement with the data and a move away from the search for essences than would be found with descriptive phenomenology. There is a strong grounding in phenomenological philosophy, particularly the work of Gadamer. As such, there is a general reluctance to formalize method, with researchers preferring to see method emerging uniquely in the context of the phenomenon being investigated. Hermeneutic phenomenological studies have been conducted on:

- client experiences of psychotherapy (Sherwood, 2001);
- living with a severe mental illness (Dahlberg, Drew & Nyström, 2001);
- exploring the beliefs and experiences of potential egg-share donors (Rapport, 2003);
- the meaning of parental bereavement (Lydall, Pretorius & Stuart, 2005).

TA is an alternative to IPA developed by Nigel King at the University of Huddersfield. Although TA is less well known than IPA, it provides similar analytical rigour and facilitates the production of similar findings, therefore making it applicable for studies exploring the meaning of some aspect of experience. TA is also based on phenomenological philosophy, but like IPA it is principally driven – methodologically speaking – by pragmatic concerns. That is, the focus here, as in IPA, is on the production of empirical findings in the hope that this knowledge may contribute to genuinely real and useful social change. The key difference between the two methods is the way in which TA studies may, although need not, start with a predetermined list of themes. Themes may come from previous research or the theoretical concerns of the analyst. A template of themes is then constructed and the data examined using this as a guide to understanding what is going on. This is not a fixed procedure, as the template is almost always going to be transformed in the process as the analyst finds it does not correspond to the data. The process is, therefore, simultaneously inductive and deductive, cycling between the meaning to be found in the data and the pre-existing, often pragmatic, concerns of the analyst. Not all TA studies employ predetermined templates, however, and those that do not are almost indistinguishable from IPA studies.

TA research has been conducted on:

- the experience of diabetic renal disease (King *et al.*, 2002);
- an investigation of different models of social and psychological functioning for facial disfigurement (Kent, 2000);
- an evaluation of an out-of-hours protocol for palliative care (King *et al.*, 2003)

## 7.1 Data collection

IPA research tends to be idiographic, with small sample sizes (the norm for student projects being five or six participants) due to the time-consuming nature of the analytical process. This is not a problem, since the work does not make general claims about larger populations. Unlike descriptive phenomenology, where maximum variation sampling is common, IPA researchers usually employ fairly homogeneous samples. The sampling is therefore purposive rather than random, the aim being to gather detailed information about the experience of a fairly specific group on a fairly specific topic.

IPA studies predominantly employ semi-structured interviews to collect data. These are designed to enable the participant to articulate as much detail about the experience as possible. Diaries can also be used, although semi-structured interviews remain the method of choice for most IPA researchers. The researcher constructs an interview schedule consisting of a number of open-ended questions on the topic being investigated. These might include questions asking the participant to describe and reflect on different aspects of their experience, such as the impact on their sense of self, family and friends and with their methods of coping, etc. Interviews are normally tape-recorded and then transcribed verbatim. The interview transcript would normally include the interviewer's questions along with the participant's responses. The transcript should focus on semantic meaning (that is, simply what people said) and so will not include detail of pauses, false starts, latched responses, etc. as one might find with transcript used in discourse analysis. Similar techniques of data collection are also used for hermeneutic phenomenological and template analytical studies with a focus on developing a conversational style of interviewing to allow meaning to emerge intersubjectively (between the interviewer and interviewee), although other forms of data collection (such as the use of diaries, written descriptions and literature) may be considered for hermeneutic phenomenological studies more frequently than for IPA or TA studies.

More recently, there has been some discussion of the possibility of using group discussions (sometimes called focus groups) to collect data for IPA studies (Smith, 2004). Whilst there are no theoretical reasons why IPA could not be used to analyse data gathered through group discussions there remains some work to be done to determine the meaning of such findings. IPA, like many phenomenological approaches, is individualistic, that is, concerned with explicating individual experience. Smith (2004) suggests a two-stage analysis of transcripts from group discussions, analysed first for group patterns and then again for individual accounts. As yet, IPA remains untested as a method for the analysis of group data, but this is an area ripe for both theoretical development and empirical investigation.

## 7.2   Method

Thematic analysis is the principal analytical approach used with IPA. Essentially, the analyst is concerned with making sense of the participant's world and, therefore, spends a considerable amount of time working through the transcript (and listening to the tape) in order to identify the major themes. The analysis begins with a single case and proceeds through the following stages. Throughout, comments are made for the entire transcript, although it is worth noting that generally this does not include the interviewer's questions. The margins are used for coding, and so the transcript should be formatted with very wide margins.

*Stage 1*: read and re-read the transcript, adding comments into the left-hand margin about the meaning of particular sections of the transcript. Not all elements will warrant comment. Comments may be summaries, associations or interpretations (based on knowledge of the extant psychological literature). Here, the aim is simply to state what is going on in the text, generally staying close to the meaning inherent in the text and less frequently making more interpretative remarks. This stage may be repeated more than once in order to maximize the likelihood that the researcher has captured the meaning in the text.

*Stage 2*: emerging themes are noted in the right-hand margin. Initial notes are transformed into more meaningful statements, reflecting a broader level of meaning in a particular section of text. These comments should reflect broader, perhaps more theoretically significant, concerns. Terms are not fixed at this stage; indeed, they are likely to change at the next stage when they are looked at together.

*Stage 3*: themes are listed separately on paper (in their original chronological order). The analyst now attempts to identify common links between themes and to reorder them in a more analytical or theoretical way. Some themes will cluster together, while others need to be broken up further. Some will appear to be more superordinate themes, subsuming others. As the analyst works to reorder and restructure the themes, he or she will need to continually return to the text to check the emerging analysis.

*Stage 4*: the analyst now produces a table of themes in a coherent order. Themes are appropriately named and each theme linked to the originating text through reference to specific quotes (given through page and line numbers). At this stage, some themes may be dropped if they do not fit well into the superordinate themes and/or because they do not add a great deal to the analysis.

Once these stages have been completed for one case, the analyst moves on to the next case (if there are more cases – it is perfectly possible to present the analysis of a single case). The analyst can either begin again from scratch, starting with stage 1, or use the table of themes generated from the analysis of the first case to guide the analysis of the next case. If the latter approach is used, then the analyst must be careful to adapt and amend the initial table of themes as he or she conducts the analysis, checking these amendments with the transcript of the first case, and then the second case, the third case, and so on. This procedure is repeated for all cases until a final table of themes is produced that represents all the cases in a study. Flexibility is important when moving from case to case, as there will be times when it is necessary to start again and completely rework themes or abandon those that appeared relevant with one case but not others. The process is cyclical and iterative, continually returning to the data to check meaning and confirm interpretations.

See Study box 7.1 for an example of an IPA study on the experience of carers of stroke survivors. The box provides detail of the methods used, which are fairly typical of research from this particular theoretical perspective, as well as a brief description of the findings. The study boxes in this chapter, and in the preceding

## Study box 7.1

**Hunt, D. & Smith, J. A.** (2004). The personal experience of carers of stroke survivors: an interpretative phenomenological analysis. *Disability and Rehabilitation*, 26(16), 1000–1011.

There are, of course, many social and emotional (as well as physical and practical) consequences for people who suffer a stroke. This paper acknowledges the importance of these sequelae but seeks to explore a much less researched area: the experience of family carers of stroke survivors. Four participants were selected on the basis of being family members of a stroke survivor on a rehabilitation ward. They were interviewed and the interview then transcribed verbatim and subject to an interpretative phenomenological analysis. As described in the main text, this involved repeated reading and re-reading, followed by systematic coding of the emergent themes on a case-by-case basis. Themes that were not significant for all participants were omitted in this study. Three superordinate themes were identified: uncertainty, personal impact and strength of relationships. The first theme (uncertainty) concerned the uncertain nature of the future for these carers, with them not knowing what the future held in relation to the recovery, or not, of their loved one. Although all the participants felt greatly for the position of their relative, they also talked about the personal impact (practically and emotionally) that the stroke had had on them (second theme – personal impact). Finally, the interviewees talked spontaneously of the strength of the relationships in their families, and with the hospital staff, and how these were vital for coping with the situation they now faced. It was clear from this study that family carers of people suffering strokes experience a great deal of distress and difficulties coping, even when their relative is still in hospital. And much as survivors of strokes need considerable time and support in adjusting to their altered way of living, so too do the families of these survivors.

and following chapters, should be seen not only as brief summaries of studies designed to further enable understanding of what can be achieved using different methods, but also as recommendations for further reading. A great deal will be gained in understanding of the methods explained in this book if it is supplemented by the original works summarized in the study boxes.

## 7.3 Presenting findings

IPA studies are written up in a fairly traditional qualitative report format, with an introduction reviewing the extant psychological literature on the topic and framing the research question. This is followed with a method section, providing some information about IPA as a method of analysis and the analytical procedure that will be followed along with detail of the sample. The analysis section follows, which presents the findings as a series of large themes (normally no more than four), with subthemes if necessary. The themes are introduced and then presented with sufficient quotes for the reader to see the links between data and analysis. The meaning of themes will be linked to appropriate psychological literature in order to interpret the meaning of the text. An IPA report will generally finish with a conclusion summarizing the work and the main findings, also discussing the implications, if not done earlier, and, possibly, suggestions for future research on the topic. Finally, as is usual in most research write-ups, there will also be sections for references and, if necessary, appendices. TA and

## Study box 7.2

**Flowers, P., Smith, J.A., Sheeran, P. & Beail, N.** (1998). 'Coming out' and sexual debut: understanding the social context of HIV risk-related behaviour. *Journal of Community & Applied Social Psychology*, 8, 409–421.

Gay men have been disproportionately affected by HIV/AIDS, with the consequence that a considerable body of knowledge has grown up over the past 20 years or so. This paper by Paul Flowers and colleagues represents a distinctly phenomenological take on the issue, with a particular focus on the social context of 'coming out' and the impact this might have for HIV risk-related behaviour among gay men living in a small town in the UK. Semi-structured interviews were conducted with 20 men, all of whom identified themselves as gay. Men were recruited through contacts of the first author and then snowballing (each interviewee providing details of further possible interviewees). There was no attempt to garner a truly representative sample, since this is somewhat meaningless when dealing with 'hidden' populations – where it is not possible to determine the norms of the population as a whole. Instead, the focus was on the experience of the men who volunteered to take part, who, demographically, appeared relatively representative of the wider community in which they lived. IPA was the method of analysis. Three themes emerged from the data, titled with direct quotes from the data: 'It's like a whole different world when you come out of the closet', ' It's like going from talking English to talking French' and 'It's not some fairy-tale romance, you're actually risking your life'. The first theme concerned the process following disclosure and self-acceptance, where these gay men first begin to live as gay men. For many, this revolved around public sex environments, and this was where they learned about gay sex and were introduced to the gay community. Entering the gay community, whether through public sex environments or the commercial gay scene, was not straightforward, however, and the second theme concerned the process of enculturation. Appropriate language use was particularly important in the process of enculturation, and these men had to learn about 'gay speak'. Finally, this paper describes the reality of early sexual encounters, in which a great deal of cultural knowledge was acquired, with initiates being particularly vulnerable because of their lack of sexual knowledge. Even among the men who knew about safer sex, they lacked the ability to initiate condom use in their earliest sexual encounters. Of greatest concern for these men was not HIV/AIDS, however, but the act of sex, loaded with importance and symbolic meaning, invariably linked with the specific social context in which the men lived. What was highlighted in this paper, in contrast to much previous research, was the importance of 'socio-sexual capital' (Bajos, 1997) – what an individual brings to sexual encounters, with the process of 'coming out' a key contributing feature of the socio-sexual capital of these gay men. In other words, the socio-biographical context provides valuable information about identity formation and the use (or not) of condoms for penetrative sex among these gay men. And finally, it is worth noting that although HIV was the focus of this investigation, 'Their experiences of loneliness, desperation, homelessness, redundancy and, amongst these participants, two suicide attempts, figured far more strongly in their lives than the somewhat distant threat of HIV infection. This underlines the importance of understanding sexual health within the wider context of gay men's lives' (p. 419).

hermeneutic phenomenological reports are also likely to be written up in a similar format. However, hermeneutic phenomenological studies are much more likely to involve the use of creative writing in an attempt to bring the topic to life, revealing the lifeworld richly in the telling. See Study box 7.2 for another IPA study, this time on human immunodeficiency virus (HIV) risk-related behaviour among gay men.

| 7.4 | Worked example of IPA: the experience of mistrust in relationships |
| --- | --- |

The data being used here come from a group project designed to explore the similarities and differences in phenomenological analysis (Finlay *et al.* 2006). A group of phenomenological psychologists met and conducted a group project on mistrust, with each of us providing an interview and conducting individual analyses before working together to produce a group analysis. In the end, we concentrated our attention on just one interview, and so the data here were not used. I conducted this interview with a mature female student, having previously asked her to participate and think of an incident where mistrust was an issue for her before the interview. This was simply to get her prepared to discuss the topic at hand, given that the method of recruitment was unorthodox (i.e. not self-selection on the basis of the topic).

The first stage of analysis was to transcribe the interview and in the process become increasingly familiar with the data. A simple form of transcription was used, where the content was transcribed verbatim but none of the additional features of talk (such as other vocalizations, pauses, stuttering, etc.) attended to, as is usual in IPA. See Data box 7.1 for part of the transcribed interview text on mistrust. Cuts have been made to the transcript, as the interview was long and very detailed. Data box 7.1 does, however, contain sufficient information for analysis (in a coherent form) and will form the basis of this example analysis. Names and places have been changed throughout to remove any identifying references.

## Data box 7.1
## Interview transcript from semi-structured interview on mistrust

**Participant 1 – female, white, British, 37 years of age, student**

I: As I said last week, the topic is mistrust and really we are just interested in understanding something about the experience of mistrust – uhm – that most of us have experienced in one way, shape or another in our lives and so I am interested in your experience of mistrust and trying to understand more about that.

R: Uh-huh.

I: OK. So I wonder if first of all you could start by – erm – telling me something about any experience really that you have had where you've – er – you've – er – experienced mistrust.

## Data box 7.1
## Interview transcript from semi-structured interview on mistrust

R: Right, OK – uhm – I think one of the most prominent ones when I was thinking about it is a while ago when me and John started out in us relationship. We'd been together a while and we'd got obviously Stuart, our youngest son – erm – and he got involved in a fracas in the city centre.

I: Stuart did?

R: No, John actually did.

I: Oh right!

R: Yeah well had happened was – erm – it's a long story but he went – erm – out on a night out with the lads and a group of lads not that we were with them started fighting. Erm and John ended up getting stabbed in the stomach and on the face.

I: Oh dear.

R: But – erm – this what happened then was the lad that did actually stabbed some people and went to court and got sent down for it. But also then it was a time when – erm – there was a lot of trouble in the inner city and anybody that got into trouble or – er – or – er – in to any sort of fighting got banned from the city centre any premises selling alcohol. So, John then got banned from the town.

I: Right.

R: Well

I: Was this Sheffield?

R: Yeah.

I: Yea.

R: So although then what happened was if ever I went out he wasn't there. I mean not only did the the incident cause him sort of psychological damage and it made him less confident and it knocked him for six basically but also it started putting doubts on our relationship – erm – although we'd gone out in town before I mean I think we were only sort of like twenty two twenty two year I were twenty two, no twenty three and John were twenty two.

I: So when was this?

R: Erm – it would be about – gosh – when would it about fifteen years ago.

I: Right, OK.

R: So even though it's such a long time ago it's I can still remember it as clear as day. And the events that led after it. Erm – he never said that he don't want me to go out drinking in town and I'd never done anything to sort of doubt the relationship ever – erm – and on one particular night I went out in town with some friends. They'd picked the night to go out and where to go out. I'd not decided and when I came out of the nightclub he was stood there. He'd not been out – er – my mum had got Stuart. And he was just stood there his face was like thunder. And I just said to him what you doing? And he said to me looked at his watch and said you should be home now. And he'd actually walked from where we live it'll be about three and a half miles. He'd been to a friend's house and then must have been talking about relationship problems and that and then he just got it into his head that he was going to come down to this nightclub and see me walk out with somebody. And I couldn't believe it and I'd never experienced anything like this before not from John anyway. So, that were that and that were fine but then it got worse. I were working at a place called Next and one of the managers had a bit of a soft spot for me. And I mentioned it to John innocently and this is and I just said to him oh gosh you won't believe it but Shaun's got a bit of a soft spot for me. And I just meant working you know he were he were nice to me and and never thought 'cause I've not much confidence I never thought that anybody fancied me or 'owt like that. It were just I thought he were genuinely nice and we got on. So, then I got a phone call weeks after from a friend at work and she

Data box 7.1
Interview transcript from semi-structured interview on mistrust

said she'd been out and she'd spoke to this Shaun and I didn't know but John were listening on the phone upstairs. And he says and she says to me I mean it couldn't have it were the worse thing she could have ever said. And she said he says if 'owt ever happened to you and John he'd be there for yer. And I were like oh fucking hell. You know I couldn't believe this not I didn't even know John were listening. But then I heard the phone go and he came storming down the steps. So he put the phone down and we had a massive blazing row and I couldn't believe that he he wouldn't believe that I that I'd done nothing nothing! And it really really upset me to the fact that then when anything ever happened if I worked with blokes or anything I'd never tell him anything about it. You know if if oh if somebody if we were getting on with somebody I'd be scared to tell him in case he got all paranoid about it and I didn't want to upset him. And that then sort of put restrictions on me then and it made me think God this is not what a relationship's about. And it really really it were it were hard and difficult. That he he I'd not done anything and I just couldn't get it over to him.

I:  Yeah, you talk about it in the past tense. Have things changed? It was hard, it was difficult?

R:  Yeah, yeah because then we had the – erm – yeah because as I say a lot of water's gone under the bridge.

I:  Right. Could we go back really to the beginning of the story again, which is the –

R:  Uhm –

I:  The you know the start, where you started, you went from the awful incident where he was stabbed in town.

R:  Yeah.

I:  And getting banned. Do you remember before that moment what the situation was like with him trusting you?

R:  That were fine and it were me. That were the problem.

I:  You didn't trust him?

R:  Yep – erm – because he's he's quite he's quite a popular guy and he were he were popular when I met him and – erm – quite good very good well I think well I think he's very good looking. Erm – and I remember – er – an incident in town that I used to meet him you see every we'd go out drinking separately but always meet up. So, therefore each each one knew what the other one were doing. And I think he'd seen me in an incident with a gentleman where – erm – I sort of pushed him away so he knew that I wasn't going to do anything and he'd seen that and I think because he were there all the time that he knew that nowt was happening.

I:  Did you talk about that incident then?

R:  Yeah, we laughed about it you know this was prior to that you know he say aw he says something like oh I thought you were going to hit him and I says well if he hadn't have moved away I probably would have done you know just joking like that. So he knew that I wasn't interested and he felt quite secure and and it was me that was probably the one that was jealous – erm – with with friends his friends girl friends who I thought were coming on to him.

I:  Right.

R:  I was quite paranoid and I've got a bit of a temper and sometimes it could get quite out of hand in the fact that I'd be threatening whoever went went anyway near him so it sort of switched completely over.

I:  Can you remember back to those – erm – situations where you were you know you were jealous you didn't trust him. Was it that you didn't trust him or – ?

R:  No I didn't trust the women.

## Data box 7.1
## Interview transcript from semi-structured interview on mistrust

I: You didn't trust the other people?

R: Yeah, I know what a woman's like you see. I used to say that to him. When women turn when women turn on tears that men go all soft and gooey. You know and I remember we'd been out in town again drinking and – erm – his friend that he he'd been out with his best friend and his best friend's girlfriend sorry this is going to become –

I: It's alright.

R: He'd been out with a friend called Paul. Paul's girlfriend Linda was out with her friend. And I'd seen them all in this particular pub in town and I was out with my friends. Erm, nowt were thought about it and he said I'll meet you at Tickles. It's a nightclub in Sheffield. Later on. So I got there and Paul was there and John wasn't. Now Paul was a bit of an alcoholic and by midnight he didn't know whether he were on this earth or he was just basically non-descript. And I knew that Linda had a bit of a soft spot for John because she once said to another friend 'What are you wasting what's John wasting his time on Sarah for' so that put me back up slightly.

I: Hmmm.

R: And I remember standing in this pub and watching Paul and thinking and he were with Linda's friend, his girlfriend's friend, who I knew that he'd slept with.

I: Right.

R: So. Obviously alarm bells are ringing over here and I'm thinking 'Where the fucking hell's he? Where's he gone?' So, I thought I'd give him ten more minutes. Erm – and I'm thinking where is he? And I'm saying to my friends I'll go and look for him. Now I knew he'd been in this bar and barrel pub round the corner. So, I am going out and it's like a dark snicket and he were walking down with her and he had his arm round her and she were crying. And I I was absolutely livid and I flew at her. I absolutely –

I: Her?

R: Yeah. I flew at her. And I really really was screaming but I wan't mad at him I were mad at I were mad at him for being so bloody gullible. You know stupid. But I knew what she were. She were a scheming little bitch. And and these tears you know and how bad a relationship she were having with Paul were to get the sympathy vote from John.

I: So – so – when you saw him with his arm round her and her in tears, what – what was your immediate feeling at that point? It was just anger or – ?

R: Hhhm, I think anger. Yeah. It's a strange feeling 'cause I I think it were I don't ever think feel that it was that I that I mistrusted him.

I: Hmm.

R: Because he's just not like that.

I: Right.

R: Well he was he wasn't like that. He still i'n't like that.

I: Hmm.

R: No, I don't think I think it were just anger. I deep in my deep down I know that John wouldn't do anything like that so I trust but sometimes I think that I can push him that he may actually do it.

I: Right. So, you trust him so that you don't expect that he would do this. But given certain situations –

[...]

R: Because, I don't I think trust is for something that's close to you. I mean if I were to say to John I am sceptical about how you are then that would sound a bit shallow and cold. You see what I am saying?

I: Hmm, so trust is – is –

→

## Data box 7.1
## Interview transcript from semi-structured interview on mistrust

R: I think trust is something you have between a very close relationship. You trust people that you love or distrust people that you love. But when it's an outsider then I don't think trust even comes into it I think it's scepticism and things like that that you're sceptical what they're saying or you don't believe them but you don't put trust into anybody outside.

I: Right, yeah. Do you not find that in some of your working relationships though that you might trust someone? You know you can trust them to do a job well. Do you understand it like –

R: Yeah yeah I understand it like that I mean I know that sometimes if I'm working that – erm – that yeah there's certain people yeah so there it just throws everything in what I've said that you can trust to do something. But then I'd say that was more reliability that I could rely on them. I think trust I use for close things.

I: Yeah, you tend to save trust for close relationships.

R: Yeah

I: It means more than just being able to rely on someone in that –

R: Yeah.

I: – simple way that you might at work?

R: Yeah.

I: Yeah.

R: Because if they were unreliable then it wouldn't affect me too much because it's on a professional they'll have they'll have annoyed me or angered me but if they've broken my trust that's a friend who's broken my trust or a partner then that would upset me and hurt me and scar me probably.

I: Yeah, something deeper.

R: Yeah, definitely so that's why I I think trust and that word is is something that I use me personally for those close to me.

I: Yeah, yeah and it's got more meaning for you personally?

R: Yeah, yeah.

I: Yeah.

R: So somebody that I don't know if they didn't do a job OK they've not done it I won't rely on them next time or I don't I don't feel that I can rely on so I don't ask them.

I: So you might use the word trust in that case but it would be a completely different level of meaning –

R: It would, yeah.

I: – to how you understand trust in close relationships?

R: Yeah, yeah it'd be just a just the language that I'm using it won't mean, have the meaning as distrust or a mistrust.

As the transcript was read and re-read, notes were made in the margin (left-hand in this case), describing those features of the experience of mistrust in relationships that appeared most salient. Analysis box 7.1 shows these for the latter part of the transcript (in the left-hand column). Following this stage, it became necessary to work through the transcript (with an eye to the notes already made in the left-hand margin) making notes in the right-hand margin of emerging themes. This process produced a number of possible themes (those of which were relevant to the latter stage shown in the right-hand margin of Analysis Box 7.1).

## Analysis box 7.1
## Part analysis of transcript on mistrust

| | Original text | |
|---|---|---|
| *Trust in close relationships* | R: Because, I don't I think trust is for something that's close to you. I mean if I were to say to John I am sceptical about how you are then that would sound a bit shallow and cold. You see what I am saying? | *Trust in close relationships versus trust in other relationships* |
| | I: Hmm, so trust is – is – | |
| *Essential in a close relationship*<br><br>*Different with 'outsiders'*<br><br>*Refusal to trust 'outsiders'* | R: I think trust is something you have between a very close relationship. You trust people that you love or distrust people that you love. But when it's an outsider then I don't think trust even comes into it I think it's scepticism and things like that that you're sceptical what they're saying or you don't believe them but you don't put trust into anybody outside. | *Two levels of meaning* |
| | I: Right, yeah. Do you not find that in some of your working relationships though that you might trust someone? You know you can trust them to do a job well. Do you understand it like – | |
| *Reliability rather than trust* | R: Yeah yeah I understand it like that I mean I know that sometimes if I'm working that – erm – that – yeah there's certain people yea so there it just throws everything in what I've said that you can trust to do something. But then I'd say that was more reliability that I could rely on them. I think trust I use for close things. | |
| *Trust saved for close relationships* | I: Yeah, you tend to save trust for close relationships. | |
| | R: Yeah. | |
| | I: It means more than just being able to rely on someone in that – | |
| | R: Yeah. | |
| | I: – simple way that you might at work? | |
| | R: Yeah. | |
| | I: Yeah. | |
| *Reliability key in professional relationships – anger the consequence of mistrust*<br><br>*Impact of mistrust deeper in close relationships – a scar the consequence of mistrust* | R: Because if they were unreliable then it wouldn't affect me too much because it's on a professional they'll have they'll have annoyed me or angered me but if they've broken my trust that's a friend who's broken my trust or a partner then that would upset me and hurt me and scar me probably. | *Impact of mistrust in close relationships versus other relationships – deeper impact of mistrust in close relationships (being 'scarred')* |
| | I: Yeah something deeper | |
| | R: Yeah definitely so that's why I I think trust and that word is is something that I use me personally for those close to me. | |

→

## Analysis box 7.1
## Part analysis of transcript on mistrust

**Original text**

|  |  |  |
|---|---|---|
|  | I: Yeah, yeah and it's got more meaning for you person-ally? |  |
|  | R: Yeah, yeah. |  |
|  | I: Yeah. |  |
| *Practical consequences of mistrust in more distant (professional) relationships* | R: So somebody that I don't know if they didn't do a job OK they've not done it I won't rely on them next time or I don't I don't feel that I can rely on so I don't ask them. | *Two levels of meaning for mistrust* |
|  | I: So you might use the word trust in that case but it would be a completely different level of meaning – |  |
|  | R: It would yeah. |  |
|  | I:  – to how you understand trust in close relationships? |  |
|  | R: Yeah, yeah it'd be just a just the language that I'm using it won't mean, have the meaning as distrust or a mistrust. |  |

Once this stage had been completed, a list of initial themes could be made and written on a separate piece of paper. These are shown in Analysis box 7.2 in the chronological order in which they emerged when reading the transcript shown in Data box 7.1. The themes were examined for similarities and links and attempts made to order them into coherent themes. During this process, it was necessary to return to the initial left-hand margin coding, and original tran-

## Analysis box 7.2
## Initial themes

**Mistrust in relationships**

1. Relationship strain leading to mistrust
2. Emerging doubt
3. Unsettling of relationship
4. Impact of mistrust – less honesty, more doubt
5. Garnering evidence for mistrust
6. External factors
7. Person–situation split
8. Two levels of trust – close versus other relationships
9. Permanent impact of mistrust on close relationships – deeper emotions

script, to ensure that the themes made sense with the data. There is a danger of continually distancing oneself from the data in the analytical process, and so it is vital to return to the original transcript and ideally also the original tape recording. Analysis box 7.3 shows the final table of themes that Z thought emerged from the data. Three major themes appeared to best reflect the meaning of mistrust in relationships here, concerned with the meaning of trust, antecedents to mistrust and the consequences of mistrust. Within these three overarching themes are a number of subthemes, which describe the substantive areas of meaning in the major themes. The original list of themes was transformed quite a lot to produce the final list of themes, but much of this represented reordering items and slight rewording. So, for instance, a number of factors were clustered together under the heading 'antecedents of mistrust', as they could all be seen to be factors providing the impetus for experiencing mistrust itself. And although there was no initial theme entitled 'meaning of mistrust', it became apparent that the initial theme 'two levels of trust' warranted further attention and unpacking to bring out the subtlety of this feature. Sub-themes (and original text) can also be included in more than one major theme. Here, the person–situation split appeared relevant to both the theme containing the antecedents to mistrust and the theme on the impact of mistrust. This participant attributed the cause of her mistrust to untrustworthy others rather than her partner (who was simply and unproblematically 'gullible') and, with this, began to feel less trust for her partner (as he might be seduced) but also ameliorated the impact of the critical incident by blaming the other and therefore still fundamentally trusting her partner.

## Analysis box 7.3
## Final table of themes

**Mistrust in relationships**

1. Meaning of mistrust
   - Two levels of trust
   - Close relationships versus other relationships
   - Deeper emotional resonance
   - Deeper (more permanent) impact ('scar')
2. Antecedents of mistrust
   - Relationship strain
   - Emerging doubt
   - Garnering evidence
   - External factors (person–situation split)
3. Impact of mistrust
   - Less honesty
   - More doubt
   - Unsettling relationship (person–situation split)

## 7.5    Hermeneutic phenomenology

This section provides detail on the method of hermeneutic phenomenology, focusing particularly on the work of Max van Manen (1990), a professor of education in Canada. Rapport (2005: 130) provides a useful list of the differences between descriptive and interpretive phenomenologists (while recognizing that some – e.g. Todres and Wheeler (2001) – have tried to draw attention to their complementarity), with the interpretivist believing that:

- meaning is unique and cannot be described;
- interpretation is vital if we are to move beyond the data.

Descriptivists, however, argue that:

- 'unified meaning can be teased out and described precisely as it presents itself' (Giorgi, 1992: 123);
- description is vital to account for variety in phenomena.

It is becoming increasingly apparent that the interpretive phenomenological position is beginning to dominate, although there is still a good deal of descriptive phenomenology being carried out on a wide variety of topics. Rapport (2005) also points out how the main judge of validity in descriptive phenomenology is the researcher, while the interpretive phenomenologist (like the IPA and TA researcher) is more likely to seek to validate his or her findings through an appeal to external judges (e.g. one's peers).

The hermeneutic (interpretivist) method of van Manen (1990), like many phenomenological methods, should be seen as heuristic – as a guide to practice – rather than as a set of rules determining the method. Many, van Manen included, follow Gadamer ([1975] 1996), with his focus on how language reveals being within particular historical and cultural contexts (see Chapter 4), understood through a fusion of horizons (here of participant and researcher – through the language of the interview) moving in a circular fashion (the *hermeneutic circle*) between part and whole, with no beginning or end. They also share Gadamer's ([1975] 1996), scepticism of method and, while recognizing that it is necessary to operationalize phenomenological philosophy, seek to steer clear of providing rules for analysis, which may prematurely foreclose possible ways of understanding, stressing the need for creative engagement with method.

Van Manen (1990: 30-31) does, however, propose six basic steps for hermeneutic phenomenological research:

1. turning to a phenomenon which seriously interests us and commits us to the world;
2. investigating experience as we live it rather than as we conceptualise it;
3. reflecting on the essential themes which characterise the phenomenon;
4. describing the phenomenon through the art of writing and rewriting;
5. maintaining a strong and oriented [pedagogical] relation to the phenomenon;
6. balancing the research context by considering parts and whole.

I have put brackets around 'pedagogical' in step 5 above because although this is van Manen's concern, it is not mine and may not be yours. Instead, I would need to insert 'psychological' into the brackets and, therefore, seek to maintain a strong and oriented psychological relation to the phenomenon that is being investigated.

As mentioned above, data collection is usually through the use of a semi- or unstructured interview. There is more flexibility in the interview process here than with IPA or TA. Following Gadamer, interviewers may contribute more of their own views to the process to better encourage the production of meaning between interviewer and interviewee. Gadamer also recommended that the researcher keep a study diary, and this is the technique used by some hermeneutic phenomenologists. Here, the researcher would record not only what was experienced as a straightforward description but also the emotional responses (for instance, to the interview and interviewee recorded immediately following an interview) and what that might mean for understanding the topic.

Data are analysed thematically in hermeneutic phenomenology, much as they are in IPA and TA. However, the process by which themes are generated is less prescriptive and guided more by the relationship between researcher and text – likened to having a dialogue with the text (Grenz, 1996). There is a deliberate move away from a mechanical application of coding to discern meaning hermeneutically, recognizing the important role of the analyst in the co-construction of meaning. Van Manen (1990) talks of needing to capture our desire (to 'accept from the stars', p. 79) for understanding, bringing our full attention to the material at hand, engaging in 'a free act of "seeing"' (p. 79). Phenomenological themes in this context are understood as the *structures of experience*, experiential structures making up the experience. Van Manen talks of how it is necessary to search – thematically speaking – for what is *universal* (the general meaning that can be derived) from the *particular* (the meaning in a specific person/situation). To assist the analyst in identifying themes, van Manen offers three methods of approaching the data: wholistic (or sententious), selective (or highlighting) and detailed (line-by-line). These involve the following (van Manen, 1990: 93, italics in original):

1. In the wholistic reading approach we attend to the text as a whole and ask, *What sententious phrase may capture the fundamental meaning or main significance of the text as a whole?* We may then try and express that meaning by formulating such a phrase.
2. In the selective reading approach we listen to or read a text several times and ask, *What statement(s) or phrase(s) seem particularly essential or revealing about the phenomenon or experience being described?* These statements we then circle, underline, or highlight.
3. In the detailed reading approach we look at every single sentence or sentence cluster and ask, *What does this sentence or sentence cluster reveal about the phenomenon or experience being described?*

It is not necessary to use all three approaches in order to analyse the text, but it does seem sensible to supplement the wholistic reading approach with either the selective or detailed reading approach. This will result in a good balance between part and whole reading and less likelihood of idiosyncratic interpretations that are beyond the data. The givens of the lifeworld (such as spatiality, temporality, embodiment and intersubjectivity) may also be used (in a similar way to a Sheffield School descriptive phenomenological analysis) as a way of interrogating the meaning of themes and engaging in theoretical discussion. Finally, it is worth mentioning the potential use of collaborative analysis to facilitate both analysis and writing. Gadamer ([1975] 1996) stressed the role of conversation and, in particular, the question–answer form, as the key to understanding. Conversation with peers about analysis and writing is, therefore, likely to increase depth of understanding and the production of rich and creative accounts of the phenomenon. See Study box 7.3 for an example of a hermeneutic phenomenological study on the meaning of parental bereavement.

## Study box 7.3

**Lydall, A.-M., Pretorius, G. & Stuart, A.** (2005). Give sorrow words: the meaning of parental bereavement. *Indo-Pacific Journal of Phenomenology*, 5(2), 1–12.

This study, based in South Africa, concerns the experience of having a child die (as an adult) through an AIDS-related illness. Participants were recruited through a support organization – The Compassionate Friends (TCF) – and a Catholic church. Three participants agreed to take part, with recruitment being very difficult due to the stigma associated with AIDS in South Africa. The authors present brief biographies of the participants in this paper, all women (although, curiously, no information about the ethnicity of the participants), along with the principal researcher's impressions of each of the participants, giving an insight into the reality of both the people involved and the research process. The interview transcripts were analysed using van Manen's (1990) approach to hermeneutic phenomenology, and a number of themes were discerned. Throughout the study, the principal researcher kept a diary and included these often painful reflections in the discussion of the findings. Themes concerned reactions to the news, relating to the dying child, the role of God, existential and spiritual aspects of grief, and the world since the loss. These themes are described in painful detail, bringing to life the difficulties of dealing with the loss of a child in the particular circumstances of their death through an AIDS-related illness in South Africa. Hope, powerlessness and helplessness were key features of these parents' experiences of caring for their child, complicated by the stigma of HIV/AIDS. The role of God and AIDS as punishment also featured in the stories told to the interviewer. This included the belief that AIDS was a punishment and/or a test but was also complicated by the inability among these women to reconcile knowledge of their children with the belief that this was a disease inflicted upon them for immoral behaviour. Life was radically transformed upon the loss of their child, prompting a deep sense of existential despair. There was a sense of emptiness, desolation and devastation among these women, with them feeling alone and deep pain at their loss. There were signs of hope, however, with all the women talking of how they have been differently struggling to find a way to survive the pain. The key source of hope for the participants was the belief that their children would always be available to them in thought. This enabled the participants to gain some sense of control and to begin the process of forging a new relationship with their deceased children.

Findings from hermeneutic phenomenological studies tend to be presented in a fairly standard qualitative report format, similar to IPA and TA. However, there is flexibility and much greater emphasis on creative writing in hermeneutic phenomenology, designed to enable the writer to reveal the richness of the lifeworld in as vivid a way as possible. Van Manen (1990), in particular, stresses the importance of writing, the power of language and the use of anecdote in phenomenological description (see Chapter 9 for more on this). As a consequence, there is a need for creativity in the presentation of findings and recognition that 'writing is an original activity' (van Manen, 1990: 173) and an essential part of the process of hermeneutic phenomenological investigation.

## 7.6   Template analysis

TA is an alternative to IPA that often involves a similar analytical procedure (King, 1998). However, the principal difference is that while IPA is always inductive and grounded in the data with themes emerging from the text, TA may, and often does, use pre-selected codes as a way of interrogating the data. That is, a template of themes is constructed before reading the transcript and then used to examine the data for meaning. Hierarchical coding is strongly emphasized, with broad themes encompassing narrower themes. IPA may similarly employ a hierarchical structure, but this is not emphasized so strongly and must be grounded in the data. Semi-structured interviews are the main source of data for TA studies, much as they are for IPA. However, TA, like IPA, can be conducted on a wide variety of data sources, including diaries and open-ended questionnaire responses.

In most cases, the first stage of a TA study involves the production of a coding template. Here some *a priori* codes are defined on the basis of previous research, theoretical knowledge or some other reason germane to the research project. Although an initial template is often produced, this is not fixed and even when it is used is very likely to change as the data are examined. Following the construction of the template, the analyst must read and re-read the data, all the time marking up segments of text that appear relevant to the research question. Where these segments relate to *a priori* themes, they will be coded as such. In studies with multiple cases (which are most usual here), amendments and additions are likely to be made to the template after coding a small subset of the total number of cases (say, 3 in a set of 20 transcripts). The template is repeatedly refined as each transcript is coded, until a final master template is derived that fits all the cases. See Study box 7.4 for an example of a TA study concerned with the experience of diabetic renal disease.

Findings are presented in TA studies in a fairly traditional qualitative report style, much like they are in IPA studies. It is normal practice to engage with the extant literature in the field, including that from quite different – even opposed – theoretical perspectives. A brief description of method is usual, including mention of the production of the template, what informed the choice of *a priori* themes, and discussion and justification of the selection of participants.

## Study box 7.4

**King, N., Carroll, C., Newton, P. & Dornan, T.** (2002). 'You can't cure it so you have to endure it': the experience of adaptation to diabetic renal disease. *Qualitative Health Research*, 12(3), 329–346.

This study sought to explore the ways in which people adapted to a diagnosis of diabetic renal disease. Diabetes is a relatively common condition, affecting at least two per cent of the population. Renal disease is a complication that affects approximately 20 per cent of people with Type I diabetes; it is a serious condition that can lead to death without dialysis or transplant. However, even when kidney failure does not occur, renal disease is likely to reduce life expectancy and impact on lifestyle (e.g. through the need to adopt a very restricted low-protein diabetic diet). Twenty people with renal disease were interviewed. They were selected to provide a cross-section of patients in terms of the stage of disease being experienced. They ranged in age from 36 to 69 years, were all white and most were from working-class or lower-middle-class backgrounds. Semi-structured interviews were conducted in order to explore a number of issues, including the impact of renal disease on their lives, their relationship with the medical system and their hopes and fears. TA was conducted on the transcribed interview data and four first-level codes were identified: immediate reactions, patient explanations, living with renal disease, and hopes, fears and expectations. Due to the rich nature of the data, the authors chose to concentrate on only two of the four major themes in this paper: living with diabetic renal disease and hopes, fears and expectations. The first theme involved discussion of the impact of the disease on the patient's lifestyle, changed involvement with the medical system and coping strategies – notably, the use of stoicism. The second theme concerned the person's future outlook, particular treatment options and the development of his or her condition. A great deal of rich description of the experience is brought to life in this paper, just one example of the value of such an approach comes with the discussion of coping. People spoke of how they chose not to think too much about their condition, not as 'avoidant coping' – identified in the extant literature as a way of not coping well – but instead as a way of adapting directly to live with the illness. The paper also includes discussion of stoicism, the dominant way of coping among these participants, and how, in spite of apparent social changes (and the growth in emotional expression), this remains the norm – and for very good reasons: principally because people with renal disease need to carry on living and avoid alienation from the healthy world through continual emotional turmoil.

Following this, it is usual to present the final template and findings theme-by-theme in a 'findings' section. This is likely to involve some discussion of what the findings mean, but most high-level discussion (e.g. links with the literature, theoretical discussion) is left for a final 'discussion' section. A short conclusion summarizing the study and implications is common, along with suggestions for future research. See Study box 7.5 for another example of a TA study, this time one concerned with the experience of people with disfigurements.

## Study box 7.5

**Kent, G.** (2000). Understanding the experiences of people with disfigurements: an integration of four models of social and psychological functioning. *Psychology, Health & Medicine*, 5(2), 117–129.

This study demonstrates how TA may be used in quite a different fashion, driven by theoretical concerns rather than simply the data, and by gathering data using a questionnaire. The author was concerned with exploring the role of four different models, which have been used to explain the personal and social effects of cosmetic blemishes, within the accounts given by people with vitiligo (depigmentation of the skin). A questionnaire package, including a battery of psychometric tests and a free-response questionnaire asking people to 'describe a situation that has occurred within the last three weeks when you felt your vitiligo affected your life in some way', was sent to members of a support group. Replies were received from 364 people; because of this large amount of data, a random sample of 30 per cent of the responses was selected for analysis (a total of 110 reports). An initial template was constructed drawing on the four theoretical models that formed the basis of the investigation: the four overarching themes were 'triggering events', 'cognitive activities', 'impression-management strategies' and 'consequences of impression-management strategies'. Coding categories were theoretically specified and then compared with the data. Additional coding categories were then added (and, if necessary, some would be deleted) as part of the analytical procedure and development of the template. In addition to the qualitative analysis, frequency counts were taken for the number of times each category was mentioned. Overall, descriptions were temporal, beginning with an event that was socially or interpersonally threatening and that increased the visibility or salience of the skin condition. This led to impression-management strategies, such as concealment or avoidance, designed to lessen the attention paid to the skin condition, but which also led to the possibility of disappointment and continuing anxiety. The findings have important implications for the design and choice of therapeutic interventions. What was clear was the need for interventions that drew on all four theoretical models, rather than just one, and that the primary intervention for social anxiety difficulties should be exposure to the feared stimuli, rather than avoidance.

## Summary

Interpretive phenomenological psychology refers to a group of phenomenological approaches more influenced by the existentialists, in particular recognizing the need for greater interpretation of data. Three approaches were outlined in this chapter: interpretative phenomenological analysis (IPA), hermeneutic phenomenology and template analysis (TA). The focus of IPA is on how people perceive an experience: a focus on the lifeworld. This chapter focused on IPA, as it is now one of the most popular forms of phenomenological psychology in the UK, and included a fully worked example of the experience of mistrust. Data are usually collected through semi-structured interviews in which the researcher seeks to explore the meaning of an experience for the participant. Like all interpretive approaches to phenomenology, thematic analysis is the main form of analysis in IPA. There are four stages: reading and re-reading while making comments, noting emerging themes, ordering themes and production of a table of themes. This process is conducted on one case and then repeated for all other cases. Two other forms of interpretive phenomenological psychology are also outlined. Hermeneutic phenomenology is mainly grounded in the work of Gadamer and involves a similar thematic analysis to IPA. TA also involves a thematic analysis but may include the production of an initial template, based on prior theoretical concerns, which is then applied to the data. Interpretive approaches to phenomenological psychology are probably the most popular forms of phenomenological psychology in the UK, and interest in them is growing all the time.

## Further reading

Dahlberg, K., Drew, N. & Nyström, M. (2001). *Reflective Lifeworld Research*. Lund, Sweden: Studentlitterateur. A detailed account of the philosophy and methods of hermeneutic phenomenology, with a focus on nursing but of great value beyond this particular discipline.

King, N. www.hud.ac.uk/hhs/research/template_analysis/index.htm (accessed 28 March 2006). A clear account of TA from the originator of the method.

Smith, J.A. (1996). Beyond the divide between cognition and discourse: using interpretative phenomenological analysis in health psychology. *Psychology and Health*, 11, 261–271. An early statement of the theoretical basis for IPA. The paper does not engage with philosophical debates in any detailed way, but it does outline the aspirations of the originator of this method for IPA and health psychology

Smith, J.A., Jarman, M. & Osborn, M. (1999). Doing interpretative phenomenological analysis. In M. Murray & K. Chamberlain (eds) *Qualitative Health Psychology: Theories and Methods*. London: Sage, pp. 218–240. A clear and succinct account of IPA, along with justification for the use in health psychology.

Van Manen, M. (1990). *Researching Lived Experience: Human Science for an Action Sensitive Pedagogy*. Albany, NY: SUNY Press. A beautifully rich description of one approach to hermeneutic phenomenology, focused on education research but still of value to all.

# 8 Narrating the lifeworld: critical narrative analysis

## Chapter aims

- Introduce a critical narrative approach to psychology

- Outline the practical issues involved in conducting narrative analyses, including data collection, method, analysis and presentation of findings

- Provide a comprehensive worked example of a critical narrative analysis

This chapter introduces critical narrative analysis (CNA), a new method I have devised built primarily on the work of Paul Ricoeur. As discussed in Chapter 4, Ricoeur sought to provide a framework for reading text that is built on the fundamentals at the heart of phenomenological philosophy while also engaging with hermeneutics and the need for methods of interpretation. Ricoeur's work has developed over time, with the central period focusing on developing a phenomenology of reading and his more recent work being concerned with time and narrative. Both of these are relevant here, as CNA translates both aspects of his philosophy into a practical methodology.

Interest in story telling has grown rapidly over the past 20 years or so and probably represents the future direction for a great deal of phenomenologically informed work. There are many different forms of narrative methods, some focused on the more micro-level conversational qualities of stories, others focused on the more macro-level and the way in which narratives allow and limit possible ways of living. Needless to say, there are many variations in between. There is no single correct way of carrying out research, and that is as true for narrative research as any other method – qualitative or quantitative. Different narrative methods have different strengths and weaknesses and so decisions about which to use must be guided by the questions for which the researcher wishes to seek answers. The form of CNA described here includes aspects of other methods, and much will be familiar to those schooled in other phenomenologically informed narrative methods. There are some differences, however, and these need to be noted. What is unusual is the way in which often disparate components are philosophically grounded and practically combined into one analytical approach, which, I argue, addresses many of the criticisms levelled at phenomenological methods while still remaining grounded in the phenomenological tradition. The key distinguishing feature between this form of narrative analysis and others is, however, the inclusion of a critical moment, where an attempt is made to interrogate the text using aspects of social theory as a hermeneutic of suspicion, albeit one modified from that of Ricoeur (1970) – more on this below.

## 8.1 The growth in story telling

> If you want to know me, then you must know my story, for my story defines who I am. And if I want to know myself, to gain insight into the meaning of my own life, then I too must come to know my own story.
>
> (McAdams, 1993: 11)

For an increasing number of psychologists, the stories (narratives) people tell of their lives are being recognized as the key object of study for the discipline. The turn to narrative occurred in the late 1980s and was heralded by a small number of books on the subject (Bruner, 1986, 1990; McAdams, 1985; Polkinghorne, 1988; Sarbin, 1986). Bruner (1986) distinguished between two forms of cognition (thinking): the paradigmatic mode (or the logico-scientific mode) and the narrative mode. The former is the stuff of science, as traditionally understood, and involves the search for universal truths about objects in the world. The latter, however, is concerned with understanding human nature and the way in which human lives become comprehensible as a whole, rather than simply a series of seemingly unconnected events. With this distinction comes the realization that treating psychology only as a natural (logico-) science, as has been the case – pretty much – for about the past 100 years, is a mistake and that instead there must be a new and vigorous focus on the mode of cognition that is distinctly human: the narrative mode.

But what is narrative? Most of us appear to be familiar with stories (narratives) and story telling and can tell the difference, for instance, between instructional communication and story telling. Narrative theorists, among others, however, have provided details of story grammar, drawing on different features of narratives and the narrative tradition in human culture. At their most basic, most stories have a beginning, a middle and an end (Becker, 1999). The story will not be finalized in everyday talk, but when the story is presented to another person, people will generally attempt to resolve the story they are telling. The obvious exception to this is, of course, psychotherapy, where clients invariably cannot resolve the story or stories they tell, with the consequence that their lives feel out of control, disrupted or in chaos. In essence, narratives involve the ordering of events into some meaningful whole. Ricoeur calls this *emplotment*, whereby episodes are organized – logically interconnected – into a whole to make a meaningful story. Through this process we also bring into being *narrative identities* – a sense of selfhood for ourselves and others (see Chapter 4). But while we might work to construct meaningful narratives for ourselves, the narratives we have access to are limited by the world we inhabit. The social imaginary – the world of stories that we inhabit – both allows and limits our possible ways of being and the identities we can construct. As Ricoeur ([1987] 1991: 437) stressed: 'We learn to become the narrator of our own story without completely becoming the author of our life'. Such work is, of course, never over, and life is a constant dynamic process of narrative emplotment and identity formation.

McAdams (1993), drawing on a number of sources, lists six features common to most stories: setting, characters, initiating event, attempt, consequence and reaction. There will normally be some *setting* in which the story takes place, enabling us to locate the story in time and place. There will also be some human (or human-like) *characters* that act as the main protagonists in the story. The characters, however, then need an *initiating event* to prompt some *attempt* to achieve a goal. This leads to a *consequence*, or series of consequences, which finally requires the character(s) to *react*. Of course, not all stories involve all of these aspects, but where they do not, it is often because the author is deliberately subverting this traditional narrative form for some literary purpose. McAdams points out that within this basic structure, there are numerous variations and methods for enriching the telling of a story. So, for instance, Aristotle suggested that as the tension mounts in a story, we experience a desire for some resolution. The tension, therefore, increases to a climax followed afterwards by the *denouement* – or resolution of the plot. I would also add that story grammar is different in different cultures and that most of that referred to here concerns Western narrative form.

The founding figure of narratology (the study of narrative structure), Vladimir Propp (1969), identified 31 structural elements underpinning the Russian fairy tale. Others, building on this tradition, have suggested that there are only a limited number of plots. Elsbree (1982), for instance, has suggested that there are only five basic narrative plots: taking a journey, engaging in a contest, enduring suffering, pursuing consummation and establishing a home. Gergen and Gergen (1986), however, argue that there are three prototypical narrative forms: the progressive narrative, the regressive narrative and the stability narrative. The progressive narrative is one in which progress towards a goal is enhanced. The regressive narrative involves the goal being impeded, and the stability narrative represents a lack of change towards the goal. Work on narratology is ongoing and, as such, will continue to inform research in narrative psychology. However, while an understanding of classic story forms can inform narrative analyses, there is a danger of imposing structure contrary to the principles of phenomenology and the desire to 'return to the things themselves'. Furthermore:

> ... attempts to create a definitive typology of plots have not been successful. The variety and combination of plot structures means that they do not conform to a categorical structure without intense abstraction of the specific features that give an individual story the power to supply a meaningful interpretation of experience. The repertoire of different plot arrays can function only heuristically for the researcher as a first-level attempt to describe the story operating in the situations being studied.
>
> (Polkinghorne, 1988: 168)

With phenomenologically informed narrative analyses, like that presented in this chapter, it is most important to let the *subject speak* – that is, to focus on the structure and form of the story as it appears in the text rather than to impose any predetermined framework of meaning. Plot form may be an aspect of the analysis (when examining the narrative tone for instance) but should not structure the analysis *a priori* without good reason. That is not to say that reference to the setting of a narrative, the characters and plot is not appropriate in a phenomenologically informed narrative analysis.

## 8.2 Data collection

Like interpretive methods of phenomenology, CNA is idiographic, with a strong emphasis on understanding the life story as presented, bounded by the research focus of the study. Case-study work from this perspective is, in many ways, ideal, but it is not the only possibility. It is perfectly possible to collect data from a number of participants in order to identify general patterns of narrative with regard to the topic being investigated. The method is, however, very labour-intensive, and this needs to be borne in mind when carrying out studies, even with very small numbers of participants.

Data can be collected in a variety of ways, but perhaps the most appropriate for psychological studies is through a semi-structured interview: a life history or biographical interview, in particular, will be helpful in facilitating the elicitation of material appropriate to a narrative analysis (see Chapter 5). Here, the focus is on encouraging the production of narrative data. This may involve just a few open questions asking the participant to tell the interviewer more about a particular aspect of their life or more complex ways of encouraging the telling of stories. McAdams (1993) provides a number of ways of generating narrative data. For instance, he suggests the following opening statement:

> I would like you to begin by thinking about your life as if it were a book. Each part of your life composes a chapter in the book. Certainly, the book is unfinished at this point; still, it probably already contains a few interesting and well-defined chapters. Please divide your life into its major chapters and briefly describe each chapter. You may have as many or as few chapters as you like, but I would suggest dividing it into at least two or three chapters and at most seven or eight. Think of this as a general table of contents for your book. Give each chapter a name and describe the overall contents of each chapter. Discuss briefly what makes for a transition from one chapter to the next. This first part of the interview can expand forever, but I would urge you to keep it relatively brief, say, within thirty to forty-five minutes. Therefore, you don't want to tell me 'the whole story' here. Just give me a sense of the story's outline – the major chapters in your life.

(McAdams, 1993: 256)

Following on from this, McAdams (1993) suggests asking about eight key events in the person's life: the peak experience (high point), the nadir experience (low point), the turning point (where the person underwent a significant change in life), the earliest memory, an important childhood memory an important adoles-cent memory, an important adult memory and another important memory. Following this, the interview moves on to ask about significant people in the par-ticipant's life. The fourth stage involves asking about future plans – the script for what is to happen next in the person's life. Following this is the fifth stage, which concerns the stresses and problems a person has experienced. The person is encouraged to focus on just two stresses and problems here. Next, there is consid-eration of personal ideology or a person's fundamental beliefs. The last section of the interview asks about an overall life theme. Although there is no doubt that this staged approach will facilitate the production of a good deal of appropriate narra-tive data, it is rather prescriptive and demanding of both interviewer and participant. There are also many occasions where the focus is not on a participant's life as a whole but rather on one particular aspect (the person's body image or ill-ness, sexual identity and experience of 'coming out', or identity as a football player) and, as such, it will be more appropriate to focus simply on the production of narrative data within the frame of the study and research question(s). To this end, a semi-structured interview designed to encourage the telling of stories, with questions asking for the 'telling of the story of …', may well be more appropriate.

Group discussions are another way of collecting data for narrative analyses. Although many phenomenological methods are focused on the individual and their experience of the lifeworld, CNA may be employed to understand the production of both individual and group narratives. Web text and other docu-mentary sources are also appropriate media for analysis (see Chapter 5 for more on this). Ricoeur (1981) stressed how the process of inscription results in *distanci-ation* and the separation of author from the text (see Chapter 4). The privileged status of the interview is thus called into question, with other sources of text providing alternative and valuable ways of gaining insight into human nature and the social world.

## 8.3 Method

There are six stages in a CNA (see Figure 8.1), none of which should really be seen as discrete, since one of the aims of CNA is the synthesis of a variety of ana-lytical tools to better enable the analyst to work critically with the data and to shed light on the phenomenon being investigated. In particular, once the researcher has worked through the first five stages, it becomes necessary to syn-thesize the findings in a final stage when presenting the research in written form. This final synthesis is not easily described, but it is hoped that the reader will be able to understand the process involved once they have read through the example detailed in this chapter. First, however, it is necessary to outline the five distinct stages leading to this final synthesis.

It should be obvious from the description provided below that CNA is a com-plex method, requiring a lot of the analyst. CNA is time-consuming and requires a high level of skill as well as a high level of openness on the part of the

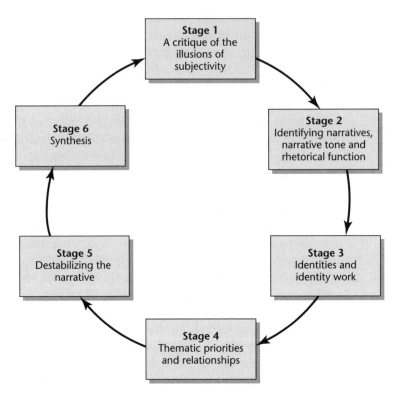

**Figure 8.1 Critical narrative analysis (CNA) – working the hermeneutic circle**

researcher. These demands should not be underestimated, and anyone considering using this method will need to factor these things into the equation when deciding on the most appropriate method for their research. Although I believe the benefits outweigh the costs, this will not be the case in all research projects, and there will be times when a simpler alternative will be a better choice. As always, any decision needs to be informed by the aims of the research and the practical constraints that we all work within (see also Section 8.6 and the discussion of these issues in Chapter 9).

### 8.3.1 Stage 1: a critique of the illusions of the subject

Stage 1 begins with the researcher subjecting him- or herself to a critique using the hermeneutic most appropriate to the topic at hand. This is effectively a moment of reflexive engagement, where the researcher thinks through their background and experience and the impact that this might have on the questions being asked, the data that they have helped to produce and that will form the basis of their analysis. Figure 8.2 identifies six possible critical hermeneutics of suspicion. However, it is important to note that all or none of these may be appropriate to any given analysis. Furthermore, other critical hermeneutics may be vital to an analysis. I will talk more about the choice of hermeneutics later when I discuss Stage 5, where the analyst turns the same hermeneutic of suspicion on the text.

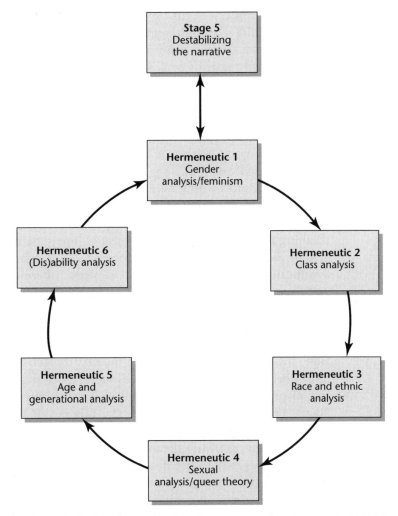

**Figure 8.2  Stage 5: destabilizing the narrative – opening the hermeneutic circle**

To begin, it is important to read through the transcript. Given that it is likely that you, as the researcher, will have chosen the topic, then it is probable that you will be reasonably familiar with the subject area. However, it is still important to be open to the text and allow for a 'fusion of horizons' (Gadamer, [1975] 1996), when attempting to appropriate meaning. Once you have a good sense of the meaning, you need to think through what this topic means to you more personally. I would recommend writing a short paragraph on your beliefs about the topic and the influence these might have on your understanding of the material – effectively, an attempt (and it will be just that – an imperfect attempt) to delineate the horizons of your world with regard to the topic at hand. It is now important to expose yourself to an appropriate hermeneutic to better critique your preconceptions about the topic and further illuminate the assumptions underpinning your particular perception of the world. It is important to realize that the requirement to engage both self and other with critical social theory implies a commitment that is relatively unusual in the research process. Most methods require a commitment to mastery, but once this is achieved their application becomes (relatively) universal. With CNA, the analyst must either engage with a limited range of topics (e.g. sexualities or ethnicity) or engage with a number of alternative, sometimes competing and often very complex, social theoretical hermeneutics. In many ways, this method requires a personal and professional commitment to theory, method and topic if the full power is to be realized. It would, of course, be possible to employ a simplified version of this method, but with CNA one is likely to lose many of the advantages over other, simpler alternatives.

It is important to note here how the hermeneutic of suspicion being advocated in this form of analysis is *not* a depth hermeneutic such as psychoanalysis or Marxism. Instead, while employing the distinction between hermeneutics of meaning-recollection (the usual project of phenomenology) and suspicion initiated by Ricoeur (1970), I make a further distinction between hermeneutic types. Specifically, I distinguish between two types of hermeneutic of suspicion: *depth* and *imaginative hermeneutics*. Depth hermeneutics are those methods of interpretation founded on the notion of needing to dig beneath the surface for the deeper meaning, often, although not always, concealed from the subject who is the focus of the investigation. The classic depth hermeneutic is psychoanalysis. Here, the analyst looks for clues in the text indicating what he or she perceives to be unconscious dynamics, such as subjects defending themselves against anxiety or projecting aspects of themselves onto others (Hollway and Jefferson, 2000). The person who produces the talk is not necessarily aware (indeed, is often expected to be unaware given that the analyst is looking for unconscious dynamics) of the meaning of his or her talk as the apparent (surface) meaning gives way to the deeper meaning, determined by the analyst rather than by the participant. Needless to say, this analytical method is controversial, with leading phenomenological psychologists arguing that such hermeneutics of suspicion mark a break with phenomenology, which privileges consciousness (e.g. Ashworth, 2003a) and understanding the lived world of the participant, as experienced.

Imaginative hermeneutics of suspicion are, by contrast, a way of moving beyond a simple focus on the apparent, through critical engagement with social theory while not subsuming the meanings of the participant to the analyst. Here, I suggest that instead of digging beneath the surface for hidden meaning, not apparent to the participant, one instead engages in a critical form of imaginative variation (see Chapter 2), using ideas from appropriate social theories. That is, by employing specific hermeneutics, the analyst aims to gain an alternative way of seeing: not a way that reveals the truth hidden beneath the surface, but rather a way of taking up an alternative position – recognizing that we always have a view from somewhere (Ricoeur, 1996), within existing ideological structures – and, therefore, enabling a critical move beyond the apparent. This move does not involve the analyst offering a superior interpretation of the meaning of the text, but rather involves a *perspectival shift* in understandings of the lifeworld, through a critical interrogation of the social imaginary of narratives they inhabit and, therefore, reproduce naturally in the stories they tell of their lives. The claim is not to have grasped some hidden 'truth' about the person, as one might with depth hermeneutics of suspicion, but rather to offer an alternative perspective on the phenomenon and specifically an alternative grounded in broader sociocultural discourse. The move is from a focus on the lifeworld of the person and his or her meanings to a critical analysis of the narrative world that both allows and limits the person's ways of speaking about his or her world.

### 8.3.2  Stage 2: identifying narratives, narrative tone and rhetorical function

Next, it is necessary to identify the distinct narratives in the text. There may be simply one narrative or several narratives in an interview. The analyst should read through the text and attempt to delineate the narrative(s). Effectively, this is a search for distinct and identifiable stories in the text. There is very likely one master narrative, invariably framed by the research aims, but within this there may be a number of other stories. By looking out for new beginnings, where there are marked shifts in content, especially involving a new setting or new characters, it should be possible to identify the clusters of narratives in an account.

The tone of a narrative also provides important insights into the meanings being expressed and thus should be examined. The tone may reveal information about the stories being told that is not apparent in the content of the text. The tone may be optimistic, pessimistic, comic or tragic; regardless, there will be a tone and that will be revealing of the meaning of the narrative(s). Although some authors have sought to outline the specific tones that one might encounter, phenomenologically speaking it is probably best to use the most appropriate descriptor available rather than attempt to slot the narrative into some predetermined framework. Furthermore, it is also important to note changes in the narrative tone. A person may begin recounting a story where the narrative is optimistic and then, as the story progresses, it becomes clear that the narrative is more tragic. Part of the work in identifying the tone(s) of the narrative is to watch out for rhetorical features of the text doing work in producing a particular tone. So, for instance, you might find the narrative peppered with excuses or justifications, criticisms – explicit and implicit. These help to highlight the tone of the narrative being analysed and should be used to strengthen the argument being made.

Identifying the function(s) of a narrative is the next stage in the analysis of the text. What does this particular story seem to be doing? What kind of story is being told? Giving opinions (that is, expressing attitudes) involves rhetorical discourse (Billig, 1997). Rhetorical discourse is argumentative talk designed to persuade and involves explanation, justification and criticism. Bakhtin (1986) argued that all talk is dialogic and, therefore, always a response to other talk. As such, the meaning of any talk (be it a brief instruction or a detailed account of a life narrative) must be understood within the wider context of other discourse and the particular conversational context in which it was produced. People invariably present a position against perceived counter-positions, at once justifying or explaining their own view and criticizing the counter-view (or views). In CNA, it is important to pay attention to the rhetorical work being done by the narrative(s) at any point. There are likely to be moments in any narrative where the talk involves the giving of an opinion (the expression of an attitude), involving the justification of one position and the implied criticism of another. The rhetorical function of a narrative may change through the course of the narrative or remain consistent but, regardless, it will be doing work to position the speaker in relation to the wider world of stories that the speaker inhabits.

### 8.3.3  Stage 3: identities and identity work

Ricoeur ([1987] 1991: 435–436) argues that 'a life examined … is a life narrated', where life is a constructive process in which we attempt to recover 'the narrative identity which constitutes us'. That is, our identities are constructed narratively through the stories we tell. The self is brought into being through the stories we construct. With this in mind, this stage of the analysis looks at the particular self being brought into being in a narrative. Once again, it is necessary to work through the transcript (which should now be quite familiar), seeking to identify the self being brought into being by the narrative(s). Who is this person? What kind of person does this particular narrative construct and how does this relate to what we know of the person (sex, sexuality, age, ethnicity, etc.) and the topic being discussed? The rhetorical function and tone of the narrative(s) are, of course, likely to be important factors in bringing a particular sense of self into being and, although Stages 2 and 3 have been separated here, the separation is somewhat artificial.

### 8.3.4  Stage 4: thematic priorities and relationships

This stage will perhaps be more familiar, as here we need to identify the themes and relationships between themes in the story (or stories) being told. However, unlike a more traditional thematic analysis (Langdridge, 2004a), it is important not to break down the text too much in the process, and so systematic coding (first order, second order or descriptive to pattern, etc.) is not usually employed. Instead, the analyst seeks to identify the major themes in the text without losing a sense of the (often coherent) narrative being presented. This requires us to work through the text systematically, as one would do in a hermeneutic phenomenological analysis (see Chapter 7), looking for themes through selective reading. The aim is to identify the key themes within the narrative(s) directly, rather than first breaking apart the text and coding every unit of meaning. Work through the text, making notes in the margins of key sentences and phrases and any ideas that emerge within the narrative(s). It is important to think back to Stage 1 here and keep in mind your own views about the topic as you engage in this process. Once you have worked through the text for the first time, you will need to go through and list your ideas on a separate sheet of paper. As you list them, try to organize them into clusters of meaning. You should also include details of the line numbers for each idea on the sheet, so you can refer back to the text. Once you have your clusters, try to work through the themes, deciding whether they are distinct or whether they can be collapsed into one category. You will also need to think through whether themes should be categorized more properly as subthemes. It is important to return to the text and the tapes many times as you engage in a cyclical process, refining your categories and examining the relationships between them.

### 8.3.5  Stage 5: destabilizing the narrative

This stage involves the analyst engaging directly in a political critique of the text. The need for a hermeneutic of suspicion when engaged in meaning-recollection is controversial but potentially very important in countering the naive phenomenology of some theories of textual analysis. As Ricoeur (1981) makes clear in his intervention in the debate between Gadamer and Habermas, we can never have 'a view from nowhere'. That is, we always speak from somewhere, from some tradition and some ideological position. A phenomenological position arguing for a transcendental subject, able to situate itself outside all ideological positions, is arguably naive (Langdridge, 2004b). We are not only physically situated and contingent, but also socially, culturally and politically situated and contingent (Ricoeur, 1981). We can try to bracket off our preconceptions and recollect meaning from the text, but this will always be imperfect. This does not mean we should abandon this aim, but perhaps it reminds us of the need to be honest about, and mindful of, the situated nature of the analyst.

Here, the researcher needs to complete the hermeneutic circle. But at Stage 5, where the researcher returns to his or her imaginative hermeneutic of suspicion, instead of turning the hermeneutic on him- or herself, the researcher interrogates the text. This stage is explicitly political and requires the researcher to engage with critical social theories. If one accepts the need to critique the illusions of the subject, and to subject the text to an imaginative hermeneutic of suspicion as well as a hermeneutic of meaning-recollection, then the question arises about what specific hermeneutic should be employed in the work. I have listed six possible critical hermeneutics of suspicion (see Figure 8.2). However, it is important to note that all or none of these may be appropriate to any given analysis. Furthermore, other critical hermeneutics may be vital to an analysis. For instance, a transsexual or cultural hermeneutic may be more appropriate, perhaps in combination with a queer or racial/ethnic hermeneutic. The list is neither exclusive nor exhaustive, but it indicates some of the most likely choices for a critical hermeneutic analysis. It is also important to note that while these hermeneutics are depicted diagrammatically as six stages, this is merely a convenient way of positioning them in relation to a CNA. Many critical hermeneutics intersect, and the points at which they do so may be particularly important for a critical analysis. Race and class, and gender and sexuality, are obvious examples where the intersection of these critical positions often proves particularly important and fruitful.

### 8.3.6 Stage 6: a critical synthesis

The final stage is the production of a synthesis of the findings. Clearly, the analysis is demanding and the production of clear findings important. Although there is no necessity for this final stage to be prescriptive, I would like to offer guidelines for the synthesis and presentation of findings. First, it is important to present the key narratives and themes contained therein, privileging the voice of the participant(s). This aspect of the analysis should, in line with other forms of phenomenological psychology, remain of paramount importance. Within the description of the narratives and themes, discussion of the narrative tone and rhetorical function becomes possible, along with discussion of the identity work being done. It is, of course, possible to discuss the way in which different narrative identities are being constructed separately from the rest of the analysis, but this has the danger of splitting off description of the narratives and themes from the subjectivity of the participant. Finally, one would present the work on the imaginative hermeneutic of suspicion. This may also be discussed alongside discussion of the narrative structure and tone, but caution needs to be exercised in order to avoid subsuming the subjectivity of the participant beneath that of the analyst and the particular social theoretical hermeneutic being employed. The critical imaginative work is likely to benefit from separate treatment, with tentative suggestions forwarded about alternative ways of reading the text.

## 8.4 Presenting findings

CNA studies are presented in a similar format to interpretive phenomenological studies. That is, they begin with a literature review and justification for the research. This is followed by some discussion of the analytical method and, if necessary, philosophy and methodology. Detail of the participant or participants is provided, either in a traditional quantitative format (with detail of the relevant demographic variables) or, ideally, through broader biographical portraits of the participant(s). The findings are then presented, structured by the main narrative(s) identified (or chosen for discussion) in the text. The narrative tone(s) and rhetorical function(s) of the narrative(s) are discussed at this stage (or later, depending on the work that these do in the analysis). The main narrative description(s) are subdivided by the themes that emerged from the thematic analysis. Finally, one presents a new section on the imaginative hermeneutic of suspicion. This includes discussion of the particular hermeneutic(s) being employed (if not already given in the methodology section earlier) along with details of the impact on the critique of the illusions of subjectivity and discussion of the implications of this hermeneutic for reading the meaning of the text.

It is appropriate to begin this section with some broad reflexive discussion about the topic and the researcher's role in producing the findings, and then provide further discussion of the impact of the particular hermeneutic of suspicion being employed on their appropriation of meaning. This can then be followed by critical discussion of the import of the particular hermeneutic(s). This format of presentation of findings is important in order to avoid the illegitimate use of hermeneutics of suspicion, which serve simply to undermine the meaning given by the participants, through the projection of the analyst's subjectivity on to the text. Finally, one wants to provide a concluding section on the implications of the findings for the topic, along with suggestions for future research. See Study box 8.1 for a study, which, although not formally employing CNA, does engage with the philosophy of Ricoeur, and the methods described herein, and so provides an insight into the way in which CNA might offer a useful alternative for psychological investigation. The study is by Dr Trevor Butt and myself and represents an early attempt – and so should not be seen as a model of CNA practice – to carry out a critical narrative study drawing on the philosophy of Paul Ricoeur.

## Study box 8.1

**Langdridge, D. & Butt, T.** (2004). A hermeneutic phenomenological investigation of the construction of sadomasochistic identities. *Sexualities*, 7(1), 31–53.

This study provides an example of narrative work that draws directly on the philosophy of Paul Ricoeur. Trevor Butt and myself sought to understand more about the way in which sadomasochistic (SM) identities are constructed. However, as we point out in this paper, although there has been some work that has focused on the voices of those within the SM communities, a very great deal of previous research has treated SM as pathological from the outset, with the voices of the medical/psychological professionals drowning out the voices of the people happily and consensually engaging in these practices/identities. This paper involves the analysis of World Wide Web text, which is somewhat unusual given the usual emphasis on interviews. However, as we state here, 'We believe – following Ricoeur (1981) – that the privileged status of the interview in providing a window to the psyche is mistaken and that the myriad textual sources available all provide valuable information about human nature and therefore warrant social scientific analysis' (p. 32). Following a systematic search of the Web, the paper identifies the key narratives (or discursive themes) present in the text. These were concerned with either rejecting the notion that SM is pathological or with the explicit negotiation of consent. Furthermore, within the first of these overarching narratives were two subthemes involving objections to the belief that SM is the product of childhood trauma and that 'SMers' cannot form satisfactory relationships. The paper explores both the detail of these narratives, and their construction in the text, as well as the implications for theoretical developments about the transformation of intimacy and rise of sexual citizenship (see Bell & Binnie, 2000; Giddens, 1992). In particular, we try to show (i) how the method of analysis may provide a way beyond the limitations of phenomenology and discursive psychology and (ii) how SM stories – with their explicit focus on openness, consent and power play – may serve to provide a critical challenge to (non-consensual and oppressive) institutional power structures through their use of parody and play.

## 8.5　Worked example: young gay men's expectations for parenthood

This example comes from a study of young gay men's expectations for parenthood. It involved interviews with 20 young gay men who did not have children. The interviews were semi-structured and concerned a series of questions about these men's experiences of growing up and their desire to father a child in the future. The motivation behind the study was the growing realization that there appeared to be a new story of parenthood for gay men emerging in these late modern times. Previous generations of gay men had had children, but even so there did not seem to be a readily available narrative of this story. We believed that this was changing and that the experience of young gay men today might be very different from that of those born only a generation ago. The interviews were conducted by a research assistant and then transcribed; part of one interview with a young white gay man aged 18 years is given in Data box 8.1.

### 8.5.1　Stage 1: a critique of the illusions of the subject

The analysis begins with reading through the transcript (see Data box 8.1). Once the transcript has been read, it is necessary to think through the meaning of the topic for you, the analyst. It is very likely that the topic is already familiar, given that the researcher will have chosen a topic of interest to him or her, and this is certainly the case here for me. Even so, there can be surprises, and it is important to be open to what the text reveals about the self and other. I would recommend writing a paragraph or two on the impact of the text and what beliefs this brings to the fore. Following this, it is necessary to engage with some critical hermeneutic of suspicion to better illuminate the assumptions underpinning the position of the analyst. In this case, this would most likely mean engaging with a gay or queer hermeneutic and possibly a feminist hermeneutic focused on the meanings of masculinity. This would require reading appropriate literature and then engaging in a process of self-analysis, which critically assesses your own particular way of being-in-the-world, paying particular attention to your understanding of men, masculinity and sexuality and the meaning of these in your own experience of the world. In this case, my reading had already been extensive on lesbian, gay, bisexual and transgender (LGBT) psychology and queer theory, but I still sought to read further and, most crucially, to engage in critical reflection about the implications for me as I read the stories of these young gay men. So, for instance, while I am theoretically drawn to queer theory and the dissolution of binary identity categories, my understanding of my own sexuality and also my political ambitions (in terms of sexual liberation and the need for an oppositional identity politics to achieve this in the current political climate) can sometimes be at odds with this. This complicated my reading of the transcript, which itself demonstrates tensions between identity and desire.

## Data box 8.1
## Abridged transcript from a study on young gay men's expectations for parenthood

**Participant 1 – Male, 18 years, interview conducted on 18 December 2001**

[First half of interview cut]

Int: Right. OK, I want to go on to now it's about expectations about fatherhood. I would now like to explore your experiences and expectations about becoming a parent. Firstly, can you imagine becoming a father at some time in the future?

Par: Definitely! Yep – erm – the current situation is that I've just bought my first home and I've just lost my job. Erm – so certainly from the financial point of view alone I wouldn't consider having a child at the moment. There's a lot of things that need to be done with the house – erm – I don't feel that... I'm certainly emotionally ready to have a child but not financially. I wouldn't want to bring a child into the world at the moment obviously because of the uncertainty in the future. Erm – certainly once I've secured employment again – erm – and I suppose really lived a bit more life, you know perhaps got myself a car so that I am mobile as well, got my house how I want it and feel that everything I really wanted to do as a single person or even in a couple, perhaps holidays, etc., that I've got all them out of the way. I mean obviously if I happen to sleep with a woman as a one-off and she became pregnant then would become my first priority and you know becoming employed again and making sure that I had money to help raise that child. Certainly the emotional support would be there that wouldn't be a problem. And the love and the affection and spending time with the child wouldn't bother me in the slightest, that would always be there.

Int: OK, can you give me examples of when you've actually being thinking and talking about this topic. You know times when you've thought...

Par: Well recently – erm – probably – err – around this time last year I found out that a gay couple of mine... two gay men that I know quite well were about to become... we'll say a dad between them – erm – they've known a couple of gay women that have been together quite a while who've for several years being unsuccessful with IVF treatment, because they so desperately wanted a child to bring up together. Fortunately for my friend, he went for the relevant tests, everything came back clear and they went to a specialist clinic, had what I would consider IVF treatment – erm – and she became pregnant and she has now had a little girl. John never expected to have children, always wanted them but always sort of like accept... more or less accepted that he'd chosen a gay lifestyle and that chances are he would probably never have children. However – erm – you know when he was approached by the two gay women that he knows – erm – he was quite happy to volunteer. He does financially help them with the child, he sees her on a regular basis, she does know who Daddy is and while his partner happy for him to be a dad and happy to spend time with the child, you know he has said you are the dad you know I... she's not got two dads, she's not got two mums. She's got a mum and a dad who happen to have partners that are of the same sex. So certainly you know like at her christening... at the little girl's christening not long since there was quite a few gay men there and we were all discussing you know would we like to have kids, do we think it's ever going to happen – erm – and I categorically stated that one day it will happen for me. I am not willing to give up on the dream of having a child just because I'm gay.

Int: Given that most heterosexual men anticipate fatherhood as the... as one of their roles in life, do you feel a lot of gay men don't see it as a role?

1

5

10

15

20

25

30

35

40

---

**Data box 8.1**
**Abridged transcript from a study on young gay men's expectations for parenthood**

Par: I think a lot of gay men realize that they're gay and automatically a light goes out in their head that you know that says perhaps fatherhood... right you will... you are likely to be a dad... right now you're gay [blows to indicate a light going out] the light goes out. It's never gone out for me, I've always when I came out to my parents my mum's first concern was that you love kids, don't you want children? 45

Int: Mmm.

Par: Erm – and my response was yes, and I'll have them one day. You know, don't think for a minute that you're never going to be a grandma through myself. It will probably be a slightly different situation from my brother who's married or my sister, who will hopefully marry and have children. Erm – but there's nothing to say that I will not have children of my own or per- 50 haps be with someone who has children. Perhaps... whether that will be erm – er – a gay partner who has perhaps been married in the past and has children. Whether I will be co-parenting with him... you know, nobody really knows what the future holds.

Int: Why do you think you have these feelings?

Par: It's just something that... something that's always been there. I've always loved and adored chil- 55 dren... right from an early age, if neighbours had babies I was always round helping them to change the babies, feed them, get them to sleep, taking them for walks. It's just something in-built in me; its not something that I've suddenly decided, ooh right, I do want to be a dad now. I've always wanted to be a dad... and, you know, it's something that will stay with me for the rest of my life. Whether I ever have children or not, I'll always love kids and I'll always crave to have a child. 60

Int: You mentioned that your mum said you'd never have children when you came out. Do you think that you have any social pressures from family or anybody?

Par: I have none at all.

Int: None?

Par: I think perhaps if I'd have been an only child, I may have felt the pressure to provide grandchil- 65 dren to pass on the surname, to keep the generations going. But I knew my older brother would one day have children as he has done and hopefully will be having another one very soon... well, announcing the pregnancy of the second baby very soon. Again, you know he absolutely adores children and my younger sister absolutely adores children, so it could just be that we've grown up in such a loving caring environment that it's just a natural feeling for us to 70 want have children.

Int: Do you think that you would be treated differently as a father or would you be given more respect? Accepted more?

Par: Er – I think a lot of people will treat me differently – er – a lot of people... a lot of people's opinion is, well, right you've chosen to be gay so you don't have the right to be a father. So far as I 75 am concerned, I have every right to be a father and while ever... so far as I am aware, I'm fertile... and while ever I stay fertile – er – there's absolutely nothing in my mind that says that I shouldn't have children. Just because I'm gay doesn't mean that I am going to be a bad parent, doesn't mean that... you know, I'm not going to care and love for that child.

Int: It makes no difference? 80

Par: It makes absolutely no difference to me at all.

Int: Have you ever thought of how you would achieve your aim to be a parent?

Par: On lots of occasions, yes. To be honest, quite recently, I've been... not so much going through a metamorphosis but beginning to doubt whether I am 100 per cent gay or not, and part of

**Data box 8.1**
**Abridged transcript from a study on young gay men's expectations for parenthood**

that has been to do with wanting to have children. Could I settle down with a woman and try to [85] make a relationship with a woman work so that I could have children? Erm – but I don't think that would be an ideal situation. I think I would rather... rather than marry somebody or have a child with a straight female and then turn round and advise her that well, really, I'm actually gay again. Not that I would ever probably ever stop being gay... you know it would either be a case [90] as my friends have done, perhaps a fellow gay female couple or perhaps a single gay woman, perhaps even a single straight woman. It's something that I have not looked a great deal into at the moment as to with regards how I would go about doing it. Certainly probably IVF would be the best bet, although I do know that my friends that have just had the baby I thinking of trying the – er – turkey baster method [laughs] for the second child. I think it's something that once I [95] was in a position to be able to look at becoming a parent that is when I would have to sit down and think right, OK, well how you going to go about doing this? Are you going to advertise for, perhaps, a gay female couple or a single gay woman that wants a child? Certainly, it would have to be a co-parenting situation, not just a case of I'm just a part-time dad. I'm just a name on a birth certificate. I'd want to be part of that child's upbringing. [100]

Int: You mentioned earlier that you've even thought about whether you're gay or not. How does that make you feel that the desire for a child makes you question your sexuality?

Par: I wouldn't necessarily say it's just because I want children. I think that's one of many factors, but certainly I wouldn't say that's the only reason. I've been on my own for quite a long time now. It's not necessarily a case of right, well, I can't find a male partner so I'll find a female partner. You [105] know one of the things my mum said was, when I told her when I was gay, was well you've always wanted to get married, you've always wanted to have children, you know a lot of gay men go through that, do you not feel that you could go through that? My opinion on that is I couldn't put a woman through it. It wouldn't be fair just to get with a girl, marry her and have a family and then think, well, then I've had the family that I want. You're not really what I want, I want to [110] be with a man. I don't feel that I could do that to any woman, it wouldn't be fair. If I'm ever going to have children, I would imagine it would have to be with someone that knew that I was gay. Either that being a lesbian or a straight woman that wants a child.

Int: As a gay man, what role do you think your sexuality plays with regards to your decision to be a parent? Can you foresee resistance to pursuing your wish for a child? [115]

Par: I don't think really being gay has got anything to do with me wanting to be a dad. I've always wanted to be a dad before I even realized I was gay. I think that was just something that was just inbred in me. I don't think its necessarily one of these male things where you automatically... right, well I'm a man and so I should father a child. There's lots of gay men that just don't have any maternal instincts at all. They're quite happy to see their nephews and nieces [120] and babysit from time to time, but they're more than happy to give the child back at the end of the day. I am quite happy to do all that but not give the child back at the end of the day. I do want the child... not for selfish reasons... I want the child you know because... Well, why does anybody want a child? You know everybody who wants a child... has a child for selfish reasons because they want a child. They feel the need to reproduce and have children to bring [125] up and love, etc. You know it's exactly the same for me. I feel the need to have a child or possibly more at some stage during the future because I want to have children. I don't see why me being gay should mean that I should never be able to have children.

Int: Do you feel that gay men are excluded from having children?

→

## Data box 8.1
## Abridged transcript from a study on young gay men's expectations for parenthood

Par: I think society in general sort of frowns upon it. Like, well, you're leading a bad lifestyle – erm –   130
you know there's certainly a lot of Christians that don't believe that gay men should become
fathers. As far as I am concerned so long as I am fertile then that is… I am not a very religious
person anyway… but I believe if I go for tests next week and I find out that I am infertile then
that's God's way of perhaps saying well I don't want you to have children. At the same time,   135
there's a lot of gay men – erm – certainly myself if I found out that I was fertile that so far as I
am concerned if God didn't want me to have children I wouldn't be physically be able to… to
reproduce and have children. Do, yeah, there's a lot of the general public that would say right,
no it's wrong to have two gay men bringing up a child or two gay women. Its utter crap! It's
just rubbish! Just because you share a bed with a person of the same sex doesn't mean that   140
you're going to be a bad mother or a bad father, that you not going to provide… that the
child is not going to be brought in a loving caring environment. Indeed, I know children that
have been brought up in gay relationships that have grown up into really wonderful young
people. Very well balanced and not prejudiced towards anybody because they have been
aware that their two mums have been prejudiced against or their two dads have been preju-   145
diced against. So it's instilled in them that perhaps you shouldn't be prejudiced against
anybody, whether you be black, white, male, female, disabled or abled.

Int: You have mentioned all the negative sides of people that all disapprove, but can you think of
anybody that if you did decide to have children that would be happy?

Par: I can think of dozens of people. Certainly my mum would be actually over the moon. She   150
knows how much I want children – erm – I think deep down she still believes that I won't ever
have them. But I just can't wait for the day when I can turn round and say, Mum, you better
get knitting because you're going to be a grandma again, but through me this time. I just
know there'd just be masses of tears, because she'd be just so pleased that she's going to be a
grandma through me when she thought she'd probably never would.   155

Int: I can see that actually moving you now.

Par: Mmm.

Int: You've… it's that deeply instilled that one day you want to say to your mum…

Par: Yeah.

Int: And she'll be that proud?   160

Par: It's… it's a day that I've dreamt about for a long time. Erm – probably even more so since –
erm – the day my… since I saw the look in her eyes and the tears well in her eyes when my
brother told her she was going to become a nan a nanan for the first time. She was absolutely
ecstatic and I think… it's not a case of well I want to top that because I'm gay and I know when
I tell you its going to top that feeling. It's not going to top that feeling at all. She's just going to   165
be over the moon for me. Concerned at the same time, worried about what people, what
other people will be but – erm – you know, my child or children will not grow up with any prejudices or they will be taught that there's nothing wrong with having two dads, nothing wrong
with having two mums. You know as I have mentioned before, there are children with no parents at all and I believe any parent is better than no parent. Whether you are gay or not makes   170
absolutely no difference.

Int: Can I just reflect on that day when your brother… how did you feel?

Par: Well, I'm – err – I was head over heels in love with the baby the minute the baby was
announced it was on its way, but I remember thinking yes, its about time that you made me an

**Data box 8.1**
**Abridged transcript from a study on young gay men's expectations for parenthood**

uncle because I thought that's the first grandchild for my mum and I know she's going to be 175
really chuffed, same with my dad. Me and my sister were to become aunty and uncle for the
first time. I just couldn't wait for the countdown to begin for the last final days when we knew
the baby was due and wanting to see what Baby looked like. Did it look anything like me? And
just holding that little bundle in my arms and knowing that was part of my flesh and blood, 180
although not my direct descendant but certainly, you know, my brother and his wife's child.
You know I can remember going out and celebrating and getting, to coin a phrase pissed as a
rat because – er – I was just so happy. I laughed and I cried – erm – but at the same time some
of the tears were for the fact well – mmm – well you know it's what I want to be able to do. I
want to be able to have children; am I ever going to achieve that? Because there are times 185
when, not so much my opinion waivers, but – erm – perhaps you get down and you wonder is
it ever going to happen? But you know, I am looking at it from a point of view of – erm – you
know, live my life for the time being, getting on with my life and then once I feel that I am
ready to be able to commit to that type of serious relationship with a child for a lifetime and
that I have got the financial backing to be able to, then it will be full steam ahead.       190

[Interview continues here...]

### 8.5.2 Stage 2: identifying narratives, narrative tone and rhetorical function

There is just a single narrative in the abridged interview transcript provided in
Data box 8.1, describing the desire for a child of this young man. There were, however, other narratives in the interview, including narratives of traditional
childhood and family roles, good and bad parenting, constructing friendship and
expressing emotion. Many of these narratives interleave, especially with regard to
sexuality and family life, which is not surprising given that sexuality and family
life were the framework provided by the researchers. In the narrative given here, it
is possible to see how this man constructs his desire for a child, how he relates this
to his own biological family and broader friendship networks and, most crucially,
how he relates this to canonical narratives (Bruner, 1990) around 'the family'.
Canonical narratives are narratives that can be found in individual personal stories
but represent broader societal stories of how lives should be lived. The narrative
links past, present and future with a clear expectation of having a child in the
future, once certain practical barriers are overcome, which will satisfy both his own
desires to love and care for a child and provide a grandchild for his mother.

The tone of this narrative shifts and changes throughout the transcript but
involves an intricate and enlightening mix of an optimistic/hopeful tone and a
somewhat tragic tone. The story begins full of optimism and hope (lines 4–17),
where the barriers to parenthood are both recognized, and put to one side, as the
desire and intention to have a child are placed centre-stage. This is made more
concrete in the next response (lines 18–38), where he ends by emphasizing his
determination to fulfil his desire:

> ... there was quite a few gay men there and we were all discussing you know would we like to have kids, do we think it's ever going to happen – erm – and I categorically stated that one day it will happen for me. I am not willing to give up on the dream of having a child just because I'm gay.

The tone of the narrative begins to change as he talks more about making this desire a reality and begins to doubt his sexuality (lines 83–114). There is a sense of pathos in this section of the narrative, with sadness around his sexuality and the perceived difficulties that this presents for becoming a parent, fulfilling his own expressed long-standing desire and also his need to provide a grandchild for his mother. Lines 105–108 include talk of his mother raising the question of marriage and children when he 'came out' to her and, with this, presenting him with a dilemma that is central in the narrative of this young man. This is stressed further in the interview (lines 148–171) when talking in more detail of the pride his mother would feel about him having a grandchild. The narrative reaches its climax here, with the denouement the presentation of a grandchild, as the story turns from one of tragedy to that of hope and possibility.

The rhetorical function of the narrative and engagement with canonical narratives also shifts throughout the interview. Throughout, however, there is an implicit (and sometimes explicit) counter to oppositional narratives against the option of parenting for gay men. The interviewer sets up the heterosexual/homosexual binary in lines 39–40, along with the possible tensions between sexuality and parenthood; in the responses, it is possible to see how the participant recognizes the canonical narratives within and outside the gay community around parenthood. These include the perception among gay men themselves that their sexuality automatically disbars them from parenthood (lines 41–45) and, later, the perception that societal opinion may be against his desire (lines 129–147).

There is also direct rhetorical engagement with a canonical natural biological narrative around explanations for parenthood and the family. The interviewer sets up the need for explanation through the use of 'why' in line 54, and the immediate response in lines 55–60 invokes a canonical narrative about an 'inbuilt' desire, which is later explicated as a natural, biological drive (lines 116–119). This becomes particularly clear in lines 130–138, where he states that:

> As far as I am concerned, so long as I am fertile then that is... I am not a very religious person anyway... but I believe if I go for tests next week and find out I am infertile, then that's God's way of perhaps saying, well, I don't want you to have children.

This bears some similarities with research on heterosexual couples and their desire for a child, where the emphasis is on love and affection as well as the desire to have a child that is biologically their own (Langdridge, Connolly & Sheeran, 2000). However, here, in contrast with research on heterosexual couples, there is a readiness to accept the will of 'God' or 'nature', should it be in opposition to the desire for a child.

There is the possibility of considerably more discussion of both the content of the narrative and the tone and implications for meaning and rhetorical function, but space precludes any further detailed discussion here. However, it is worth noting briefly that there is rhetorical work being done to justify his desire in lines 83–85 and 116–118, where his desire for a child is constructed as more essential than his own sexuality, the deliberate separation of sexuality and desire for a child (lines 114–119), and to construct and defend against a complicated story of sibling rivalry (lines 47–53, 65–71, 150–152, 161–166 and 173–190).

### 8.5.3 Stage 3: identities and identity work

There is a great deal of identity work being done in the transcript, much of it related to the narrative work detailed above. He constructs his identity in a variety of ways, but consistently in relation to his family. In the very first section (lines 4–17), he presents himself as responsible, needing to be financially secure before having a child, in spite of his sense of emotional maturity, caring nature (lines 173–190) and the intensity of his desire for a child. The sublimation of his desire, accepting the possibility of 'an accident', serves to construct him as a responsible, considered young man, mature beyond his years. Later, in lines 41–45, he presents himself as different from many other gay men, refusing to accept the canonical narrative in the communities he inhabits and, instead, being strong and determined enough to find an alternative path. However, much of the identity work being done relates to his family (particularly his mother) and his desire to be 'a good son', like his brother (lines 47–51), maintaining the family into the future (lines 65–71). This identity leads to some level of conflict, and much of the rhetorical work revolves around a need to find a way to bridge the gap between his identity as a gay man and identity as 'a good son'. At one stage, this involves the separation of sexuality, fatherhood and the family (lines 114–120), although more generally it involves the complex interweaving of sexuality, fatherhood and the family (see, for instance, lines 150–159 and 161–171).

### 8.5.4 Stage 4: thematic priorities and relationships

This stage should be familiar (see Chapter 7) and so will receive less attention than the others here. There are a number of themes in the narrative, including themes about the construction of 'the family', gay identities and fatherhood, parental expectations and sibling rivalry. These have all been touched upon above, and this stage simply involves working systematically to identify the themes and explore the meanings. So, for instance, while he finds it necessary to critically rework his notion of the family due to his sexuality, he constructs family life in a rather traditional way, based on flesh-and-blood relationships and drawing on canonical narratives of hegemonic masculinity. The theme around sibling rivalry also provides some interesting insights into the desire for parenthood and the pressures felt to match one's brothers and sisters. This stage, therefore, involves brief coding of the text, summary of the themes and linking to the extant literature on this topic as one explores the meaning of the themes, drawing on quotes throughout to support the argument (much as one would do in interpretive phenomenology).

### 8.5.5   Stage 5: destabilizing the narrative

The final stage is where the narrative is subjected to critique, from an appropriate hermeneutic. The most obvious hermeneutic here would be one grounded in existing lesbian, gay, bisexual (affirmative) theory and research that seeks to identify successful outcomes for lesbian, gay or bisexual individuals. An alternative that is arguably more radical would be to engage a queer hermeneutic within the analytical process. That is, one would expose the text (through a hermeneutic of suspicion) to a critique from queer theory (Butler, 1991; Fuss, 1991; Sedgwick, 1991). There is not the space here for a thorough discussion of queer theory (see Seidman (1996) for an introduction and discussion from a social scientific perspective) and the meaning is itself contested but, in brief, queer theory is concerned with providing a challenge to fixed identities: heterosexual, bisexual and homosexual alike. The notion of a stable sexual subject is contested and traditional identity politics challenged as forms of disciplinary regulation. A stable homosexual subject consolidates a heterosexual–homosexual binary, which reinforces particular sexual and social boundaries. Instead, it is argued that identities are always multiple and unstable. Incorporating a queer hermeneutic, therefore, provides a radical challenge to texts concerned with lesbian, gay and bisexual identities (as well as those concerned with heterosexual identities, for that matter).

Many of the canonical narratives drawn on in the text are problematized when interrogated through a queer-theoretical lens. The discourse around 'the natural' is obviously, and notably, questionable as a way of understanding desire. By invoking 'flesh and blood' (line 180), the narrative emphasizes the biological as a causal explanation for the desire for a child. This canonical narrative stands in opposition to the other canonical narrative being invoked with regard to sexuality – the desire for a child (and the right to choose). The attempt to bridge this gap involves a great deal of rhetorical work in the text and, arguably, is not resolved satisfactorily. Given that imaginative suspicion should be teleological rather than archaeological – opening up future possibilities for the narrative rather than digging down to uncover the hidden meaning – critically reworking these two narratives may offer liberatory potential. That is, by resisting the natural narrative, and a simple biological reductionism, with both sexuality and the desire for a child – and, instead, understanding meaning as constructed and the desire for a child, like all desire, emerging from a lack or, more specifically, a 'nothingness' at the heart of human existence (cf. Sartre, [1943] 1956), rather than biology or nature – offers up an alternative to flesh- and-blood reductionism that is both radical and progressive. This alternative queer narrative of sexuality, parenthood and the family opens up possible ways of being for young gay men, breaking down the limits founded on a fixed notion of identity and biology, which no longer require them to perform the complex rhetorical work being done in this text in order to justify their own desire.

### 8.5.6  Stage 6: synthesis

This young man was 18 years of age, white British and 'out' about his gay sexuality to friends and family. He had a very clear idea about parenthood and definitely wanted children. He told a story of always loving children and feeling that this particular trait was 'in-built'. He began his story by talking about his happy and rather traditional childhood and his particularly close relationship with his mother. Much of his story represented the expression of a rather traditional view of parenting and the family. He then moved on to state that he believed gay men should have the right to have children and that he believed they could be good parents, just like heterosexual parents. This statement was constructed rhetorically in response to a perceived counter-discourse denying this possibility.

His narrative of wanting a child was themed around the notion of 'flesh and blood' and the connection between biology and family lineage. He articulated this through his 'natural' 'in-built' 'need to reproduce' and provide his mother with a grandchild. The tone of the narrative was variously optimistic and pessimistic, beginning with the former and becoming more tragic when the impact of his sexuality on his decision-making process came to be discussed. In particular, the tone changed when he considered whether he might be '100 per cent gay' and whether he could perhaps have children with a woman, and when he talked of dreaming of the day when he could say to his mother that she would be a grandmother again.

I interrogated the narrative(s) with a queer hermeneutic of suspicion and made a number of tentative suggestions. Through the use of my knowledge of queer theory, and the arguments therein about the dissolution of binary categories, especially concerning identities and a process of imaginative variation, I thought that the narrative was being employed to provide a bridge between the story of gay identity being constructed and the biological narrative of 'the family'. Through the motif of giving his mother a grandchild that is their 'flesh and blood', the narrative demonstrates the need to work on the narrative boundaries of a heterosexual–homosexual binary divide. The narrative tension being expressed appears to be a result of the way the story attempts to bridge the apparent gap between the story of gay identity being told here and 'the family'. An alternative, with both sexuality and the desire for a child constructed as a lack, rather than biological drive, has been presented as a way of opening up possible narratives of being for all young gay men.

## 8.6  Final thoughts

As may be obvious by now, CNA is a particularly demanding method. Although I believe it offers a way of working with narratives that is particularly enlightening, the method can (and, arguably, should) be adapted to one's needs. In particular, the first and final stages can be left out or simplified, especially in the context of student projects. The core of any narrative analysis is presented through Stages 2–4, and a study will be rigorous and enlightening if these alone are employed. Although I do believe it important to engage with broader socio-political concerns, this need not be a requirement for all research projects. Research is always a process of compromise, and methods should be a way of helping to discover/construct knowledge; if this is facilitated by adapting the methods in this chapter, and the book as a whole, then that is justification enough. No method is perfect or appropriate for all situations, and, as long as they are adapted wisely and with explicit justification, then the research should remain rigorous and persuasive.

## Summary

Interest in story telling and the way in which we use narratives to express our experiences has grown a great deal over the past 20 years and probably represents the future for a great deal of phenomenological informed work. This chapter outlined a critical narrative analysis (CNA), which is based on the philosophy of Ricoeur and involves a series of stages similar to those of other methods of narrative analysis but with some key differences. A fully worked example from a study on young gay men's expectations for parenthood was presented. Data may be collected in a variety of ways, but perhaps the most appropriate for psychological studies is through a life history or biographical interview. There are six stages to a CNA: a critique of the illusions of the subject, identifying narratives, tone and function, identities and identity work, thematic priorities and relationships, destabilizing the narrative and critical synthesis.

## Further reading

**Polkinghorne, D.E. (1988).** *Narrative Knowing and the Human Sciences.* **New York: SUNY Press**. A classic text on narrative research stemming from the phenomenological tradition.

**Ricoeur, P. (1970).** *Freud and Philosophy: An Essay on Interpretation* [trans. D. Savage]. **New Haven, CT: Yale University Press** and **Ricoeur, P. (1992).** *Oneself as Another* [trans. K. Blamey]. **Chicago, IL: University of Chicago Press.**

These two books represent probably the most important pieces of work that Ricoeur produced in his lifetime. The first book introduces the distinction between the hermeneutics of meaning-recollection and suspicion, along with the argument that both are needed in order to fully understand the meaning of a text. The second book concerns Ricoeur's move to narrative and his engagement with analytical philosophy. The book also, importantly, includes detail of Ricoeur's notion of narrative identity as well as his attempt to produce an ethical philosophy grounded in the narrative tradition.

**Ricoeur, P. (1981).** *Hermeneutics and the Human Sciences* [ed. and trans. J. B. Thompson]. **Cambridge: Cambridge University Press**. Probably the most readable collection of Ricoeur's writings and certainly the one of most relevance to the social sciences. This collection includes important essays on distanciation, the critique of ideology, explanation versus understanding, human action as text and narrative.

# 9 Key issues, debates and rebuttals

## Chapter aims

- Critically discuss key issues and debates surrounding phenomenological psychology

- Provide further detailed discussion of validity in phenomenological research

- Explore the distinction between description and interpretation

- Outline a possible future for phenomenological psychology: a 'post-phenomenology'

For some, phenomenology, and, indeed, even phenomenological psychology, is something that should always be referred to in the past tense: it is something that belongs to the history of continental philosophy, having little or no part to play in contemporary debates and developments in the field. The fact that I have written this book, and the fact that you have (probably) just read it, clearly suggest this may not be the whole story, especially when considering the application of phenomenological philosophy in the social sciences. Although there is some truth that phenomenological philosophy appears to have had its day, the reasons for this and the possibility of a return to this approach in the social sciences deserve to be interrogated further. This chapter seeks to offer such an interrogation and also explores some of the criticisms levelled at phenomenological psychology in particular, and, I hope, provides some answers to these criticisms. There are undoubtedly limitations to phenomenological psychology, but these are not insurmountable; I believe that phenomenological psychology offers a rigorous and systematic – theoretically grounded – approach to qualitative research in the social sciences and, as such, demands the attention needed to address these limitations.

## 9.1 Challenging existing perspectives

Phenomenological psychology, in all its forms, is without doubt most popular in social and applied psychology, in the UK at least. This is not surprising, since adopting a phenomenological approach in cognitive or, to a lesser extent, developmental psychology would require (most) researchers to reject completely their existing ways of working. In social and applied psychology, however, we have witnessed the growth of qualitative methods, and there phenomenological methods have found a home. It is worth noting that while there has been considerable growth in qualitative methods in the UK, this has not been the same in the USA. There have been (and continue to be) important developments in qualitative methods in psychology in the USA, but quantitative methods still dominate and this looks unlikely to change in the near future. The growth in qualitative methods in the UK effectively began with what is now termed the 'crisis in social psychology', a period in the 1970s marked by a critical challenge to mainstream, predominantly quantitative social psychology. The crisis marked the beginning of a philosophical and methodological challenge to the assumptions underpinning most quantitative social psychology, notably the *a-historical/a-cultural*, *essentialist*, *dualist* and *scientistic* nature of, predominantly experimental, social psychology. That is, critics, starting in the 1970s, questioned first the tendency of much social psychology, especially cognitive social psychology, to rely on an a-historical and a-cultural notion of people, failing to recognize the way in which all human life is embedded in a particular history and culture that shapes life in the most profound way. Second, questions were raised, and indeed continue to be raised, about the view central to a great deal of social psychology that there is an essential (information-processing) system at the heart of human nature. Third, it was argued that the dualist separation of mind and body, person and world, still central to most social psychology, discussed in Chapter 2, was philosophically naive. Finally, it was, and is, argued that the use of natural science methods with a human science discipline has failed to take account of the object of study. That is, using scientific methods with subjects (people) rather than objects fails to account adequately for the complexity inherent in human subjectivity (for more on these criticisms, see Burr, 2003; Butt, 2004; Gergen, 1999; Harré & Gillett, 1994; Henriques *et al.*, 1984; Parker, 1992; Potter & Wetherell, 1987; Smith, Harré & Van Langenhove, 1995). However, although these challenges have been formidable and, arguably, not refuted, cognitive social psychology still remains dominant. So, although the challenge has not demolished traditional social and applied psychology, it has had an impact, in the UK at least, opening up a space for alternatives. And, even though it is not new, one of the most successful alternatives has been qualitative work informed by phenomenological philosophy.

## 9.2   Validity and phenomenological research

Although the criteria for judging validity in quantitative studies are well established, there is considerably more debate about the criteria for judging validity with qualitative research. The validity of findings produced through qualitative research is an important topic, both within and outside this particular subdiscipline of psychology. Not only is it important for those of us working qualitatively to establish guidelines for best practice, but it is also necessary to make available such guidelines to quantitative psychologists interested in qualitative research so they have clear criteria for evaluating the quality of the work. In many ways, the ongoing debates are due to the relative novelty of qualitative methods, especially in psychology, but they are also, more problematically, due to the diversity of methodologies, apparently all requiring different methods of judgement (Yardley, 2000). As Yardley points out, however, this diversity is both a necessity and a strength of qualitative methodologies, and the ways of judging validity will, therefore, also need to be similarly diverse and methodologically appropriate:

> The unwillingness of qualitative researchers to converge on a unitary set of methods, assumptions and objectives can lead to confusion and scepticism about the validity of their work. But a pluralistic ethos is central to the non-realist philosophical traditions underpinning most qualitative research... But if this is the case, there can be no fixed criteria for establishing truth and knowledge, since to limit the criteria for truth would mean restricting the possibilities for knowledge, and would also privilege the perspective of the cultural group whose criteria for truth was deemed 'correct'.

(Yardley, 2000: 217)

There has not been a great deal written specifically on validity in phenomenological psychology. What has been written tends to emphasize the Husserlian position with respect to validity (e.g. Giorgi, 2002; Moustakas, 1994). That is, knowledge does not exist in itself but is correlated with subjectivity and so can only be claimed in the context of a subject apprehending the world. The question then, which Giorgi (2002) seeks to answer, is how do we know whether the knowledge that has been apprehended and claimed is valid – apprehended as it really is – rather than invalid – distorted through the over-imposition of subjectivity? The key, for Husserl and, therefore, most, if not all, descriptive phenomenologists, is for the researcher to be fully present to the phenomenon being investigated, such that the researcher is able to derive a structural understanding of the experience being described. Knowledge that is valid is self-evident, in that if someone experiences something as self-evident, then someone else is not likely to experience it as absurd. The phenomenological reduction (or, more accurately, reductions, for Husserl) is the key for being present to experience in such a way that our knowledge of it – with regard to its structural properties – should be self-evident. Polkinghorne (1989: 57) builds on this position somewhat, producing a list of five guidelines for validity:

1. Did the interviewer influence the contents of the subjects' descriptions in such a way that the descriptions do not truly reflect the subjects' actual experience?
2. Is the transcription accurate, and does it convey the meaning of the oral presentation in the interview?
3. In the analysis of the transcriptions, were there conclusions other than those offered by the researcher that could have been derived? Has the researcher identified these alternatives and demonstrated why they are less probable than the one decided on?

4. Is it possible to go from the general structural description to the transcriptions and to account for the specific contents and connections in the original examples of the experience?
5. Is the structural description situation-specific, or does it hold in general for the experience in other situations?

Although the guidelines from Giorgi (2002) and Polkinghorne (1989) may be useful in the context of descriptive phenomenology, they are not terribly appropriate for more interpretive or narrative approaches. They are also, arguably, unlikely to convince researchers working outside the phenomenological tradition (or, for that matter, many within the tradition – myself included), for they rely exclusively on the philosophical precepts of Husserl for their justification. If there is doubt about phenomenology itself, especially that of Husserl, which is likely among those outside this perspective, then these arguments about validity are likely to do little to assuage doubt.

Yardley (2000), however, writing in the context of health psychology, has produced a very useful set of guidelines for judging the validity of qualitative research from a variety of different methodologies. She highlights four broad topics likely to be of concern for all qualitative researchers: sensitivity to context, commitment and rigour, transparency and coherence, and impact and importance. Context comprises a number of different aspects of the qualitative research process. First, there is the need to be sensitive to the theoretical context of the study and findings from previous research using similar methods or on a similar topic. In part, because of the frequent need to theoretically critique the extant literature, it is also important to have a good grounding in the philosophy underpinning the methodology being employed. In addition, Yardley (2000: 220) points out how it is important to be sensitive to the broader socio-cultural context of the study and the way in which 'normative, ideological, historical, linguistic and socio-economic influences' interplay with the beliefs and behaviours of participants and researchers. Finally, for this first aspect of validity, Yardley argues that it is important to be aware of the way in which the relationship between researcher and participant, including the balance of power, affects the collection of data and meaning therein.

The second and third criteria concern the need to demonstrate commitment and rigour and transparency and coherence. These are more familiar concepts, being concerned, in the main, with the research process and the need for thoroughness in data collection, analysis and reporting of findings. Commitment relates to the competence and skill of the researcher and the time engaged with the topic (long-term and in the context of any specific study). The completeness of a set of data, in terms of whether the sample is adequate for the task, whatever that might be, and the completeness of the interpretation are the key criteria of rigour for Yardley. That is, both the data-collection process and the analysis need to be thorough and systematic, taking account of the complexity of the data, such that the work transcends superficial understandings. Transparency and coherence relate primarily to the presentation of findings, which need to be clear and cogent. This includes the need for the findings to be persuasive, both to other researchers and to people knowledgeable about the topic being investigated. Yardley does not say much about this aspect of validity, but I think it is one of the most important criteria. With no ability to make grand truth claims about the nature of reality, the communication of our findings to our peers, and their critical interrogation of them, is a vital part of the research process. Ricoeur (1981) likens this process to judicial judgement, where one presents one's evidence before the court for judgement. The case must be internally coherent and the most plausible of all possible interpretations, and if it is not, then it should be refuted. That is, a case is made that must be falsifiable (Popper, 1963) and that must, therefore, be not only a probable interpretation but also the most probable (i.e. persuasive) interpretation of the data. The core principle underpinning this criterion for validity, for Ricoeur, is that although texts (and, hence, all data) can be read in multiple ways, interpretations of the text are not limitless. The need for transparency also relates to this idea, since a case is more likely to be persuasive if the reader can see (i) how the data were collected and analysis conducted, (ii) the evidence in support of the claims being made, in the form of the part-presentation of original data (i.e. transcript) and (iii) the influence of the researcher on the production of the findings, through a discussion of reflexivity (see Chapter 5).

The final criterion that Yardley (2000) discusses, and, for her, the most decisive, concerns the impact and importance (i.e. utility) of the findings. Having an impact on the wider world, in terms of an affect on people's beliefs or behaviour, for Yardley, is the ultimate way of judging the value of any piece of research. She recognizes that this impact may be delayed and indirect of course, but she still argues that it must have some impact. I am somewhat less convinced by this particular criterion and wary of the need for research to have utility (in a way that is apparent and, therefore, suitable for judgement). Although Yardley is not making this point herself, I think that, in the light of the increase in the commodification of knowledge and pressure for findings to have practical, unfortunately often ultimately monetary, value, this leads to an unwanted and unnecessary emphasis on applied research. I have no objection to applied research, of course, and the contribution it can make, but I have noticed the growth in pressure (principally from funding bodies) for all research to be applied. With this in mind, while there is no doubt that research findings should be important to someone other than the researcher – and should impact on their thinking – I remain unconvinced that they should also have practical impact, directly or indirectly, such that we might be able to judge the validity of the research in these terms.

## 9.3 Description versus interpretation

Classical approaches to phenomenology (i.e. descriptive phenomenological), which draw very directly on the work of Husserl, stress the need for a descriptive approach to psychological research. And, on the basis of this, critics have argued that phenomenological approaches to psychological research are too descriptive, staying too close to describing meaning as expressed by the participants and failing to take this further through interpretation. In other words, descriptive phenomenology does not do enough work – analytically speaking – to satisfy the demands of many qualitative researchers.

There are a number of responses to this criticism, but it is important to first detail the distinction between description and interpretation a little further. Ricoeur (1970) has drawn a clear distinction between description and interpretation that is particularly useful in the context of this discussion. In Chapter 4, I outlined his ideas about the hermeneutics of meaning-recollection and the hermeneutics of suspicion. The classic approach for phenomenology is a hermeneutics of meaning-recollection, with the researcher remaining close to the participant, attempting to give voice to the participant's experience with as little of the researcher as possible. This is an imperfect exercise, even with a researcher engaging fully with the notion of epoché. Clearly, phenomenological psychology privileges the former, unlike, for instance, psychosocial methods informed by psychoanalysis (e.g. Hollway and Jefferson, 2000, 2005), which privilege the latter.

Accepting this distinction, one could argue that describing the things in their appearing is a valid enterprise in itself, and that the call for interpretation is drawing on a false scientific discourse, where interpretation and explanation are privileged over and above description and understanding. Husserl, after all, stressed the need to establish the fundamentals of a discipline through description. It is all too easy and probably too appealing to move from description to interpretation in search of quick answers to the complexities of human nature. But phenomenology is about understanding experience, and the belief among many in the area is that this is more than enough to keep psychology occupied for many years to come. Staying close to experience is both philosophically justified and methodologically sound, as I hope you have appreciated from reading Chapters 2 and 6.

However, not all phenomenological psychologists are ready to accept this particular understanding of the phenomenological project, preferring instead to follow the later phenomenological philosophers and explore the possibility of a phenomenological psychology that is more interpretive. These phenomenological psychologists accept the argument that descriptive phenomenological psychology is too descriptive and, instead, work to incorporate a more interpretive perspective within their own research programmes. IPA, TA and hermeneutic phenomenology are good examples of approaches that are phenomenologically informed and that have sought explicitly to be more interpretive than the classic descriptive approaches. So, for instance, while IPA has not yet been theorized adequately, and indeed appears to be too ready to accept a dualist cognitive position, there is a clear attempt here to work more interpretatively with the data. Indeed, this was a specific aim with the creation of this particular analytical method:

> IPA also emphasizes that the research exercise is a dynamic process with an active role for the researcher in that process. One is trying to get close to the participant's

personal world, to take ... an 'insider's perspective', but one cannot do this directly or completely. Access depends on, and is complicated by, the researcher's own conceptions; indeed, these are required in order to make sense of that other personal world through a process of interpretative activity. Thus, a two-stage interpretation process, or double hermeneutic, is involved. The participants are trying to make sense of their world; the researcher is trying to make sense of the participants trying to make sense of their world.

(Smith and Osborn, 2003: 51)

CNA goes a stage further and, specifically building on the distinction between a hermeneutics of meaning-recollection and suspicion made by Ricoeur, seeks to work interpretively with the data using both. This includes an analysis grounded in the participant's meaning, as one might find with any interpretive phenomenology, and also an analysis grounded in specific hermeneutics of suspicion. It is important to note, however, how the hermeneutic of suspicion being advocated here is not a depth hermeneutic such as psychoanalysis but rather an 'imaginative' hermeneutic, where the researcher seeks to engage with critical social theory to effect a perspectival shift in ways of understanding the narratives (especially canonical) being employed (see Chapter 8). The charge that phenomenological analysis is too descriptive carries no weight here. Indeed, the charge is really appropriate only with descriptive phenomenology and, if made now, reflects a lack of knowledge about contemporary developments in the field. The use of hermeneutics of suspicion is not without controversy among phenomenological psychologists. There are those who see this as a move away from the core Husserlian project of the description of experience that is phenomenology. I think there is a need for care but that it is possible to work dialectically with hermeneutics of meaning-recollection and imaginative suspicion, as long as the latter is always subservient to the former. Heidegger demonstrated that all description is interpretative and there is, therefore, no way of arriving at something that is pure description, untainted by the interpretative frame of the human being producing the description. Employing hermeneutics of suspicion is a major move away from the focus on description, but I hope I justified this sufficiently in Chapter 8, with the need for a wider theoretical perspective on phenomena, in the light of the influence of the social world on our possible ways of narrating our being-in-the-world.

## 9.4   Postmodernism and the turn to language

Assuming we accept the claims that we are currently heading towards or already in a postmodern period, in which the certainties of much of life in the West are called into question, then it becomes important to examine the impact of this postmodern turn for phenomenological psychology. Postmodernism heralds a brave new world, in which there are no transcendental universal criteria of truth (science), judgement (ethics) or beauty (aesthetics). The philosophy of enlightenment, reason and rationality is retreating, as is the consensus regarding the 'grand narratives' of progressive knowledge, increasing understanding, emancipation and perfection. The rejection of belief in a unitary system of knowledge and truth, the emphasis on the 'will to truth', recognition and celebration of diversity in all areas of life, capture some of the essential elements associated with postmodernism (Lyotard [1979] 2004). However, perhaps the single most important shift with postmodernism, at least as far as methodology is concerned, is the turn to language.

The rise of discursive psychology (Henriques *et al.*, 1984; Parker, 1992; Potter & Wetherell, 1987) reflects this postmodern turn and has led social and applied psychologists to rethink the role of language in their attempts to understand what is going on in conversation. That is, for most, it is no longer acceptable to see language solely as a way of expressing one's inner reality. Discursive psychologists have drawn on different strands of philosophy, from Wittgenstein and Austin to Foucault and Derrida, to question the taken-for-granted assumption that language is a transparent medium in which a speaker simply seeks to communicate (internal psychological) content. Indeed, for many discursive psychologists, this has meant an almost total shift from understanding the content of language to the function of language (e.g. Potter, 2005). This clearly poses a challenge for phenomenological psychology, given the reliance on language to communicate experience (albeit, not cognitions). Phenomenology has not been naive about the need to account for the construction of meaning through language, however, and there are a number of responses to the charge that phenomenological psychology fails to account for the complexity of language (and, hence, has failed to take up the postmodern challenge – preferring to remain doggedly in the past).

But, before outlining these responses, I would like to make a meta-point about the claims being made by some, although not all, of those engaged most centrally in promoting the turn to language in psychology. Although I have considerable sympathy for the arguments from discursive psychology, simply because there has been a turn to language – or, more accurately, text – in a great deal of continental philosophy does not mean that the equivalent step must necessarily follow in psychology, as if all developments in continental philosophy represent progress (an enlightenment idea itself). Philosophy is a discipline of contestation and, furthermore, if we are to take the claims of the postmodernists seriously, then newer will not always be better or – perhaps more pertinently – what is more fashionable will not always be superior to that which is not fashionable. I think it is ironic indeed that some of the most relativist of psychologists apparently seek to impose a methodological hegemony upon the discipline through their unquestioning acceptance of a select group of continental philosophers (and it is a very select group). The recent call to abandon the interview and/or treat data in discursive/conversation analytical terms, before considering any other means of appropriating meaning, by Potter and Hepburn (2005a) is one such example. In their reply to the critical responses to their paper, they claim:

> CA [conversation analysis] and DP [discursive psychology] can help highlight features of interview interaction that present issues for any researcher doing analysis

within any theoretical frame and with any psychological ontology (narrative, unconscious, phenomenological, etc).

(Potter & Hepburn, 2005b: 319)

For me, the most striking thing about this claim is the certainty of the authors about the claim. Rather than reflecting the relativist ontology, which the authors espouse, it appears realist in the extreme. They have found the truth, and if other qualitative psychologists do not allow for this – by first analysing the micro-conversational aspects of their participants' talk – then their work is not valid or meaningful. I do, of course, believe that some of the findings from discursive psychology have been insightful, valid and useful. But their findings no more represent the truth than do those from phenomenological psychology. Our alleged 'truths are illusions of which one has forgotten that this is what they are – metaphors that have become worn out' (Nietzsche, 1979: 314). It seems to me quite incredible that (some) discursive psychologists have forgotten this so quickly in their desire to evangelize.

Existential and hermeneutic phenomenological philosophers have, of course, considered the role of language and the way in which meanings are communicated through language, as well as, more recently, the implications of postmodernism for phenomenology. Heidegger ([1927] 1962), in *Being and Time*, raised the issue of language – or, rather, discourse – recognizing that we need to understand ourselves as discursive entities. Most importantly, here, Heidegger does not think language acts as a bridge between private spheres. Like Wittgenstein (1953), Heidegger thought that language does not provide the means to access a person's private cognitions; however, unlike Wittgenstein, this is not because there is nothing but language games – where the meaning of a word or phrase is no more than the set of (informal) rules governing the use of the expression in actual life – but rather because we are already 'outside', enmeshed in a meaningful world. Language, and, more particularly, communication, is, in these terms, simply a way of making our shared experience of the world more explicit. Later, in his 'Letter on humanism', Heidegger ([1947] 1993) takes up the challenge of language again, this time through a focus on poetry. It is here that his most famous phrase about language – 'language is the house of being' (Heidegger, [1947] 1993: 217) – is written. For Heidegger, language is not something to be fixed as a tool for communicating unambiguous meaning. A universal unambiguous language is impossible for Heidegger, given the way in which meaning is culturally and historically contingent. Even simple phrases carry very different meanings in different cultures and at different times in history. Furthermore, language is not simply a tool for communicating meaning, since language is fundamental in revealing the world and our relationship to it. Poetic language (rather than ordinary prose) is, for Heidegger, fundamental, in that it is the most elementary way of disclosing the world:

> ... even relatively original and creative meanings and the words coined from them are, when articulated, relegated to idle talk. Once articulated, the word belongs to everyone, without a guarantee that its repetition will include original understanding. The possibility of genuinely entering into discourse nevertheless

exists... discourse, especially poetry, can even bring about the release of new possibilities of the being of *Dasein*.

(Heidegger [1925] 1985)

Most existence is inauthentic and derivative and, hence, most talk *idle prattle*. Moments of revelation are few and far between, both for the individual and for the history of a people. Poetic language is, however, the means for showing authentic original living. In spite of the somewhat romantic nature of the claims made by Heidegger, there is an important point about our very existence being constituted in and through language, and poetry being the means for revealing being: 'Language is not just a human construct or human act, but a deeper "Saying" that should always be understood as showing – an event of unconcealment' (Polt, 1999: 178).

Gadamer ([1975] 1996), while taking his inspiration from Heidegger, deviates from the focus on poetry revealing being and, instead, emphasizes the commonality of language constructed through the dialogical act of question and answer. Language, being, culture and history for Gadamer, like Heidegger before him, are all intrinsically interrelated – through 'tradition' – and all, therefore, are implicated in understanding. Conversation is the key to understanding for Gadamer, for it is here that experience happens and is revealed in speech, not by or to any individual but, rather, between people. Understanding is the core of existence and this occurs intersubjectively – between people – in the 'play' of language, where, like Wittgenstein, the shared social nature of language is key. There are limitations with Gadamer's philosophy, however: notably, his failure to provide a means to decide the 'truth' of any consensual understanding and, crucially, his failure to account for the way in which dialogue may involve power and oppression (see Moran (2000) for more on this). Ricoeur's (1981) intervention in the debate between Gadamer and Habermas over these issues is, I think, the most sophisticated hermeneutic phenomenological philosophical position on language as tradition and critique (see Langdridge (2004b) for more on this debate and the application of Ricoeur's ideas to psychotherapy). I discussed Ricoeur's philosophy at some length in Chapter 4, but I return to one key aspect of it below when discussing the development of a *postphenomenology* by Don Ihde, based in the main on Ricoeur's philosophy.

One of the criticisms of the turn to language also worth highlighting very briefly here – before moving on to discuss the development of a *postphenomenology* – has been the loss of the body from the psychological research project. Phenomenological psychology has probably been the most ready of all psychological perspectives to take embodiment seriously and to work to incorporate this into the research process (see Chapter 3). For many phenomenological psychologists – following Merleau-Ponty ([1945] 1962) – there is much that is pre-reflective and, therefore, outside language (see Butt & Langdridge (2003), for more on this). That is, we are immersed in a social world before we have had time to reflect on it through language. When someone tickles us, we feel this immediately and pre-reflectively as pleasure (or not) and only later may come to reflect on this as we try to express the sensation – imperfectly – in language.

Although recent work in interpretive phenomenology and narrative has recognized the importance of language for communicating understanding, this has not resulted in a loss of everything outside language. With Merleau-Ponty[1] ([1945] 1962: 408) and all those phenomenologists inspired by him, for instance, we see the lived body placed centre-stage, as we move from being subjects with bodies to body-subjects:

> . . . when I reflect on the essence of subjectivity, I find it bound up with that of the body and that of the world, this is because my existence as subjectivity is merely one with my existence as a body and with the existence of the world, and because the subject that I am, when taken concretely, is inseparable from this body and this world. The ontological world and body which we find at the core of the subject are not the world or body as idea, but on the one hand the world itself contracted into a comprehensive grasp, and on the other the body itself as a knowing-body.

Don Ihde (1993), in his book entitled *Postphenomenology*, engages directly in the philosophical debate about the turn to text espoused by a number of postmodern philosophers, most notably Jacques Derrida. Ihde first notes, somewhat playfully drawing on Foucault's (1973) delineation of *epistemes* in *The Order of Things*, how the turn to language – or, more properly, the turn to text – of many postmodern philosophers is actually a return to the pre-modern:

> I suggest that the 'book metaphor' is itself a return to an older and essentially *pre-scientific* tradition, whose roots are to be found in the medieval and early Renaissance traditions. Could it be that this drift of Euro-American philosophy, not unlike its cousins in analytic essentialism, . . . who have discovered in medieval logic a new interest, is in the continental context equally a revival of the primacy of reading and writing?
>
> (Ihde, 1993: 73)

Ihde (1993) goes on to stake out an alternative, grounded in phenomenology and, particularly, the work of Ricoeur: a *postphenomenology*, in which speech is once again prioritized and perception reinstated. Ricoeur (1981) had engaged in the debates about structuralism (see Chapter 4), which today have become the debates about poststructuralism, arguing that the problem was the emphasis on synchrony over diachrony. More recently, Ricoeur (1984, 1985, 1988, 1992) has again been engaged in debate, this time around the postmodern turn to text. In this later work, Ricoeur himself recognizes the importance of language and reflects this in his turn to narrative. But, as Ihde (1993) points out, his decision to turn to narrative, rather than text, is itself instructive, for narrative (deliberately) implies a more agentic and dynamic process than text. Ricoeur is typically phenomenological, with his focus on the human–world relationship at the heart of narrative. So, unlike structuralism but in the existential tradition of Heidegger, there remains a referential quality to language, not a sentential one with

---

[1] See Grosz (1994), Chapter 4, for an excellent exposition on Merleau-Ponty's arguments about embodiment, which includes discussion of his very difficult later work on the 'flesh' and a feminist critique.

language reflecting some inner state but rather reference founded on the multiple dimensions of metaphor and the (public) relationship between person and world. The noema–noesis correlation is, therefore, shifted to a correlation between writing and reading, not so the world is reduced to text but rather so that understanding action is hermeneutic, based on a phenomenology of reading, rather than structural and based on an analysis of text. Ihde (1993) supplements Ricoeur's work further by reinstating perception as the crucial process in the phenomenology of reading and writing. By highlighting the polymorphy of perception, through an analysis of perception – reading, in particular – through history and across cultures, he argues that while:

> ... it makes a good deal of sense to utilize the reading metaphor widely, it does not make sense to forget its involvement in the unspoken and unwritten domain of perception and bodily action within a material world.

> (Ihde, 1993: 102)

Here we see a phenomenological alternative to the postmodern turn to text, a postphenomenology, where the speaking subject is not lost, while recognizing the vital role of language as the 'house of being'. There remains a considerable amount of work to be done to develop this position, but, while phenomenology might be dead, philosophically speaking, there is the possibility of a postphenomenology that can inform phenomenological psychology and facilitate the development of new methods grounded in the phenomenological tradition.

Phenomenology, and, therefore by implication, phenomenological psychology, has also, quite justifiably, been accused of being politically naive, paying insufficient attention to the sociocultural conditions in which the phenomenon being investigated is embedded. If the postmodern critics are right, as I think they are, that all life is ideological and, therefore, all forms of analysis must pay heed to politics – and the culturally and historically situated nature of researcher and participant – then phenomenological approaches have a long way to go in order to deal adequately with this charge. Deleuze and Guattari (1984), for instance, argue that all psychotherapy (and, by implication, I think one could say all psychology) is inherently political, being marginal, subversive and even potentially revolutionary. So, even if a psychologist sought (and claimed) to be neutral, Deleuze and Guatarri argue that they are making a political choice: a choice to support a traditional, arguably conservative, ideology. Descriptive (although, to a lesser extent, interpretative) phenomenological psychologies are predominantly individualistic approaches to research, with surprisingly little work or engagement with the wider social forces involved in the production of the psychosocial subject. The exception is, of course, CNA, which involves a deliberate attempt to deal with the politics of social research and the broader sociocultural context. This approach works hard to engage politically in an open way, rather than to assume that the researcher's political aims and aspirations can be bracketed off or simply ignored. It is true that phenomenological psychology gets messy when we bring politics into the equation. Much more is at stake and many more judgement calls become necessary. But with this complexity comes recognition of the political reality of life as lived.

## 9.5 The codification of methods: variation/integration, creativity and methodolatry

Although this book has provided detail on a number of 'pure' forms of phenomenological psychology, it is perfectly possible to add to or amend existing methods and/or combine them in any single research project. One possibility, for instance, would be to conduct an IPA study and then supplement the analysis with the seven fractions of the lifeworld, as a heuristic, as used by the Sheffield School. Similarly, these fractions could be used in the thematic stage of a critical narrative analysis. See Study box 9.1 for a research paper describing a good example of a phenomenological research programme, which drew on

### Study box 9.1

Todres, L. and Galvin, K. (2005). Pursuing both breadth and depth in qualitative research: illustrated by a study of the experience of intimate caring for a loved one with Alzheimer's disease. *International Journal of Qualitative Methods*, 4(2), www.ualberta.ca/~ijqm (accessed 14 March 2006).

This paper describes the methodology involved in a programme of study of just one person's experience, the experience of M, who had been caring for his wife as a result of her developing Alzheimer's disease. The participant approached the researchers to volunteer to participate as he knew of their work. The researchers had two phases to their programme of research: phase 1, in which they conducted an interview study designed to generate a (broad) thematic analysis of the caring narrative, and phase 2, in which they undertook a descriptive phenomenological study of a number of concrete experiences related to caring. In the first phase, the researchers conducted an open-ended generic qualitative interview. The interviewee was given maximum freedom to tell his story so that the researchers could get a sense of his story as a whole. The analysis of this interview was in two stages: first, a thematic analysis; second, a narrative analysis of his changing identity and role. The findings from this phase of the study are reported elsewhere in detail (Galvin, Todres & Richardson, 2005), but the authors briefly report them here. They note three thematic clusters, which they title 'something is wrong', 'the challenging shared journey – being the carer' and 'coping through meaning making – advocacy'. They also provide some detail about the way in which M acted as a complex mediator between public and private worlds and how his identity was constructed as someone who is both 'intimate participant and interpreter'. In the second phase of the programme, the researchers focused on six experiences, named in the first interview, to consider each as a lived experience in its own right. To achieve this, they conducted further descriptive phenomenological interviews, which were more focused, designed to garner as much concrete information about the experiences as possible. The six experiences on which they focused were: living with L's memory loss, the experience of adjusting to more limited horizons, caring engagements with changes in self-care behaviour and everyday routine, the change in their emotional relationship, the transition to living apart, and advocacy sustained by passion and know-how. In this paper, they provided detail of only the first experience, given the limits on space. The authors reflect on the pros and cons of each phase of the programme and the way in which breadth and depth might be achieved through these two similar, but different, methods of data collection and analysis, and how this might enable the researchers to gain a greater understanding of the complexity of lived experience than through using either one alone.

different methods to enrich the work. On other occasions, one might choose to focus on just one or two of the givens of the lifeworld, for theoretical or practical reasons. Van Manen (1990), for instance, talks of just four givens rather than seven and shows how these might be used in descriptive phenomenology. It may also be appropriate to incorporate methods or particular aspects of other methods from outside the phenomenological tradition. There are, for instance, a huge variety of approaches to the study of narrative (see Mishler (1995) for an excellent theoretical – if partial and now inevitably rather dated – review), and it may be appropriate in the context of a study to work together two different models of analysis. This form of variation/integration, of course, requires much more care, given the potential for the methods to be incompatible – philosophically (in terms of epistemology) as well as methodologically. However, the possibilities are endless, and while there is merit in all of the approaches outlined in this book, none should be viewed as untouchable and all should be considered open to modification, as long as the variation/integration is valid and theoretically justifiable.

It is also important to realize that while I have striven to provide very clear and structured guidelines, these need not be adhered to rigidly. One of the wonders of the phenomenological method is the potential for creativity in data collection and analysis but perhaps most especially in the presentation of findings. Max van Manen is a particularly important figure in phenomenology in this regard, highlighting the way in which writing is a crucial part of the analytical process and one that rewards creativity. He emphasizes the way in which it is important to be attentive to the subtlety of language, to listen to 'the deep tonalities of language that normally fall out of our accustomed range of hearing' (van Manen, 1990: 111) and, most importantly to listen 'to the language spoken by the things in their lifeworlds, to what things mean in this world' (van Manen, 1990: 112), which may include the need to listen to silence:

> Phenomenologists like to say that nothing is so silent as that which is taken-for-granted or self-evident... Silence is not just the absence of speech or language. It is true that in our own groping for the right words we sense the limits of our personal language. Speech rises out of silence and returns to silence, says Bollnow (1982). Not unlike the way that an architect must be constantly aware of the nature of the space out of which and against which all building occurs, so the human scientist needs to be aware of the silence out of which and against which all text is constructed.
>
> van Manen (1990: 112)

Van Manen (1990: 116) also talks extensively about the storied nature of human sciences research and the way that *anecdotes* show 'that the human being not only stands in a certain conversational relation to the world – the human being *is* this relation'. Anecdotes are not, therefore, simply ways to liven up some dull writing, but ways of revealing what was previously concealed (cf. Heidegger, [1927] 1962) – ways of making something comprehensible. Drawing on a number of other writers, van Manen (1990: 119–120 abridged here) identifies a number of functions for anecdote in phenomenological writing:

1. Anecdotes form a concrete counterweight to abstract theoretical thought.
2. Anecdotes express a certain disdain for the alienated and alienating discourse of scholars who have difficulty showing how life and theoretical propositions are connected.
3. Anecdotes may provide an account of certain teachings or doctrines which were never written down.
4. Anecdotes may be encountered as concrete demonstrations of wisdom, sensitive insight and proverbial truth.
5. Anecdotes of a certain event or incident may acquire the significance of exemplary character.

Anecdote may, therefore, have particular value in phenomenological writing, showing fundamental truths through an engaging story of a particular incident. Anecdotes are powerful ways of encouraging readers to attend and reflect, in a very real and personal way, upon the issue, such that it may transform them in the process (van Manen, 1990). Writing is a crucial part of the research process and should not be seen as the mere representation of one's findings. For in writing, one discloses the world, the heart of the phenomenological project, and the manner of one's writing, therefore, impacts not only on what is revealed and how clearly it might be understood but also on the mood (cf. Heidegger, [1927] 1962) of the reader in relation to the phenomenon represented in the text.

Finally, I want to emphasize that no method provides the tools to find all answers to all questions (assuming we ever had the knowledge and insight to ask them), and it is important, therefore, not be too obsessed with methodology. There is a tendency in psychology, in particular, to think that by rigidly following a particular method, we will conduct good-quality (i.e. valid) research. Although this may be true for quantitative research (although even here, I think this position is questionable), it is certainly not true for qualitative research, where the role of the researcher is central and the need for understanding, reflection and insight crucial. So, while it is important to be rigorous and systematic, this should not mean the unquestioning and rigid adoption of methods. Furthermore, there is often fruitless argument over methodologies and methods, as if some superior claim to truth can be made. Janesick (1994: 215) came up with the term 'methodolatry' (a combination of 'method' and 'idolatry') to refer to the 'preoccupation with selecting and defending methods to the exclusion of the actual substance of the story being told'. This term and Janesick's (1994) concerns rightly reflect the way that interest in method can become obsessional, with a consequent loss of sight of the meaning of the findings. What is important is simply that the method is fit for purpose and that it is employed rigorously – in its own terms – so that the world is revealed in as rich and fruitful way as possible.

## 9.6 What future for phenomenological psychology?

The future is looking promising for phenomenological psychology. The rapid growth in qualitative methods, especially in social and applied psychology, clearly signals the need for approaches that prioritize understanding and focus on the meanings of experiences for participants. Furthermore, this rapid growth is not simply confined to psychology; there has been tremendous interest shown in phenomenology in nursing and education, in particular in recent years and a considerable body of knowledge is emerging from these disciplines that is of relevance to researchers, theoreticians and practitioners, both inside and outside the disciplines. Descriptive phenomenology continues to demonstrate its value and influence through the steady and continued application of the method to a very wide variety of topics (see the *Journal of Phenomenological Psychology* and the *Indo-Pacific Journal of Phenomenology* at www.ipjp.org for the latest research), while the growth of newer variations (such as the Sheffield School, among others) show its vitality and willingness to change. Interpretive methods of phenomenological psychology, such as IPA, hermeneutic phenomenology and TA, have been taken up very rapidly in recent years, especially among applied psychologists. A great deal of work is emerging in qualitative health journals as well as in more mainstream social psychology journals, and this particular approach to phenomenological psychology is very much in the ascendancy.

And, although phenomenology may no longer be such an active form of philosophy, the developments in continental philosophy – such as the turn to narrative – have been taken up by phenomenological psychologists and used to further develop methods of enquiry appropriate to the needs of the social sciences and study of human nature. CNA is just one example. The rise in narrative research, more generally, the production of an increasing number of books on the subject, a journal dedicated to the topic (*Narrative Inquiry* – formerly the *Journal of Narrative and Life History*) and dedicated narrative conferences all show the vitality and growth of this approach to human sciences research. I have no doubt that we are at the beginning of a new era of research, focused on the description or interpretation of experience and narrative, and that the future for phenomenology is very bright indeed.

## Summary

Although some may believe phenomenology to be something belonging to the past, the recent surge of interest proves that there is a real need for a psychological perspective that focuses on lived experience. Phenomenological approaches to psychology provide insight into human nature in a way that few others can match. The validity of these findings is something that has troubled critics, however, and in this chapter I have discussed a number of ways of assessing the validity of phenomenological findings, which, I hope, would satisfy even the harshest critic. Critics have also been ready to charge phenomenological psychology with being too descriptive. Not only does this fail to recognize the value of description, but it also fails to recognize the wide range of phenomenological approaches, some of which are deliberately engaged in more interpretive ways of working (e.g. CNA). The core of this chapter, however, involved an engagement with postmodern philosophy and the application of these ideas to psychology. Rather than simply concede that this is a superior philosophy, I have sought, drawing on the philosophy of Paul Ricoeur and Don Ihde, to provide a direct rebuttal and, in the process, to outline a postphenomenology that offers a possible future for phenomenological philosophy and psychology alike.

## Further reading

Cresswell, J. W. (1998). *Qualitative Inquiry and Research Design: Choosing Among Five Traditions*. London: Sage. A very comprehensive comparison of five traditions of qualitative research. Very useful for grasping the finer points of the differences between descriptive phenomenology, biographical research, grounded theory, ethnography and case study research.

Ihde, D. (1993). *Postphenomenology: Essays in the Postmodern Context*. Evanston, IL: Northwestern University Press. A particularly lucid and insightful exploration of perception, technology, postmodernism and the turn to text by one of the leading living phenomenological philosophers.

Kvale, S. (ed.) (1992). *Psychology and Postmodernism*. London: Sage. An interesting collection of essays on postmodernism and psychology. Of particular note are the chapters by Ken Gergen, Kvale and Polkinghorne.

# References

Aanstoos, C. M. (1983). A phenomenological study of thinking. In A. Giorgi, A. Barton & C. Maes (eds) *Duquesne Studies in Phenomenological Psychology*, Vol. 4. Pittsburgh, PA: Duquesne University Press.

Aanstoos, C. M. (1985). The structure of thinking in chess. In A. Giorgi (ed.) *Phenomenology and Psychological Research*. Pittsburgh, PA: Duquesne University Press.

Akrich, M. & Pasveer, B. (2004). Embodiment and disembodiment in childbirth narratives. *Body & Society*, 10(2–3), 63–84.

Anthony, K. & Lawson, M. (2002). The use of innovative avatar and virtual environment technology for counselling and psychotherapy. www.kateanthony.co.uk/InnovativeAvatar.pdf (accessed 1 November 2005).

Ashmore, M. (1989). *The Reflexive Thesis: Wrighting Sociology of Scientific Knowledge*. Chicago, IL: University of Chicago Press.

Ashworth, P. (2003a). The phenomenology of the lifeworld and social psychology. *Social Psychological Review*, 5(1), 18–34.

Ashworth, P. (2003b). An approach to phenomenological psychology: the contingencies of the lifeworld. *Journal of Phenomenological Psychology*, 34(2), 145–156.

Ashworth, A. & Ashworth, P. (2003). The lifeworld as phenomenon and as research heuristic, exemplified by a study of the lifeworld of a person suffering Alzheimer's disease. *Journal of Phenomenological Psychology*, 34(2), 179–205.

Ashworth, P., Freewood, M. & Macdonald, R. (2003). The student lifeworld and the meanings of plagiarism. *Journal of Phenomenological Psychology*, 34(2), 257–278.

Austin, J. L. (1962). *How to Do Things With Words*. Oxford: Oxford University Press.

Bajos, N. (1997). Social factors and the proces of risk construction in HIV sexual transmission. *AIDS Care*, 9, 227–237.

Bakhtin, M. M. (1986). *Speech Genres and Other Late Essays* [trans. V. W. McGee]. Austin, TX: University of Texas Press.

Bargdill, R. (2000). The study of life boredom. *Journal of Phenomenological Psychology*, 31(2), 188–219.

Barthes, R. (1977). *Image – Music – Text* [trans. S. Heath]. Glasgow: Fontana.

Baudrillard, J. (1993). *Symbolic Exchange and Death* [trans. I. Grant]. London: Sage.

Becker, G. (1999). Narratives of pain in later life and conventions of storytelling. *Journal of Ageing Studies*, 13, 73–87.

Bell, D. and Binnie, J. (2000). *The Sexual Citizen: Queer Politics and Beyond*. Cambridge: Polity.

Billig, M. (1997). *Arguing and Thinking: A Rhetorical Approach to Social Psychology*. Cambridge: University of Cambridge.

Bollnow, O.F. (1982). On silence: findings of philosphico-pedagogical anthropology. *Universitas*, 24(1), 41–47.

Bruner, J. (1986). *Actual Minds, Possible Words*. Cambridge, MA: Harvard University press.

Bruner, J. (1990). *Acts of Meaning*. Cambridge, MA: Harvard University Press.

Burr, V. (2003). *Social Constructionism*, 2nd edn. Hove: Routledge.

Butler, J. (1991). *Gender Trouble*. New York: Routledge.

Butt, T. (2004). *Understanding People*. Basingstoke: Palgrave Macmillan.

Butt, T. & Langdridge, D. (2003). The construction of self: the public reach into the private sphere. *Sociology*, 37(3), 477–494.

Chapman, E. (2002). The social and ethical implications of changing medical technologies: the views of people living with genetic conditions. *Journal of Health Psychology*, 7, 195–206.

Cohn, H. (1997). *Existential Thought and Therapeutic Practice: An Introduction to Existential Psychotherapy*. London: Sage.

Colaizzi, P. (1971). Analysis of the learner's perception of learning material at various stages of the learning process. In A. Giorgi, W. Fischer & R. von Eckartsberg (eds) *Duquesne Studies in Phenomenological Psychology I*. Pittsburgh, PA: Duquesne University Press.

Dahlberg, K., Drew, N. & Nyström, M. (2001). *Reflective Lifeworld Research*. Lund, Sweden: Studentlitteratur.

de Beauvoir, S. ([1949] 1997). *The Second Sex* [trans. H. M. Parshley]. London: Vintage.

Deleuze, G. & Guattari, F. (1984). *Anti-Oedipus: Capitalism and Schizophrenia*. London: Athlone Press.

Edwards, D. (1997). *Discourse and Cognition*. London: Sage.

Edwards, D. & Potter, J. (1992). *Discursive Psychology*. London: Sage.

Elsbree, L. (1982). *The Rituals of Life: Patterns in Narrative*. Port Washington, NY: Kennikat Press.

Finlay, L. (2003). The intertwining of body, self and world: a phenomenological study of living with recently diagnosed multiple sclerosis. *Journal of Phenomenological Psychology*, 34(2), 157–178.

Finlay, L. (2006). The body's disclosure in phenomenological research. *Qualitative Research in Psychology*, 3(1), 19–30.

Finlay, L., King, N., Ashworth, P., Smith, J.A., Langdridge, D. & Butt, T. (2006). 'Can't really trust that, so what can I trust?': a polyvocal, qualitative analysis of the psychology of mistrust. *Qualitative Research in Psychology*, 3, 1–23.

Fischer, W. F. (1974). On the phenomenological mode of researching 'being anxious'. *Journal of Phenomenological Psychology*, 4(2), 405–423.

Fischer, W. F. (1985). Self-deception: an empirical phenomenological inquiry into its essential meanings. In A. Giorgi (ed.) *Phenomenology and Psychological Research*. Pittsburgh, PA: Duquesne University Press.

Fiske, S. & Taylor, S. (1991). *Social Cognition*, 2nd edn. New York: McGraw-Hill.

Flowers, P. & Langdridge, D. (in press) Offending the other: deconstructing narratives of deviance and pathology. *British Journal of Social Psychology*.

Flowers, P., Smith, J. A., Sheeran, P. & Beail, N. (1997). Health and romance: understanding unprotected sex in relationships between gay men. *British Journal of Health Psychology*, 2, 73–86.

Flowers, P., Smith, J. A., Sheeran, P. & Beail, N. (1998). 'Coming out' and sexual debut: understanding the social context of HIV risk-related behaviour. *Journal of Community & Applied Social Psychology*, 8, 409–421.

Foucault, M. (1973). *The Order of Things: An Archaeology of the Human Sciences*. New York: Vintage Books.

Fuss, D. (ed.) (1991). *Inside/Out*. New York: Routledge.

Gadamer, H. ([1975] 1996). *Truth and Method*. London: Sheed and Ward.

Galvin, K., Todres, L. & Richardson, M. (2005). The intimate mediator: a carer's experience of Alzheimer's. *Scandinavian Journal of Caring Sciences*, 19, 2–11.

Gergen, K. J. (1999). *An Invitation to Social Construction*. London: Sage.

Gergen, K. J. & Gergen, M. (1986). Narrative form and the construction of psychological science. In T. Sarbin (ed.) *Narrative Psychology: The Storied Nature of Human Conduct*. New York: Praeger.

Giddens, A. (1992) *The Transformation of Intimacy: Sexuality, Love and Eroticism in Modern Societies*. Cambridge: Polity Press.

Giorgi, A. (1985). Sketch of a psychological phenomenological method. In A. Giorgi (ed.) *Phenomenology and Psychological Research*. Pittsburgh, PA: Duquesne University Press.

Giorgi, A. (1992). Description versus interpretation: competing alternative strategies for qualitative research. *Journal of Phenomenological Psychology*, 23(2), 119–135.

Giorgi, A. (2002). The question of validity in qualitative research. *Journal of Phenomenological Psychology*, 33(1), 1–18.

Giorgi, A. & Giorgi, B. (2003). Phenomenology. In J. A. Smith (ed.) *Qualitative Psychology: A Practical Guide to Research Methods*. London: Sage.

Gough, B. (2003). Deconstructing reflexivity. In L. Finlay & B. Gough (eds) *Reflexivity: A Practical Guide for Researchers in Health and Social Science*. Oxford: Blackwell.

Grenz, S. J. (1996). *A Primer in Postmodernism*. Grand Rapids, MI: William B. Eerdmans.

Grosz, E. (1994). *Volatile Bodies: Toward a Corporeal Feminism*. Bloomington, IN: Indiana University Press.

Guba, E. G. (ed.) (1990). *The Paradigm Dialog*. Newbury Park, CA: Sage.

Gurwitsch, A. (1964). *Field of Consciousness*. Pittsburgh, PA: Duquesne University Press.

Harré, R. and Gillett, G. (1994). *The Discursive Mind*. London: Sage.

Heidegger, M. ([1925] 1985). *History of the Concept of Time: Prolegomena* [trans. T. Kisel]. Bloomington, IN: Indiana University Press.

Heidegger, M. ([1927] 1962). *Being and Time* [trans. J. Macquarrie & E. Robinson]. Oxford: Blackwell.

Heidegger, M. ([1947] 1993). Letter on humanism. In *Basic Writings* [ed. by D. F. Krell]. London: Routledge.

Heidegger, M. (1978). *Basic Writings*. [ed. D. F. Krell]. London: Routledge.

Heidegger, M. (2001). *Zollikon Seminars: Protocols – Conversations – Letters* [trans. F. Mayr & R. Askay]. Evanston, IL: Northwestern University Press.

Henriques, J., Hollway, W., Urwin, C., Venn, C. & Walkerdine, V. (1984). *Changing the Subject: Psychology, Social Regulation and Subjectivity*. London: Methuen.

Hinchliff, S. (2001). *Female Experiences of the Body in Club Culture*. Unpublished PhD dissertation. Sheffield: Sheffield Hallam University.

Hollway, W. and Jefferson, T. (2000). *Doing Qualitative Research Differently: Free Association, Narrative and the Interview Method*. London: Sage.

Hollway, W. and Jefferson, T. (2005). Panic and perjury: a psychosocial exploration of agency. *British Journal of Social Psychology*, 44(2), 147–163.

Hunt, D. & Smith, J. A. (2004). The personal experience of carers of stroke survivors: an interpretative phenomenological analysis. *Disability and Rehabilitation*, 26(16), 1000–1011.

Husserl, E. ([1900] 1970). *Logical Investigations* [trans. J. N. Findlay]. New York: Humanities Press.

Husserl, E. ([1931] 1967). *Cartesian Meditations* [trans. D. Cairns]. The Hague: Nijhoff.

Husserl, E. ([1936] 1970). *The Crisis of European Sciences and Transcendental Phenomenology* [trans. D. Carr]. Evanston, IL: North Western University Press.

Hutchby, I. & Wooffitt, R. (1998). *Conversation Analysis: Principles, Practices and Applications*. Oxford: Polity Press.

Ihde, D. (1986). *Experimental Phenomenology: An Introduction*. Albany, NY: SUNY Press.

Ihde, D. (1993). *Postphenomenology: Essays in the Postmodern Context*. Evanston, IL: Northwestern University Press.

Janesick, V. J. (1994). The dance of qualitative research design: metaphor, methodolatry, and meaning. In N. K. Denzin & Y. S. Lincoln (eds) *Handbook of Qualitative Research*. London: Sage.

Kearney, R. (1994). *Modern Movements in European Philosophy*, 2nd edn. Manchester: University of Manchester Press.

Kent, G. (2000). Understanding the experiences of people with disfigurements: an integration of four models of social and psychological functioning. *Psychology, Health & Medicine*, 5(2), 117–129.

King, N. (1998). Template analysis. In G. Symon & C. Cassell (eds) *Qualitative Methods and Analysis in Organizational Research*. London: Sage.

King, N., Carroll, C., Newton, P. & Dornan, T. (2002). 'You can't cure it so you have to endure it': the experience of adaptation to diabetic renal disease. *Qualitative Health Research*, 12(3), 329–346.

King, N., Thomas, K., Bell, D. and Bowes, N. (2003). *Evaluation of the Calderdale and Kirklees Out of Hours Protocol for Palliative Care: Final Report*. Huddersfield: Primary Care Research Group, School of Human and Health Sciences, University of Huddersfield.

Langdridge, D. (2003). Hermeneutic phenomenology: arguments for a new social psychology. *History and Philosophy of Psychology*, 5(1), 30–45.

Langdridge, D. (2004a). *Introduction to Research Methods and Data Analysis in Psychology*. Harlow: Pearson Education.

Langdridge, D. (2004b). The hermeneutic phenomenology of Paul Ricoeur: problems and possibilities for existential-phenomenological psychotherapy. *Existential Analysis*, 15(2), 243–255.

Langdridge, D. (2005). The child's relations with others: Merleau-Ponty, embodiment and psychotherapy. *Existential Analysis*, 16.1, 87–99.

Langdridge, D. & Butt, T. (2004). A hermeneutic phenomenological investigation of the construction of sadomasochistic identities. *Sexualities*, 7(1), 31–53.

Langdridge, D. & Butt, T. W. (2005). The erotic construction of power exchange. *Journal of Constructivist Psychology*, 18(1), pp. 65–73.

Langdridge, D. & Flowers, P. (2005). Resistance habitus and the homophobic social psychologist. *Lesbian & Gay Psychology Review*, 6(1), 53–55.

Langdridge, D., Connolly, K. J. & Sheeran, P. (2000). A network analytic study of the reasons for wanting a child. *Journal of Reproductive and Infant Psychology*, 18(4), 321–338.

Latour, B. (1988). The politics of explanation: an alternative. In S. Woolgar (ed.) *Knowledge and Reflexivity: New Frontiers in the Sociology of Knowledge*. London: Sage.

Lydall, A.-M., Pretorius, G. & Stuart, A. (2005). Give sorrow words: the meaning of parental bereavement. *Indo-Pacific Journal of Phenomenology*, 5(2), 1–12.

Lyotard, J.-F. ([1979] 2004). *The Postmodern Condition: A Report on Knowledge* [trans. G. Bennington & B. Massumi]. Manchester: Manchester University Press.

Mann, C. and Stewart, F. (2000). *Internet Communication and Qualitative Research: A Handbook for Researching Online.* London: Sage.

McAdams, D. (1985). *Power, Intimacy, and the Life Story: Personological Inquiries into Identity.* New York: Guilford Press.

McAdams, D. P. (1993). *The Stories We Live By: Personal Myths and the Making of the Self.* New York: The Guilford Press.

Merleau-Ponty, M. ([1945] 1962). *Phenomenology of Perception* [trans. C. Smith] London: Routledge.

Mishler, E. G. (1995). Models of narrative analysis: a typology. *Journal of Narrative and Life History,* 5(2), 87–123.

Moran, D. (2000). *Introduction to Phenomenology.* London: Routledge.

Morley, J. (1998). The private theater: a phenomenological investigation of daydreaming. *Journal of Phenomenological Psychology,* 29(1), 116–134.

Moustakas, C. (1994). *Phenomenological Research Methods.* London: Sage.

Muldoon, M. (2002). *On Ricoeur.* Belmont, CA: Wadsworth/Thomson Learning.

Murray, C. D. (2004). An interpretative phenomenological analysis of the embodiment of artificial limbs. *Disability and Rehabilitation,* 26(16), 963–973.

Nietzsche, F. (1979). Werke. Band III. Munich: Ulstein. [Cited in Cooper, D. E. (1996). Modern European philosophy. In N. Bunnin & E. P. Tsui-James (eds) *The Blackwell Companion to Philosophy.* Oxford: Blackwell.]

Parker, I. (1992). *Discourse Dynamics: Critical Analysis for Social and Individual Psychology.* London: Routledge.

Polkinghorne, D. E. (1988). *Narrative Knowing and the Human Sciences.* Albany, NY: SUNY Press.

Polkinghorne, D. E. (1989) Phenomenological research methods. In R. S. Valle & S. Halling (eds) *Existential-Phenomenological Perspectives in Psychology: Exploring the Breadth of Human Experience.* New York: Plenum Press.

Polt, R. (1999). *Heidegger: An Introduction.* London: UCL Press.

Popper, K. (1963). *Conjectures and Refutations: The Growth of Scientific Knowledge.* London: Routledge.

Potter, J. (2005). Making psychology relevant. *Discourse and Society,* 16(5), 739–747.

Potter, J. & Hepburn, A. (2005a). Qualitative interviews in psychology: problems and possibilities. *Qualitative Research in Psychology,* 2(4), 281–307.

Potter, J. & Hepburn, A. (2005b). Action, interaction and interviews: some responses to Hollway, Mishler and Smith. *Qualitative Research in Psychology,* 2(4), 319–325.

Potter, J. & Wetherell, M. (1987). *Discourse and Social Psychology: Beyond Attitudes and Behaviour.* London: Sage.

Pretorius, H. G. & Hull, R. M. (2005). The experience of male rape in non-institutionalised settings. *Indo-Pacific Journal of Phenomenology,* 5(2), 1–11.

Propp, V. I. (1969). *Morphology of the Folk tale* [ed. L. A. Wagner]. Austin, TX: University of Texas Press.

Rapport, F. (2003). Exploring the beliefs and experiences of potential egg share donors. *Journal of Advanced Nursing,* 43(1), 28–42.

Rapport, F. (2005). Hermeneutic phenomenology: the science of interpretation of texts. In I. Holloway (ed.) *Qualitative Research in Health Care.* Maidenhead: Open University Press.

Ricoeur, P. (1970). *Freud and Philosophy: An Essay on Interpretation* [trans. D. Savage] New Haven, CT: Yale University Press.

Ricoeur, P. (1971). The model of the text: meaningful action considered as text. *Social Research*, 38, 529–562.

Ricoeur, P. (1981). *Hermeneutics and the Human Sciences* [trans. J. B. Thompson] Paris: Edition de la Maison des Sciences de l'Homme/Cambridge: Cambridge University Press.

Ricoeur, P. (1984). *Time and Narrative*, Vol. 1 [trans. K. McLaughlin & D. Pellauer] Chicago, IL: University of Chicago Press.

Ricoeur, P. (1985). *Time and Narrative*, Vol. 2 [trans. K. McLaughlin & D. Pellauer] Chicago, IL: University of Chicago Press.

Ricoeur, P. ([1987] 1991). Life: a story in search of a narrator. In M. Vlades (ed.) *A Ricoeur Reader*. Toronto: University of Toronto Press.

Ricoeur, P. (1988). *Time and Narrative*, Vol. 4 [trans. K. McLaughlin & D. Pellauer]. Chicago, IL: University of Chicago Press.

Ricoeur, P. (1992). *Oneself as Another* [trans. K. Blamey]. Chicago, IL: University of Chicago Press.

Ricoeur, P. (1996). *Lectures on Ideology and Utopia* [ed. G. H. Taylor]. New York: Columbia University Press.

Ricoeur, P. (1998). *Critique and Conviction*. New York: Columbia University Press.

Ryle, G. (1949). *The Concept of Mind*. London: Hutchinson.

Sarbin, T. (ed.) (1986). *Narrative Psychology: The Storied Nature of Human Conduct*. New York: Praeger.

Sartre, J.-P. ([1943] 1956). *Being and Nothingness: An Essay on Phenomenological Ontology* [trans. H. Barnes]. New York: Philosophical Library.

Sartre, J.-P. ([1943] 2003). *Being and Nothingness: An Essay on Phenomenological Ontology* [trans. H. Barnes]. London: Routledge.

Searle, J. R. (1969). *Speech Acts: An Essay in the Philosophy of Language*. Cambridge: Cambridge University Press.

Sedgwick, E. (1991). *The Epistemology of the Closet*. Berkeley, CA: University of California Press.

Seidman, S. (ed.) (1996). *Queer Theory/Sociology*. Oxford: Blackwell.

Sherwood, T. (2001). Client experience in psychotherapy: what heals and what harms? *Indo-Pacific Journal of Phenomenology*, 1(2), 1–16.

Smith, J. A. (1996). Beyond the divide between cognition and discourse: using interpretative phenomenological analysis in health psychology. *Psychology and Health*, 11, 261–271.

Smith, J. A. (1999). Towards a relational self: social engagement during pregnancy and psychological preparation for motherhood. *British Journal of Social Psychology*, 38, 409–426.

Smith, J. A. (2004). Reflecting on the development of interpretative phenomenological analysis and its contribution to qualitative research in psychology. *Qualitative Research in Psychology*, 1, 39–54.

Smith, J. A., Harré, R. & Van Langenhove, L. (1995). *Rethinking Psychology*. London: Sage.

Smith, J. A. & Osborn, M. (2003). Interpretative phenomenological analysis. In J. A. Smith (ed.) *Qualitative Psychology*. London: Sage.

Spinelli, E. (2005). *The Interpreted World: An Introduction to Phenomenological Psychology*, 2nd edn. London: Sage.

Suler, J. (1999). The psychology of avatars and graphical space in multimedia chat communities. www.rider.edu/~suler/psycyber/psyav.html#Physical (accessed 7 March 2005).

Todres, L. (2002). Humanising forces: phenomenology in science; psychotherapy in technological culture. *Indo-Pacific Journal of Phenomenology*, 2(1), 1–11.

Todres, L. and Galvin, K. (2005). Pursuing both breadth and depth in qualitative research: illustrated by a study of the experience of intimate caring for a loved one with Alzheimer's disease. *International Journal of Qualitative Methods*, 4(2), Article 2. www.ualberta.ca/~ijqm (accessed 14 March 2006).

Todres, L. and Wheeler, S. (2001). The complementarity of phenomenology, hermeneutics and existentialism as a philosophical perspective for nursing research. *International Journal of Nursing Studies*, 38, 1–8.

Turner, A. J. and Coyle, A. (2000). What does it mean to be a donor offspring? The identity experiences of adults conceived by donor insemination and the implications for counselling and therapy. *Human Reproduction*, 15, 2041–2051.

van Deurzen-Smith, E. (1997). *Everyday Mysteries: Existential Dimensions of Psychotherapy*. London: Routledge.

van Manen, M. (1990). *Researching Lived Experience: Human Science for an Action Sensitive Pedagogy*. Albany, NY: SUNY Press.

Warnock, M. (1970). *Existentialism*. Oxford: Oxford University Press.

Wertz, F. J. (1985). Method and findings in a phenomenological psychological study of a complex life-event: being criminally victimised. In A. Giorgi (ed.) *Phenomenology and Psychological Research*. Pittsburgh, PA: Duquesne University Press.

Wetherell, M., Taylor, S. & Yates, S. J. (eds) (2001a). *Discourse as Data*. London: Sage.

Wetherell, M., Taylor, S. & Yates, S. J. (eds) (2001b). *Discourse Theory and Practice: A Reader*. London: Sage.

White, S. (1997). Beyond retroduction? Hermeneutics, reflexivity and social work practice. *British Journal of Social Work*, 27(6), 739–753.

Wilkinson, S. (1988). The role of reflexivity in feminist psychology. *Women's Studies International Forum*, 11, 493–502.

Willig, C. (2001). *Introducing Qualitative Research in Psychology: Adventures in Theory and Method*. Buckingham: Open University Press.

Wittgenstein, L. (1953). *Philosophical Investigations*. Oxford: Blackwell

Yardley, L. (2000). Dilemmas in qualitative health research. *Psychology and Health*, 15(2), 215–228.

# Index